Librarians as Learners, Librarians as Teachers:
The Diffusion of Internet Expertise in the Academic Library

Edited by
Patricia O'Brien Libutti

Association of College and Research Libraries
A division of the American Library Association
Chicago 1999

The paper used in this publication meets the minimum requirements of American National Standard for Information Sciences–Permanence of Paper for Printed Library Materials, ANSI Z39.48—1992.∞

Library of Congress Cataloging-in-Publication Data:
Librarians as learners, librarians as teachers : the diffusion of
    Internet expertise in the academic library / edited by Patricia
    O'Brien Libutti.
        p. cm.
    Includes bibliographical references.
    ISBN 0-8389-8003-1
    1. Academic libraries--United States. 2. Internet (Computer
network)--United States. 3. Computer literacy--United States.
4. College librarians--United States. 5. Library information
networks--United States.   I. Libutti, Patricia O'Brien.
Z675.U5L415 1999
027.7--dc21   99-13042

Printed in the United States of America.

03 02 01 00 99   5 4 3 2

Table of Contents

Foreword

Anne Woodsworth

In many respects, this work is a trailblazer with lessons for a wider array of librarians than those who work in colleges and universities. In almost all settings, the librarian is increasingly seen as having a teaching or training role, particularly in connection with navigation of the Internet and the information technologies. As is pointed out by many of the contributors to this book, as teachers of topics that are almost ethereal and certainly fleeting, librarians have had to become continuous learners. Fortunately, the ethos of continuous and self-directed learning has been part of the profession for some time.

Each of us acquires different knowledge from what we read. The lessons I took from this work were many. For example, as librarians become trainers, (or more), they need to have a better understanding of how adults learn. As David W. Carr's article illustrates, there is a powerful body of literature (and underlying research) on which we can draw, particularly in the fields of education and cognition. Happily, this is directly transferable to the field of library science. In addition to the literature review by Laurie J. Lopatin, the Web sites identified by Irina Poznansky and Harriet A. Hagenbruch offer shortcuts for further self-directed learning and for teaching Internet and related skills.

This book focuses on the "training" role of the academic librarian at a point in time when the Internet and certainly Web search engines are pretty young. As they mature, I foresee an opportunity for academic librarians to assume a stronger and probably more formal teaching role within the academy. What they teach will be far beyond today's hands-on, skill-building workshops. Students in colleges and universities will need to graduate with basic knowledge that will enable them to work in an increasingly digital world. No matter what work arena graduates wish to enter, the core curricula they take will have to incorporate areas such as introduction to information science, information storage and retrieval, database searching, metadata management, knowledge management, information processing, human–computer interaction, electronic records management, indexing, and information systems management, to name a few.

Who is better equipped to teach these subjects than librarians? Yes, software to perform some of these tasks will no doubt emerge, but it will be too complex for most people to use without formal instruction. Thus, academic librarians will have an unprecedented opportunity to build themselves into the center of the educational processes in colleges and universities and function as true peers among the faculty.

The research reported in this book sets the stage for further exploration as we make the transition from bibliographic instruction to the broader arena of information literacy instruction. The needed research includes identifying the following: factors that have changed, and will change, the role of librarians in higher education; how to measure the efficacy of using the Internet in teaching and learning experiences; the impact of laboratory and classroom design on technological training; the relationship of diffusion of technology on campus and its rate of adoption in the teaching–learning process; the uses of technology for Internet searching and its relationship to library-based research and library use; the growth of programs that deliver courses (or segments of courses) that are independent of place and time; and not least, the extent to which schools of library and information science can best model and prepare librarians to assume teaching roles in all kinds of settings.

The literature of education will help us as we begin to pay attention to curriculum and syllabus design, learning theories, facility design, and outcomes assessment. The examples of training programs that are described in the book (Columbia and METRO) tell us what did and did not work and what changed as the 'Net evolved. The example offered by Heather Blenkinsopp as faculty in a graduate program offers a glimmer of the potential connections for learners outside the classroom. The The chapter on new librarians (Anderson and Franz), the leaner's complement to the practioners' chapters (Moslander and Johnsen-Seeberger, Carroll-Mathes), reinforces the notion that any group of learners includes a wide array of experience that has to be accommodated in any classroom. Again, this is where the 'Net itself can be harnessed to provide individualized learning modules that allow for faster or slower knowledge acquisition.

Although this work will be helpful to librarians in all types of settings, academic librarians may have more obstacles to overcome in providing instructional and technological leadership on campuses and here is why. K–12 is getting a massive infusion of funds for technologies use in the educational process from the federal government and foundations. However, this is not happening in higher education. As a result, colleges and universities will be caught short when students experienced in the information technologies reach them. The students will come with expectations that will be unmet both pedagogically and in terms of information resources. They will expect fast and easy access to their information needs via the Internet and will be increasingly frustrated to be pointed to metadata about books that are not in digital form. They will opt not to fetch a book from the stacks and choose, instead, to substitute anything that can be downloaded or printed from the Web.

There will be problems in the classrooms in higher education as well. The speed with which teachers in K–12 schools are adapting and using the Web and other distance delivery systems in the teaching–learning process is not being matched in higher education. And yet, the institutions that are adapting and using the technologies such as the University of Phoenix, are growing by leaps and bounds. Here again, massive amounts of money are being made available to place technology into K–12 schools, to retrofit physical plants, and to teach teachers how to incorporate the power of technology and the Internet into their classrooms. In higher education, there has not been a similar mass effort to date.

The information technologies are being infused into the teaching–learning process across the entire curriculum in the K–12 sector. There, the librarian has become the teacher's partner in a formal teaching role. The average academic librarian is not used or perceived this way in most places. Colleges and universities are bound up in traditions, such as having discipline-based academic department structures, that mitigate against easy, across-the-board curricular changes. In addition, faculty control of the curricula does not encourage the capacity to change curricula quickly.

Schoolchildren and a growing number of adults (including college students) view any information on the Web as "good." Librarians' penchants, however, to just point to information in authoritative print sources will not work in the Web environment, nor will the tradition of not evaluating the information that librarians pass on to users. Thus, changes in roles and outlook will be needed. In addition, librarians will have to provide tools that enable people to evaluate the information that is found via the Web.

Academic libraries and their parent institutions should be—but are not—organizations that reward the acquisition of knowledge by librarians. The institution values the production of knowledge by its faculty and the teaching–learning interaction in the classroom. It values service (and in some settings, scholarship) on the part of its librarians. But if the library wants to enable and recognize continuous learning as a valuable asset in its librarians and staff, it will have to do so without institutional support and an enabling organizational culture. Thus, funds will have to be carved out of the library's budget to support this activity. Most libraries spend more on preserving their print collections than on staff training and development. This will have to change. Perhaps spending the proportionate amount relative to the campus's computing/technology centers will be necessary. This is one place where continuous learning is supported and funded.

Another tough hurdle will be the institutional frameworks that categorize librarians variously as faculty, quasi-faculty, or professionals. Sometimes librarians are placed in the faculty tenure stream and sometimes not. The systems that determine pay and comparable worth will creak and moan when librarians become truly active partners with computing and telecommunications staff. Again, this is an area that needs more research

Although these may appear to be insurmountable obstacles, the emerging role of the librarian as teacher is a welcome and needed one. As teacher, mentor, "info-mediary," and expert on technology-intense information access systems, the librarian is seen as an increasingly desirable professional role. As a result, a stronger pool of applicants will apply to schools. The quality of graduates will be such that employers will compete for the best and pay higher (and well-deserved) salaries—at last.

Anne Woodsworth, Ph.D.
Palmer School of Library and Information Science
March 30, 1999

Acknowledgments

This volume is a historic endeavor in which an entire ACRL chapter collaborated in a publication. It would not have been assembled without the librarians and library educators who gave of their experience and expertise in preparing their contributions. Many told their own story of approaching and learning the Internet. Others provided research projects to develop an understanding of librarians' needs for training during this rapidly changing work environment. Librarians collated and annotated resources for others in the field to consider in their own continuing education. The librarians, library educators, and university faculty who acted as peer reviewers for contributors helped develop ACRL/NY as a publication preparation community.

The editor wishes to acknowledge the support of the Association of College and Research Libraries for an Initiative Fund, awarded for 1994–1995. This fund made possible the research project that began an examination of the Internet as it affected librarians in the New York Metropolitan area. The support of the Association of College and Research Libraries, New York Metropolitan Chapter, 1994–1999, was crucial to the development of this volume. The support was evident in e-mailed proposal ideas through manuscripts and eventually into a volume replete with their contributions. Also important in this process were Cecile Hastie, President, ACRL/NY, 1998; Ree DeDonato, President of ACRL/NY, 1994; and Marilyn Rosenthal, member of the ACRL/NY Executive Board, 1994. These three individuals provided constructive critiques of the original proposal for research as well as the manuscript proposal.

The evolution of this volume began with the collaboration of the members of the Internet Training Program team, led by Catherine M. Thomas, without whose cooperation, collaboration, and information the ITP study would not have occurred. Their continued willingness to answer many questions this investigator had as the process continued and their invitations to planning meetings provided background information helpful in understanding the development of the program. Particularly important were the expertise and openness of Catherine M. Thomas, Daniel J. Caldano, and David S. Magier, who have contributed to this volume. The skills of Joseph McNicholas, textual transcriber, also must be recognized. The permission of Pierian Press to reprint David W. Carr's 1988 article "The Situation of the Adult Learner in the Library" is gratefully acknowledged. The editor thanks Fordham University Libraries for the released time for the observation phase of the research at Columbia University Libraries, as well as for provision of textual analytical software used in the ITP study.

Patricia O'Brien Libutti, Ph.D.
Editor
April 6, 1999

Part I

Foundations of Internet Expertise in the Academic Library

The Diffusion of Internet Expertise in the Academic Library: An Overview

Patricia O'Brien Libutti

he grounding of Librarians as Learners, Librarians as Teachers: The diffusion of Internet Expertise in Academic Libraries is in the daily impact of the Internet on librarians and their transactions with learners in the library. In American academic libraries, the Internet has resulted in dramatic shifts in work content, process, and flow, crowding the traditional aspects of the library institution. Currently, the frontline librarian is learning and teaching technology advances, and integrating them into instruction, reference, and collaborative curricula at a rapid pace. How librarians teach the Internet and what they learn are concerns for practitioners who wish to develop instructional expertise in Internet education. This volume addresses these topics through research and reflection by practitioners who have experienced the advances that the Internet has propelled in academia.

Origin of *Librarians as Learners, Librarians as Teachers*
The beginning of this volume was research developed with an ACRL Initiative Fund awarded to the ACRL/NY chapter for the year 1994–1995. The fund supported a study of librarians' learning and teaching processes with the Internet, which is the primary purpose of this book. Research on the same issues by other librarians between 1994 and 1998 was thematically integrated with individual reflections in this publication. The secondary focus was to bring forward for critical thought the change process in areas important to librarians: everyday instructional

and reference jobs, technology-driven institutional relationships, and values embedded in instructional practice.

These reflections were influenced by the thinking of Schon in *The Reflective Practitioner: How Professionals Think in Action* (1983). The Greater Metropolitan New York ACRL chapter presented the book proposal to the ACRL New Publications Board in February 1998, and it was accepted for publication in March 1998.

Contributors and Organization of the ACRL/NY Publication Venture. The contributors to this volume include frontline librarians, administrators, and library school educators. They come from large and small libraries, universities, four-year colleges, community colleges, and consulting agencies. The editor of this volume developed the basis of contribution responsibility by following the tenet of The WELL— "You own your own words"— and served ACRL/NY by developing each article as an advisor when needed, as well as organizing the manuscripts for publication. Such a responsibility could not have been undertaken without the collaboration of the ACRL/NY chapter members who contributed as authors, editors, and peer reviewers.

Organization of Librarians as Learners, Librarians as Teachers: The Diffusion of Internet Expertise in Academic Libraries

This volume is organized thematically into four parts, intended to present the reader with issues as lived by librarians. Part I, Foundations of Internet Expertise in the Academic Library, focuses on the adult learner, for whom all is planned, independent of any technology. Part II, Enlarging the Internet Literate: Early Training and Learning Experiences, documents the program planning in academic libraries in the early 1990s. Part III, The Present Tense: The Diffusion of the Internet into the Work Flow of Academic Librarians, examines research and reflections on the influx of new work patterns, tasks and positions due to Internet impact. Part IV, Preparing Librarians to Teach the Internet, documents instructional expertise for Internet education through reflections and resources. Research includes both quantitative and qualitative analyses; reflections are narrative essays rooted in the meanings of learning and teaching the Internet for each librarian.

Diffusion of Internet in Academic Libraries

The experience of disequilibrium seen in conferences replete with sessions such as "Leading and Engineering the Future," "Changing Roles," or "Putting the Pieces Back Together" illustrates the flurry of concern generated by the presence of the Internet (http://www.ala.org/events/dc98/programs/satpm.html). No longer is a librarian necessarily depended on to know a precise answer when asked. Gumpert, in his 1987 chapter "The Last Person to Know Everything," provokes discomfort in the very thought of current aspirations to be such a person, and perhaps lessens the pressure felt by some librarians to "know it all." Instead, as many reflect, librarians are scurrying to keep in touch with light-speed knowledge expansion. Many will argue that what is available is hardly "knowledge," some will advocate the instructional novelties possible, but all will admit that the Internet has radically changed the way they work and teach in the library.

The central invention that spurred rapid Internet dispersal was the personal computer. Donald A. Norman gives us the good news and the bad news about the development of technology due to the computer.

> The good news is that technology can make us smart, in fact, it already has. The human mind is limited in capability. There is only so much that we can remember, only so much we can learn. But among our abilities is that of devising artificial devices—artifacts—that expand our capabilities. We invent things that make us smart. Through technology, we can think better and more clearly. We have access to accurate information. We can work effectively with others, whether together in the same place or separated in space or time. Three cheers for the invention of writing, reading, art, and music. Three cheers for the development of logic, the invention of encyclopedias and textbooks. Three cheers for science and engineering. Maybe. The bad news is that technology can make us stupid. The technology for creating things has far outstripped our understanding of them. Things that can make us smart can also make us dumb. They can entrap us with their seductive powers—as with commercial television—or frustrate us through their artificial complexity (1993, 3).

Diffusion of Innovation Theory

Librarianship is not the only occupational field that has experienced essential redefinition of functions by technology. The effect of convergence of technologies, as seen by Ithial de Sola Pool (1990), presented turmoil in all sectors of our society. Educators, communicators, and all merchants are irreversibly affected by technology-driven methodologies in accomplishing basic tasks. The Internet has changed the speed of information access, the purchasing patterns of commerce, the rate of news dissemination, and the possible audiences for cultural events.

Rogers (1995) developed a theoretical orientation to explain innovation and its incorporation into society. The differing stages of incorporation of innovation are explained by personality factors in acceptance of novelty. Initially, Rogers saw those who would be the first to try and use innovation of any kind as pioneers and risk-takers, willing to explore what is new. Rona L. Ostrow and Debra Randorf's article expresses Rogers's theorized diffusion process in marketing terms, explaining the customer's buying patterns as similar to the spread of "buying" the Internet.

Diffusion Theory Applied to Internet Infusion into Academic Libraries

Institutional Adaptation of Internet

Each institution has a unique learning history, seen in its organizational structure and the transmission of information throughout the structure (Senge 1990). At this point in time, most academic library systems and all librarians are conversant with the Internet (LARC Fact Sheet No. 26: http://www.ala.org/library/fact26.html). The American Library Association reports that, in academic libraries, users have access to the Internet from terminals in 93 percent of doctorate-granting institutions, 82 percent of master's degree–granting institutions, 76 percent of baccalaureate degree–granting colleges, and 61 percent of Associate degree–granting institutions. There are institutions where the Internet is not available.

Academic institutions do reflect society's uneven acceptance with respect to Internet diffusion, as seen in individual observations. The reflection by Eleanor R. Kulleseid describes the beginning social structures affecting the diffusion of Internet training in the metropolitan New York agency (METRO). The organizational evolution of training at METRO is a sample of similar Internet training provisions seen outside librarianship.

Librarians' Introduction of Internet to the Institution
First Stage: Innovators

Factors leading toward Internet adaptation, connected to institutional involvement, bring into focus a larger picture, a context for the librarian's involvement. Rogers's theory was used to examine library change by Koval-Jeboe (1996). She captures some of the "early explorer" characteristics in library managerial options. Except for the earliest innovators, it is likely that the individual librarian developed within the library environment. Initiators, who had learned the Internet largely on their own, knew that they were exploring conceptual territory with no clear boundaries. Catherine M. Thomas observed, with respect to Columbia University Libraries, Internet Training Program, "We realized we were doing something no one had done before."

Second Stage: Early Adopters, Early Majority

The followers of the first wave of exploration, similar to the settlers who followed the pioneers, staked out early instructional programs. However, the diffusion was considered tumultuous, as described by Dervin (1996), emphasizing the difficulty of integrating the Internet into academic work (http://edfu.lis.uiuc.edu/allerton/96/wl/Dervin96c.html). The confusion of early adaptation is reflected across libraries in the narratives in this volume. The Internet Training Program study (Libutti) documents the reliance on known teaching behavioral patterns coupled with the questioning of their effectiveness by the teachers and students themselves.

The report on the 1994 Internet Training Program at Columbia University Libraries focuses on specific behavioral patterns that emerged from observations that appear important for demonstrations in classrooms and accompanying comprehension. Rogers (1995) includes characteristics of early learners as people who were not incorporated into institutional values through recognition. This characteristic does not describe many of the contributors to this book, perhaps due to the different settings of the theoretical development and the library learning. It is plausible that an institution that has an entrenched value system would not welcome new technology for some time, no matter how it was presented by an early learner, as Charlotte D. Moslander relates in her chronological reflection.

Some libraries supported training librarians as the beginning step (Thomas, Caldano), others began by initiating relationships with the faculty (Carroll-Matthes), and still others made liaisons with the academic computing center. The variety of institutional liaisons can be inferred from Moslander, Johnsen-Seeberger, Magier, and Ostrow and Randorf. In some institutions, the sole enthusiastic librarian faced indifference in the library (Moslander). Others, coming into the library, found the Internet technology in place and needed to adapt to decisions made prior to their employment in the library (Harris, Franz). New librarians (Anderson) found ways to use the technology that surprised them and overcame their resistance to the learning curve. Caldano, Magier, and Thomas's descriptions of the Internet Training Program depict the evolution of such different methodologies.

The transition state from traditional lecture and presentation modes of instruction to participatory learning is seen in many chapters. Carroll-Matthes's model of collaborative teaching is one example of a program approach that is effective and will coexist with other approaches as they are discovered and documented.

Third Stage: Late Majority, Laggards, and Nonadapters.

The final stage of diffusion of an innovation occurs when the innovation is commonplace, a "taken-for-granted" part of the society's operations. In academic libraries, it is likely that Internet presence is taken for granted. Thomas observed that "It is clear that using the Internet is a way of life." The proliferation of many Internet education models that are available on the Internet itself, as seen in Libutti's listing of resources for Internet instructional expertise, indicates that librarians are using the Internet and trying new methods to teach it.

It cannot be inferred that Internet is totally diffused throughout academic libraries. It is likely that much more exploration of effective teaching, effective integration of the Internet in course work, and development of resources of high quality will be needed for final adaptation of the Internet in academic libraries. Comparisons of technological evolutions that have affected educational institutions as significantly as the Internet appears to be doing are seen in the literature of educational technology history. Television, computers, and the telephone have resulted in significant work change and similar diffusion stages (de Sola Pool 1990; Saettler 1990; Kozma 1991).

Authors in this volume experienced the pervasiveness of myths about the Internet's power that is similar to the beginning stages of television diffusion. Everyone Knows How to Use the Net is one belief that can be rejected by the sheer amount of support requests made by library users. David J. Franz's reflection provides examples of this thinking in current library use, in which attitudes have causes not explained by age or experience.

Librarians as Learners of the Internet

Thinking about what exactly is learned and what processes are involved in learning the Internet is relatively new. The Internet is a synthesis of all antecedent technologies and involves new skills, such as decoding electronic text (Costanzo 1989). These new skills may be an extension of critical thinking, reading, and language literacy applied in an electronic environment. Exploration is the stage for learning theorists at this point in the evolution of new ways of learning and knowing. Although librarians who prepared reflections for this volume did not refer to explicit theory in their reconstruction of Internet learning and teaching, decisions on the basis of their choices reveal implicit hypotheses about learning processes. Several perspectives will be reviewed briefly, because they are relevant to Internet education in higher education.

Adult Learning: Construction of Knowledge

The most relevant current theory applicable to Internet education is dialectical constructivism" (Brandt 1997; Harapnuik 1999). Simply put, dialectical constructivism occurs when a learner constructs knowledge from the environment or conditions, and this knowledge is then modified by continuous interaction with new information. The concepts explored by both Brandt and Harapnuik are not new; in fact, they appear to be a rearticulation of the basic tenets of John Dewey (1933) applied to Internet teaching and learning.

In each of the reflections in this volume, the librarian provides a portrait of learning as needed, of exploring a wide availability of opportunities, and of using hands-on experimentation to learn about the Internet. The chronology of each reflection appears to follow a similar pattern of involvement, as one would expect from activity emanating from curiosity, puzzlement, and interest. Piaget's (1985) concept of disequilibrium and the need to regain equilibrium through construction of new knowledge structures seems to be rearticulated in the constructivists' approach. The teacher and the learner are confronted with situations demanding a new mental structure to proceed further with learning. Each learner is stopped until specific tasks are mastered, then an inquiry may proceed. This observation is seen in Thomas's reflection, in which she notes the necessity of sequence in learning the Internet, which is then built into the Internet training program through suggested modules.

It is assumed that children and adults learn in different ways and for different purposes, and employ different methodologies, due to chronological development and its consequences. Some of these assumptions are open to question, as seen in the proliferation of resource-based or active learning experiences in the K–12 environment. It is possible that the Internet may provide for similar active learning for both children and adults, as seen in the Web-based tools prepared by children and adults. Two organizations demonstrate the range of possibilities for instructional resources with Internet. ThinkQuest (http://www.thinkquest.org), an organization sponsoring Web learning applications prepared by children aged 12–18, illustrates the possible shift in relationships between teachers and students through the products prepared in collaborative teams. Libraries for the Future (http://www.lff.org), a grassroots public library advocacy organization, has numerous projects in which the teacher of the information varies from librarian to community leader to children with the technological savvy to prepare Web-based databases.

It is obvious that despite the capability of children, the choice of learning content is guided by those who have prepared curricula and selected significant experiences for the students to progress through for mastery. Some of this methodology is just as appropriate for adults learning the Internet. However, the factor of choice of learning methods and content is resolved differently for adults who are in a job. Because advances in androgogy (Caffarella 1994) include the expansion of the capacity (and the necessity) of learning well beyond the traditional early adult years, adult learners are responsible for many such choices during their careers.

Teaching methods best suited for adult learning styles include learner control (Cross, 1991). The Internet is a vehicle for self-directed learning and due to the features of asynchronous, location-independent opportunities would seem to fulfill the qualities needed for adult learners, librarians in particular. One has to reflect that each reference interview produced the same result, as seen in the oldest pedagogical relationship—that of tutor and student. Internet technology adds the dimension of the self as intermediary, which is true of anyone in a library browsing the stacks.

Situational Factors Affecting Construction of Knowledge Using the Internet

Jana Varlejs categorized kinds of self-directed learning (SDL) likely to occur for librarians and identified several triggers that initiated such learning. These included the presence of new technology, new training, and department changes in position, interest in topics, and needs for technology awareness and use. Part of the support in workplace learning comes from opportunity variables for development. These opportunity variables include such factors as higher levels of institutional support as seen in e-mail provision, availability of library and information science literature, and released time for research and courses. Workplace learning encompasses formal continuing education activities (courses, seminars, and workshops), yet librarians spend more time in informal training than in formal training. Paradoxically, Varlejs found that released time and financial assistance do not affect librarian's participation in self-directed learning. Her findings on academic librarians as self-directed learners need to be seen in juxtaposition with a collection of resources for professional development offered over the Internet, as reported by Libutti.

The Attitude of the Librarian Toward Adult Learners

Carr's essay on "the situation of the adult learner in the library" highlights the early adult educator's learning theories with close observations of the specifics of adult learning within the context of the library. Being aware of "the questions of the learner," noting the qualities of the "learners who touch us," and reflecting on "pursuit skills" are basic to developing a relationship with learners who use the Internet as their medium of query. The context in each library needs the closer examination suggested by these viewpoints.

Has the reference function shifted toward accommodating increased instructional demands for Internet access? Is such a shift worth the expense, energy, and time? Does the following of "customer demand" mean leaving behind the librarian's capacity as learning leader?

These and other issues seen in narratives in this volume leave little doubt as to the conceptual (as well as resource allocation) conflicts often coexisting with enthusiastic diffusion through library outreach and programming of Internet instruction.

The Levels of Knowledge the Librarian and the Student Bring to the Learning Situation

Perhaps most pragmatic and true for a librarian is Carrroll-Mathes's observation: "In order to teach Internet, the librarian has to learn it." This statement, echoed across other reflections in this book, brings to light the fact that there is a leveling factor in the possession of knowledge. Teacher and student may have much to offer each other.

The ways learning occurring in the early 1990s included workshops, "surfing the Net," trial and error, and self-taught strategies (Ostrow and Randorf). Librarians used vivid descriptors to express the struggle with both learning and teaching. Terms such as "groping," "hack" (at the technology), and "scramble" were seen in various articles and provide a picture of rocky beginnings to learning the Internet.

The Rapidity of Access to Information and the Nature of Understanding

The crucial difference in Internet diffusion as it affects learning may be in the kinds of resources one can obtain and at what rate one can obtain them. What is equally true, and not often examined, as expressed by Norman (1993), is the rate at which a learner can assimilate new information, see connections, and make valid inferences. The Internet may have sped access and connections, but the learner has yet to make such an evolutionary comprehension leap. The "on-the-horizon" possibility of such rapidity of learning is enticing. Yet, an observer of learning has to examine what is curtailed with rapidity of information as it becomes more sophisticated. Authors in this volume express these concerns, usually at the end of their chronological account of their development, which may take the form of questioning the cognitive costs of the changes experienced.

Differing Perceptions of the Teacher in Internet Education

With Web-based learning in place in most institutions, the changes in structure, expectations, and possibilities will change the very nature of "teacher" (Brandt 1997; Galbraith 1991). Technology use makes different instructional relationships with learners possible, such as mentor, colearner, coteacher, facilitator, collaborator, and team member (Kozma 1991). Are these relationships taken seriously by users of the library and the academic community? Do teaching faculty also change their traditional podium style for technology-enabled roles? Librarians in individual institutions are likely to have different answers to these questions, as seen in different reflections.

Different methods to effect such role changes have evolved in different locations, if role changes are part of the institution's value system. Carroll-Mathes, Moslander, Magier, and Thomas illustrate differences in the perceived role of "teacher of Internet" in an institution, including seeing learners as potential teachers.

Teaching the Internet
Early Calls for Increased Instruction on the Internet
The alarm about the coming flood of instructional demand for the field was sounded often and loudly in the early 1990s. Who is responsible for teaching the Internet on a campus to both librarians and end users? In the early 1990s, there were divided responses from librarians about this task: the library, the academic computing center, and teaching faculty have all been seen as capable, and perhaps responsible, for providing training (Ostrow and Randorf). Different institutions began at differing training origins: some began with the people who would be involved in distinct roles (librarian–faculty collaboration of Carroll-Mathes). Other institutions were director initiated in implementation. In other libraries, new administrative configurations, such as uniting libraries and academic computing centers, proved to be important to the ensuing partnerships for Internet training.

In 1998, Marilyn Rosenthal and Marsha Spiegelman documented the need for restructuring continuing education for librarians. The increasing need for Internet and technology instruction demonstrated in their study warrants a redesign of post-MLS education that would provide for on-the -job needs of instructional librarians.

Emergence of Training Formats: Train the Trainer
Columbia, Ulster, and METRO are examples of training programs that aimed at enabling others to pass along the expertise. Parts of presentations learned were to be used in librarians' information literacy instruction sessions in their institutions. The formats that evolved from initial presentations took different shapes: workshops, seminars, pro-

grams, consultations on a one-to-one basis, and e-mail instruction evolved, among other hybrid delivery modes. Early models were nonexistent, except for former instructional practice, seen in Libutti's observation of the 1994 Internet Training Program at Columbia University Libraries.

The unifying capacity of the Web provided many instructional options not available before. However, one still had to learn how to use e-mail before doing a file transfer protocol. Interestingly, the Web was not part of the first ITP syllabus. Libutti, noting that resource materials to increase instructional expertise abound, examined models at many institutions where there was an absence of such merely five years ago (Grassian, 1991).

Content and Process in Internet Training

Teachers and students see the same phenomena. Yet, in the specific instance of Internet education, teacher and student were often the same person. The librarians who initiated their their "learning the Net" were candid about their points of beginning. Moslander expressed her beginning point: "I had to learn what .com, .org, .edu, and their kin meant." She also found that she had to learn citation style for Internet sources. Magier documented the progressive development of content differentiation from beginning with basics to including HTML as part of training options. His reflection includes current topics, gathered from training experience with more than 3,000 librarians.

Other practitioners began at different points in their approach to content and subsequent determination of what others needed to know. The field is far from being able to determine a universal Internet education standard, despite many attempts to do so. This is in evidence in the visibility of evolving curricula on the Internet. Using the transitory nature of the Internet can accommodate decision revisions. The curriculum outlines in this volume also demonstrate the rapidity of thought about instructional priorities. The changes seen in these curricula reflect concentration on the ever-changing Internet combined with the stable elements needed for successful use of the medium.

Assessment of outcomes

The evaluation of quality of content, design of Web pages, and effectiveness of communication of educational information are often the substance of Web pages and journal articles. Kulleseid calls for objective, rather than self-reported, assessment of student learning. Tools for such assessment are in constant development at several levels of education, most prominently at the K–12 level. The evolution of the Internet will pose problems for those using such objective measures for learning. The Internet may not be stable enough to provide time for prolonged development of measures. This remains a challenge for educators, as well as an opportunity to change one's mind about learning outcome information validity.

Factors Involved in Successful Internet Training

Franz has an immediate priority in relating to learners' needs: "The biggest challenge I face every day is making people feel comfortable with computers. PERIOD." The factors cited in a recent article on Internet instruction (Withers & Sharpe 1999) included limitations on content, topics, and processes in single classes. Other factors were noted in many of the contributions in this volume and presented as tips learned from experience (Thomas, Magier, and Johnsen-Seeberger). Teaching over the Internet itself has increased exponentially, as seen in the collated resources by Lopatin, Libutti, Hagenbruch, and Poznansky.

Continuing Issues for Librarians and Internet: An Uneasy Co-Existence or A Liberating Opportunity?

The Internet is still far from an entrenched component of the library. Many of the contributors have issues that are important to explore as the organization develops the technology to serve learners. Roger T. Harris questions: "Is what was appropriate last year (or last month) still appropriate today? Are users fully conscious of their shift away from traditional sources of information, or have they simply been conditioned: it will all be on the Internet." Kulleseid raises the crucial issue of allocation of resources: "How much training is needed and for how long?" Magier ponders the changing role of the library. Harris wonders if the evolving role of the librarian will be that of navigator. He also raised the issue of self-assessment: "to question ourselves habitually about this degree of confidence we have in all available resources."

However, the library is unlikely to be able to contain so powerful a phenomenon as the Internet. The entire academic institution is compelled to forge collaborative relationships with "significant others" in industry, government, communities, and the public sector for "best practices." All interested in using the Internet need to maintain a concentrated focus on the forceful impact of the Internet on our learning.

These developments are visible in citizen movements in the proliferation of community networks. Information is organized according to the needs of the particular constituency, sometimes with the help of librarians, often as citizens took the existing technology and developed their information locally (e.g., Libraries for the Future).

Such perspectives are likely to be relevant to the evolving teaching library, in which consideration of community is crucial. However, as Senge (1990) and others have noted often, changing one aspect of a learning environment necessitates reevaluating other aspects of the same environment. The Library as a Learning Institution is posed as the logical evolution with Internet-changed relationships, positions, and possibilities. It sounds likely. It leads to inspiring rhetoric. It may develop in diverse manners depending on the institution and the constituency.

This volume is itself a focus on the daily impact of Internet seen over a course of time. The ACRL/NY publication project provides much to be learned from what each contributor has documented on the accomplishment of ordinary tasks in extraordinary ways. The resulting Internet education scenarios in academic libraries can provide a depth to the perspectives we each bring to our teachable —and learnable— moments in the library.

References

American Library Association. LARC Fact Sheet No. 26. Available at: http://www.ala.org/library/fact26.html.

Brandt, D. S. 1997. "Constructivism: Teaching for understanding of the Internet." *Communications of the ACM* 40(10): 112–17.

Caffarella, R. S. 1994. *Planning programs for adult learners: A practical guide for educators, trainers, and staff developers.* San Francisco: Jossey-Bass.

Costanzo, W. V. 1989. "Reading the electronic text." In W. V. Costanzo, ed., *The electronic text: Learning to read, write, and reason with computers.* Englewood Cliffs, N.J.: Educational Technology Publications.

Cross, K. P. 1991. *Adults as learners.* San Francisco: Jossey-Bass.

Dervin, B. 1996. "Given a context by any other name: Methodological tools for taming the unruly beast." Paper presented at ISIC '96: Information Seeking in Context. Conference on Research in Information Needs, Seeking, and Use in Different Contexts. Available at: http://edfu.lis.uiuc.edu/allerton/96/wl/Dervin96c.html.

Dewey, J. 1933. *How we think.* Lexington, Mass.: D. C. Heath.

Galbraith, M. W. 1991. "The adult learning transactional process." In M. W. Galbraith, ed., *Facilitating adult learning: A transactional process.* Malibar, Fla.: Krieger Publishing.

Grassian, E. 1999. February 1999 Internet resources: Information literacy. *College & Research Libraries News* 60(2): 78–81. Available online at: http://www.ala.org/acrl/resfeb99.html.

Gumpert Harapnuik, D. 1999. "Inquisitivism or the 'HHHMMM??? What does this button do?' Approach to Adult Education." [Article in syllabus, University of Alberta, Can]. Available at: http://dte6.educ.ualberta.ca/tech_ed/.

Koval-Jarboe, P. 1996. "Quality improvement: A strategy for planned change." *Library Trends* 44(3): 605–30.

Kozma, R. B. 1991. "Learning with media." *Review of Educational Research*, 61(2): 179–211.

Norman, D. A. 1993. *Things that make us smart: Defending human attributes in the age of the machine.* Reading, Mass.: Addison-Wesley.

Piaget, J. 1985. *The equilibration of cognitive structures: The central problem of intellectual development*, trans T. Brown and K. J. Thampy. Chicago: University of Chicago Pr.

Pool, I. 1990. *Technologies without boundaries: On telecommunications in a global age.* Cambridge, Mass.: Harvard Univ. Pr.

Rogers, E. M. 1995. *Diffusion of innovations*, 4th ed. New York: Free Press/Simon & Schuster.

Saettler, L. P. 1990. *The evolution of American educational technology.* Englewood, Colo.: Libraries Unlimited.

Schon, D. A. 1983. *The reflective practitioner: How professionals think in action.* New York: Basic Bks.

Senge, P. M. 1990. *The fifth discipline: The art and practice of the learning organization.* New York: Doubleday/Currency.

The WELL. [Online bulletin board]. Available at: http://www.well.com.

Withers, R., and J. F. Sharpe. 1999. "Incorporating Internet resources into bibliographic instruction." *College & Research Libraries News* 60 (2): 75–76.

The Situation of the Adult Learner in the Library

David W. Carr

My true work over the last several years has been to think about adult learners in libraries and museums. I think about the institutions themselves, what they contain, and what they mean to the culture that sustains them. But most important, I think about the moments that adults invest in them; I anticipate the objects they use, the thinking they do, the ways they might change as a result of these moments, how they might be different—more reflective as thinkers, more informed as communicators, more powerful as actors—when they leave. I also think about the qualities of those invested moments and how well they invite the adult learner to continue to learn when the moment passes, to return with new interests and new expectations, and to come to understand the library, the librarian and the learner as an alliance for learning that is defined by the situation, intellect, and desire of the learners; the extent of the information given; and the attention of the librarian.

In all of these reflections, the learner in my mind is like me, since the projections of thinking and experience I describe in my notebooks all begin in my head. I have constructed a learner in my own image, and I think about that learner a great deal of the time. This may be both a

When this presentation was first made at LOEX in 1988, its author was a member of the faculty at the School of Information and Library Studies at Rutgers University. The author is now a member of the faculty at the School of Information and Library Science, University of North Carolina–Chapel Hill. Permission for this reprint was obtained from both the author and the publisher.

strength and an error, but I think that everyone who examines questions of thought and learning—and everyone who practices in institutions devoted to them—designs that practice for the learner inside the head. Of course we modify that practice for the actual learners inside our institutions, seeing them as they stand before us, hearing them as they articulate their questions, and working exactly for them as we attempt to fit information to inquiry. But much of what we know about practice we learn from ourselves as learners and the virtual worlds we create.

Who is the adult learner in my mind? What is the design of the world that learner occupies? What is the need the learner brings to the library? What do they mean—both the need, and that it has been brought here? How does the world of the learner (private, personal, informed by invisible sources) enter the life of the institution (public, general, structured by ageless, infinite systems of knowledge)? How does the learner confirm and act on an inquiry? What does this mean to one life? What does this learner, this needful adult, mean to us as agents, actors, and witnesses, touched as we are by that one life?

The Learner Who Touches Us

When we work for adult learners, we are participants in learning that is not casual; it is learning that comes from or anticipates an event or situation of continuous importance in the life of the adult before us: for example, adjustment, preparation, fulfillment. It is learning that is undertaken cautiously; its commitments may be fragile at first. But it is rooted in one life and its situation. We are dealing with human beings who are embedded, engaged, entwined in situations. As the early theorist of adult learning Eduard Lindeman wrote in 1926, the situation, not the subject matter, is what we most need to understand.

> Life is confronted in the form of situations, occasions which necessitate action. Education is a method for giving situations a setting, for analyzing complex wholes into manageable, understandable parts, and a method which points out the path of action which, if followed, will bring the circumstance within the area of experiment (179–80).

> Situations arise when our aims or purposes are impeded, when our wishes fall beneath our present capacities (181).

At the end of an article published in *Library Trends* (Carr 1983), I once alluded to Grace Clements, my favorite among the voices captured by Studs Terkel in *Working* (1974, 384–89), and the multiple informing contexts of her life, each capable of supporting an inquiry of depth and meaning. It is useful to imagine the multiple dimensions in such lives—especially those spent in numbing work on luggage factory assembly lines, as Grace Clements's is. Our need is to understand the latent strands of information need in every situation, in every life. The learner in my mind has picked up and is spooling one of those strands.

In a summary of research on information seeking and use, Brenda Dervin lists the following major conclusions:

> • information cannot be treated like a brick being thrown from system to user but like clay the user can use for constructing his or her own sense;
> • the questions people have about the situations they are in constitute their information needs; information needs are always personalized, as there is no other way for them to be;
> • information seeking and use can be predicted more powerfully by knowing the kind of situations users are in rather than knowing their personality or demographic attributes;
> • people seek information when their life situations are such that their old sense has run out;
> • people are in charge of how they use the information they attend to (1983, 173).

I am most drawn to the third and the fifth of these: that "information needs are always personalized, as there is no other way for them to be" and that "people seek information when their life situations are such that their old sense has run out." These are important to me for the implications they hold for how we see the learner: as an individual actor in need of a new sense of things, and able to recognize that moment of need. The adult learner I envision is a competent, authoritative, but probably tacit theorist and decision-maker about self and knowledge. Understanding that a need exists in a personal situation, the learner moves ahead to face it, willing to make commitments and changes in order to respond.

These commitments are not trivial, but they may begin with common statements: Isn't this interesting? How does this happen? I must know more about this. Or an open-ended sentence beginning with the words: I need . . . . These are commitments in the sense that they use language in open, direct ways to create an agenda and identify an initial focus. Every good question does this. If librarianship were to be redesigned—away from tools and technologies to human information needs—the question in the situation ought to stand at the center of its concerns, since everything we do bears in mind the questioner and the questions that lead to learning.

Questions

In a taxonomy of twelve semantic categories Arthur Graesser et al. have demonstrated the generic questions at the heart of inquiry. Some seek verification (Is X true or false?); some seek concept completion (Who? What? When? Where?); some seek causality (What caused some event to occur?); some seek enablement (What is needed for an agent to do some action?); and some seek judgement (What should an agent do?) (Graesser, Lang, and Horgan 1988, 7). To these we may add critical—but probably unspoken—questions about specific behaviors and processes in libraries: What kind of information is here? How can I select from this array? What must I do to learn here? What is expected of me?

The learner I envision is the principal actor in one life given meaning by questions. Some of these are experiential, growing out of the everyday. Some are contextual, informed by values, styles of work, and striving. These questions draw on the repertoire of events and meanings, and the history one bears as a learner. They grow out of the desire to make one varied life coherent. The situation of the adult learner in the library is characterized by the expectation of making a difference by using information, and by the intention to make that life better.

This learner also is both a participant and author in multiple social realities, each with its own definitions, relationships, and engagements. In each of them we construct meanings, conduct dialogues, adjust toward stable partnerships In these settings we strive *for* and *among* others, and we risk ourselves. As our risks and strivings increase, our situations and so our questions—become more complex. Lindeman asks:

In what areas do most people appear to find life's meaning? We have only one pragmatic guide: meaning must reside in the things for which people strive, the goals which they set for themselves', their wants, needs, desires and wishes (1926, 13).

As I think librarians will quickly confirm, even lives of routine can have texture and passion. In little boats, we feel the currents and respond. In this situation, only actions matter; as Lindeman writes: "We do not 'think through' problems; we act through" (1926, 192). The learners who touch us are likely to be learners like us. We are all in situations and contexts where our plans are always incomplete, where our theory is always tempered by immediacy, where our ideals are tempered by limits and we have no other ways to find meaning except to work and think and ask questions that mean something to us.

Images of Mind in the Library

In these situations the acts that matter most are invisible. They are intellectual acts of grasping that reflect the dimensions of thinking and problem solving described as cognitive style. Alan Knox (1977) lists nine of these dimensions, and their pertinence to educative acts in the library is striking. Librarians will recognize them instantly, perhaps in themselves. They will recognize the tensions created by having to tolerate incongruous information and the challenge of sustaining its ambiguity. They will understand how the desire to reflect is overwhelmed at times by the rush toward closure. And who of us in the library is not susceptible to distractions, the battle between constricted versus flexible control over our attention? We will see in this cognitive mirror images of our focussing or scanning intelligences, our roving or poring attentions, our sharpnesses and, as we age, our blurs.

Another dimension of style has to do with dealing with difficult ideas: a dimension of complexity and simplicity—not a linear concept at all. How well do we use categories, themes, classes, or functions to organize and differentiate our perceptions? How well do we see the forest, how well do we see the trees? How broadly do we think, how narrowly do we exclude some thinking? (Knox 1977, 447–48)? I think of thinking in the library as the challenge of carrying out cognitive acts in a linear field. That is, in libraries there are no lines to guide us, no patterns or routines that will tell us our journey; and at any moment our inquiry may burst with unexpected implications.

Were we to create a cognitive landscape for the independent learner, what would it look like? It would be a map more than a landscape, of a mazelike problem that is sometimes a narrow channel, and sometimes opens to a broad space. It would be configured as well by sideways passages connected naturally to equally mazelike and limitless other problems.

In this landscape the learner would be shown in motion: examining and interpreting information through a personal lens, or a private exploratory system; devising and revising telling images as new information appears; breaking through, overcoming obstacles to new information; finding an almost aesthetic appreciation for the rich net of connections; marking the meanings and uses of mistakes; experiencing dullness and confusion; staring in boredom; quitting for awhile; perhaps reorganizing the whole field into new patterns as an effect of one moment's insight.

My thinking about learning in libraries has been influenced by three formative models of mentality: learning in the proximal zone as described by Lev Vygotsky; the personal construct theory of George Kelly; and the work of Jerome Bruner, especially his concept of going beyond the information given.

Vvgotsky, the Soviet psychologist—whose brief life (1896–1934) has caused him to be called the "Mozart of psychology" by Stephen Toulmin—defined an area he described as the "zone of proximal development":

> The distance between the actual developmental level as determined by independent problem solving and the level of potential development as determined through problem solving . . . in collaboration with more capable peers (Vygotsky 1978, 86).

Vygotsky applied this to the relation between the child and the teacher, describing "those functions that have not yet matured but are in the process of maturation . . . the 'buds' or 'flowers' of development" (86) rather than the completed products or fully developed skills, those functions helped to fruition by the "more capable peer" or an adult agent. If we apply this concept to the relation between the librarian and the learner, the zone of proximal development is the distance between the learner's independent ability to pursue an inquiry and the quality of the inquiry with assistance. Whenever we work with a learner in the library, it seems to me, we are working in Vygotsky's zone of proximal development.

The second formative model is the psychology of personal constructs, a theory developed by George A. Kelly and now being tested and developed in library settings by my colleague Carol Kulthau. A personal construct is an individually developed set of anticipatory ideas about a situation, the ways we have of interpreting, predicting, and organizing events in order to give them meaning and call them experience. "It is not what happens around him that makes a man experienced; it is the successive construing and reconstruing of what happens, as it happens that enriches the experience of his life" (Kelly 1963, 73). Constructs are the channels in which one's mental processes run. They are two-way streets along which one may travel to reach conclusions. They make it possible to anticipate the changing tides of events. Constructs are the controls that one places on life—the life within him as well as the life that is external to him. Forming constructs may be:

> considered as binding sets of events into convenient bundles which are handy for the person who has to lug them. Events, when so bound, tend to become predictable, manageable, and controlled (Kelly 1963, 126).

Library searching and thinking are processes of construction—sequences of observation and reflection, decision and confusion, suggesting and testing, supposing and confirming. When librarians encounter learners, they are witnesses to the evolution of constructs grounded in experience within a knowledge system.

The third model for minds in libraries is suggested by Jerome Bruner in two ways. The first of these is his important statement that "one constantly goes beyond the information given" (1973, 218) in order to carry out mental life. We assemble information, codify, recombine, and interpret it; we develop it and apply it in new circumstances; and we construct it to make and possess new knowledge. The real intention of a librarian's informing acts is to assist the learner not just *to* information, but to assist the learner to go beyond the information as it has been discovered, and to make it endure in new and original meanings.

The second perspective I draw from Bruner is found in *Actual Minds, Possible Worlds*.

> A culture is constantly in process of being recreated as it is interpreted and renegotiated by its members. In this view a culture is as much a *forum* for negotiating and renegotiating meaning and for explicating action as it is a set of rules or specifications for action. Indeed, every culture maintains specialized institutions or occasions for intensifying this 'forum-like' feature. Storytelling, theater, science, even jurisprudence are all techniques for intensifying this function—ways of exploring possible worlds out of the context of immediate need . . . . It is the forum aspect of a culture that gives its participants a role in constantly making and remaking the culture—an active role as participants rather then as performing spectators (1986, 123).

Bruner suggests that culture is an "ambiguous text that is constantly in need of interpretation by those who participate in it" (122). To me, the library is one of the forums Bruner mentions, and the agency of the librarian is, in part, to help the learner to interpret the ambiguous texts of our culture—the "ways of exploring possible worlds out of the context of immediate need."

The request for assistance implicates librarians deeply in the processes and activities of the learner's mind, and the meanings of asking for help emerge from these three images of mentality. The librarian is a proximal other who can expand the behaviors of the inexperienced learner. The librarian is a participant in the development of mature constructs. And the librarian is an agent in the interpretation and negotiation of cultural meanings.

The most important kinds of help address the situation of the learner by assisting in the articulation of meanings at three levels.

First, the librarian assists the learner to articulate the need for information at the personal level: by asking questions, by developing contexts, by fitting search processes to cognitive styles, and by helping to anticipate outcomes.

Second, assistance articulates an inquiry process, a way of going about, pursuing, making, and evaluating order. This process includes incidents and encounters that move the learner toward insight, change, and closure. This is an epistemic—that is, knowledge-generating—and a heuristic—that is, problem-solving—process,

Third, assistance helps to articulate the library as a forum for the construction of meanings, as a system of knowledge structures, assembled for the processes of discovery, integration, and construction that we call learning.

These are collaborative achievements and they are largely processes of language, intimately involving librarians as mentors and models. When they are effective, they confer power and control over a complex environment. These engagements also may engender competence because they display the librarian's range of expert thoughts and behaviors in the presence of information. They allow the learner to see and interpret the librarian's skills of analysis and action as possible, adaptable behaviors in an individual process of intellectual becoming. In this way, the librarian may be the critical source of the learner's image of the adult mind in the library.

Language Acts

The paperless society seems not to have taken hold in libraries very well, if the number of notebooks, notecards, or scrap paper citations is any evidence. And despite the dominant stereotype, I find libraries to be places where conversations occur constantly, often at the instigation of librarians. These papers and conversations testify to the language-based reality of library acts. In libraries, learners are always documenting: writing citations, taking notes, collecting data, making copies, gathering references, planning the gathering of more references, keeping track of their paths, organizing, systematizing, categorizing what they have uncovered, keeping it in order, organizing it for use, annotating it for reuse, and assembling pieces into wholes. In conversation, learners ask for directions and advice, explain their needs and intentions, define their tasks and expectations, compare discoveries and progress, clarify difficult ideas, collaborate, commiserate, and complain.

(Even the photocopy transfers ownership of information in a sort of mechanical language act: for one thin dime we can purchase, possess, incorporate, and store data in a life without the immediate exertion of intellect.)

Acts of language are complex engagements. They involve self-presentation, and this involves self-construction. They involve self-confidence, and that involves self-esteem. They often occur out of need, implying vulnerability and confusion. By their nature, language acts communicate about mastery and competence and so they reveal our accomplishments, and perhaps our limits. Every speech is in some way a self-portrait, and everything we write describes a fragment of our intellect. Every question tells part of our story—the narrative of growth we trail with us everywhere.

Acts of language have complex effects. They give a sense of location and intimacy, power and legitimacy. They inform others and ourselves of our purposes. They confirm the worth and substance of our inquiries. They expose infirm foundations or invite admiration for their coherence and authority. They are acts of construction and meaning. Assembled from fragments of an infinite language, coherent statements select images from a vast array. Elaborated in combinations and recombinations, language acts help us to go beyond the isolated word. Mindful of Bruner, we can see that language causes us to go beyond the information given, to interpret to draw inferences, to combine, to reflect from new perspectives, to innovate to make our lives more complex. Except for the mind of the librarian, language is the primary instrument of librarianship. As Bruner (1975, 76) writes, quoting Sapir's 1921 work, *Language*: "The instrument makes possible the product, the product refines the instrument" (81). In the library, acting with language implies the power to apprehend a concept in the abstract and so to have the power to do things, perform functions with it: to transform and combine it, and to juxtapose it to another concept for comparison. Our language here is not just useful for capturing or keeping dates; these are actions of thought we can do solely because we have language. Language is the instrument of intellectual exploration and the exploration of tools. Our techniques for using electronic databases and controlling thesauri that are grounded in our abilities to handle language as a structure of hierarchies (Bates 1979). Determining both broad relationship and specific relevance appear to be language acts of a sophisticated kind. Language documents the path and the circumlocutions of the searcher, separates the learner from randomness in order to attend to regularities and deviations in experience. Language is a kind of place-holder; it permits the learner to think, even momentarily, beyond experience, to move meanings and then to speculate about those meanings in other contexts.

A problem cannot be fully understood until it is fully described, nor can it be concluded until language is found to summarize the journey. My feeling is that librarians need to understand more about libraries as places for language and they need to attend especially to how they talk to learners. Every encounter, it seems to me, offers opportunities for sensitive language use, and the foundation of dialogue.

Some advice to librarians: learn how to discuss inquiries and their parts, since these compose the intellectual business of the library. Explore the situation of the learner, and how it leads to the topic of the inquiry. These *situations* have entered the library—not simply an assortment of human beings. Determine the learner's comfort with inquiry as well as the level of literacy needed to resolve the problem in hand. Use all of this information to describe experimental acts in the learner's construction of a search process. Be prepared for conversations that discuss how, in the process of inquiry, the learner's assumptions are challenged and situations are changed (Lindeman 1926, 193).

Language is useful to librarians for the same reasons it is useful to learners—librarians are adult learners too, and so language is an instrument of the librarian's thought as well. Buy a notebook, document what you do and think. Tape-record your observations and conversations. See how you use language to invite, encourage, adapt, comprehend, and generate independent heuristic acts—or not. Pay attention to paying attention. As the metaphor suggests, paying attention is a form of investment.

Heuristic Acts

I have for most of the last fifteen years been thinking in detail about a heuristic approach to library learning as problem-solving. This approach is embodied for me, in the following questions: For any given inquiry: What is the unknown and how can I recognize it? What is known now and how can I confirm it? What is possible to be known and how can I explore it? What might be known next and how can I decide? What steps must be taken toward resolving this? Through a heuristic of this kind, the construction of an inquiry evolves.

The word *heuristic* deserves some attention. The mathematician G. Polya in his book *How to Solve It* addresses the need for an understanding of the "mental operations typically useful" in solving problems. Polya writes

> Experience in solving problems and experience in watch-
> ing other people solving problems must be the basis on

which heuristics is built. In this study, we should not neglect any sort of problem, and should find out common
features in the way of handling all sorts of problems; we
should aim at general features, independent of the subject
matter of the problem. (1957, 130)

I am most interested in the heuristics of everyday life: how we
know what information we need when we need it; how, in Polya's
words, we look at the unknown; how, when we encounter the information we need, we know where and how it fits, never having seen it
before; how we in some sense might be said to own the information
we use, by the power of our investment in it, how our possession of
information is in some way a significant modification of it—assuming
that there is an impress of ourselves in the information we possess,
like a fingerprint in clay.

I am especially interested in questions with infinite futures, because I think that they are stable instruments in our lives—questions
like the one asked by a sixth-grade student of mine seventeen years
ago, How do poets think? I hope she is asking that question still, wherever she is, and answering it in a different way each time. These are
the questions that moment by moment help to lead us toward less
accidental lives. Although I doubt that we should ask for a show of
hands, I think that each adult has or should have such leading questions
embedded somewhere in mind. They are formative for us, even if
they are never articulated. Not incidentally, one of mine is, What is
useful behavior in the presence of an unknown?

The *ideal* setting for the understanding of this general heuristic in
the lives of adult learners is the library; the *ideal* experience for the
observation of others solving information problems is the experience
of the librarian. This is the only setting that assists individual learners
to create their own breakthroughs; this is the field where acts at the
edges of the intellect can best be witnessed. In assisting learners and
preparing them for their search, the most instructive question to ask
is, What is the unknown and how might I respond to it?

Pursuit Skills

In answer to my question about useful behavior in the presence of an
unknown, I have developed a little list of pursuit skills. These are the
applied aspects of inquiry especially necessary for going beyond the

abstract question at hand, for making sense of it and—to use an idea of Michael Polanyi (1958)—for dwelling within it. We dwell within our inquiries much as the informing knowledge and technical grace of the musician can be said to dwell only within her living performance. Pursuit skills guide the grasping intellect. They are the ways the mind progresses, uses experience to continue inquiry, and prepares the learner for things which have not happened yet. So here is my list of pursuit skills: useful behaviors in the presence of an unknown.

First, learners should be encouraged to spend time where information can be found, since that will increase the likelihood of finding some.

Second, I think it is useful to assist learners to mark off a problem, or a significant fragment of a problem, by using identifiable categories or segments that define boundaries. This should be written down. It takes time, but is an essential act because boundaries permit the search of a specific territory.

Third, the learner should draw a map for, design a path toward, or consider inquiry to be an adventure about, an unknown territory. Concentrate on the idea of exploration, expanding the boundaries of the problem, reaching beyond the conventional path. To expand a problem, rather than strive to resolve it, probably runs counter to every inquirer's instincts, but ultimately it is useful because it confers a sense of context.

Fourth, as the strands of information lead the learner on, connecting information known to information nearer to the unknown, the problem at hand should be set in a network of other problems as they are found. Draw this too. It will help to develop an awareness of the relationships between problems. It is even possible to trade up to a better problem.

Though it is difficult to teach or demonstrate this, I think it is especially useful, fifth, to know how to use accidents well: accidental discoveries, miserable discoveries, unplanned diversions. Serendipity is an operative principle in libraries, but it can occur only to people who are prepared and present for it. Accidents will happen, but some accidents are more just than others. A well-prepared learner deserves a good accident now and then. But when it occurs, the learner has to understand that it occurs because the learner has been in the right place for it to happen.

Sixth, it is always useful to have an understanding of patterns and their meanings: the recognition of names in association with topics, observations of borrowings from other disciplines and literatures, identification of new angles through informal citation analysis.

Seventh, it is useful to know how to reassemble information and reconfigure it in new contexts or reconstruct it in a new order and with new dimensions and weight. That is, to know how to possess information fully by immersing oneself in it—by becoming deeply informed, as though there were no other information. Learning can become a useful obsession.

Eighth, it is useful to know how and when to move on to a new question. Though we may not recognize it readily, closing down and moving on is an information skill.

And the ninth of these pursuit skills follows: It is useful to know that some questions do not end, but simply expand the unknown toward infinity, inviting one further. How *does* a poet think?

Even so, the tenth of these pursuit skills is vitally useful: how to pause, be cool, and wait for another question to come along.

Thinking of Polanyi and the concept of indwelling, it occurs to me that we do not often think of inquiry as a process of the senses, but a progress of the mind. I think that this is unfortunate. In a sense, remembering Brenda Dervin's summary, it is important to see that an inquiry is as individual an experience as the musician's performance or the brushstrokes of a painting. Researchers in my experience, especially new ones, have expressed a form of satisfaction that can best be described as aesthetic. The aesthetic senses in question must involve a perspective over the passage of time, the achievement of control and order, the satisfactions of sudden insight and discovery, the weight and reality of a product, and the way we are touched, and almost disappointed, when we feel closure at hand. I might summarize it this way: the more sensuous the progress of the inquiry—the more vivid and tactile one's grasp of it—the clearer the image of what is sought, and the richer one's arrival at it.

Library Wrestling

I think that our truly permanent questions possess us like wrestling opponents: every encounter is an attempt to gather useful information about our problem without making too large an impression on the mat. In every encounter we feel the power of our questions. We may know and love them intimately, but we have to watch for their strangleholds. And these impervious questions are like wrestling opponents in the sense that Roland Barthes uses to make this distinction: "A boxing match is a story which is constructed before the eyes of the spectator; in wrestling, on the contrary, it is each moment which is intelligible, not the passage of time" (1982, 19).

Wrestling with questions rarely leads to victory or defeat; the real, heartfelt inquiry is not about a championship, but about the notion of our passions, the collisions of meanings from moment to moment, with no clear prospect of triumph and only rare glimpses of conclusion. It absorbs us because it is our match. Adult inquiry is about mastery rather then victory; by the time the event is over, though we may savor our achievement, we may also regret the imminent loss of the struggle, because it has engaged us so.

My competence as a librarian does not wholly lie in the quality of my answers, but in how well I give them, and very much in how well I attend, how well I read those moments of collision and use them to nurture and develop the learner's question. My competence lies in how well I understand the dimensions of my ignorance at any moment, how well I can understand what to do next, and how well I develop processes in response.

Barthes also says something else that reminds me of the links between librarians and wrestlers: "Each sign in wrestling is therefore endowed with an absolute clarity, since one must always understand everything on the spot. . . . Each moment in wrestling is therefore like an algebra which instantaneously unveils the relationship between a cause and its represented effect" (1982, 20, 22). At every moment we have to know what is relevant, what is important, what is the meaning of this in relation to that; and yet like the wrestler, have to know how every bit of information changes the equation, and so the balance, in the progress of a question from moment to moment.

If boundaries are to be transcended in libraries, in the presence of librarians—and because of, rather than despite, the presence of those librarians—it seems to me that they will occur because the library as an institution and all of the people who design and populate it, together strive intently to create settings where change is invited, settings that invite such breaking through. These are libraries where the dominant professional economy—deep order, low risks, brief encounters accurate fit—may have to be overturned in favor of a more nurturant economy, where the very questions a librarian or mentor asks the learner in the presence of information serve to mirror the expanding instrumentalities that define adult growth.

Are you finding what you need? How does this look to you? What do you think of this? How has what you examined been of use? How well does this fit with what you have seen before? How is your question different, now? Where to, next? Only by questions can questions become better. Overturning the economy of library encounters implies a frame of mind centered no less on the qualities of questions than it is on the qualities of answers. Every question bears assumptions, has implications, takes directions, accepts variations—and anticipates the conditions of its own answer. In the presence of a question, think of what Whitehead (1929; 1967) says somewhere: "It requires a very unusual mind to undertake the analysis of the obvious." But that is the task that matters. That, and the creation of a coherent and trustworthy domain.

The Needs of Strangers

Librarianship is for me the most difficult of all educative tasks because the librarian must invest in the thoughts and uncertainties of another human being. Most often these encounters involve intimate engagements with strangers; they must refer to the stranger's meanings, and must enter the stranger's context and situation—must occupy the stranger's world. But these investments are made at a certain distance and with a certain cost. In Vygotsky's zone of proximal development, the learner and teacher are stable, continuous presences for each other. The librarian, however, remains a virtual bystander whose participation as actor, agent, witness—or educator—is episodic and perpetually incomplete.

How do we prepare ourselves to meet the needs of adult strangers in libraries? Allen Tough suggests that professional helpers should interview five of the people they help in order to understand the situations of one life and the contexts they provide for adult change. "It is important to give each person an hour or two to reply at leisure and in some depth. Five or ten hours spent at this listening can transform a helper" (Tough 1982, 102–3). I believe that this transformation will cause librarians to see learners less as generic strangers, and more as individual strangers, sharing a field with other strangers, yet with the desire to know or change held in common. It will also bring about a sense of adult learning needs not as isolated symptoms or indicators of distress, but as problems driven by a context, and so to be responded to in a context. Another important professional question librarians must answer is this: What is the life of the stranger who needs me?

Librarians encounter learners, and learners most need librarians, at the moment when cognitions explode with vividness and novelty. Whitehead (1967, 17) calls this the "stage of romance" in the rhythm of education, when knowledge is not dominated by system or process, when connections lie unexplored and when relationships, or possibilities of relationships, entail the imagination. While based on the "immediate cognizance of fact," learning here begins with the imagination of possibilities—what Dewey calls "the suggestion of something not observed" (1933, 9). Librarians offer mastery over the setting where all of these things—connections and relationships, and inviting possibilities of relationships—are waiting to be assembled. It is not accidental that we know the library—this forum for mediation between the learner and his possibilities—as a cultural institution, because this is where culture is made possible.

In fact, in a time when cultural literacy is at risk of being mistaken for a canon of unblended knowledge, the first two sentences of Whitehead's essay, "The Aims of Education" should be inscribed above the library door: "Culture is activity of thought, and receptiveness to beauty and humane feeling. Scraps of information have nothing to do with it" (1967, 1). It is a statement of remarkable similarity to one I have found in Eduard Lindeman's work: "To be educated is not to be informed but to find illumination in informed living" (1926, 171). And that is what adult learning in the library means to me.

References

Barthes, Roland. 1982. The world of wrestling. In *A Barthes Reader*, ed. Susan Sontag. New York: Hill and Wang.

Bates, Marcia J. 1979. Information search tactics. *Journal of the American Society for Information Science* 30: 205-14.

Bruner, Jerome. 1973. Going beyond the information given. In *Beyond the Information Given: Studies in the Psychology of Knowing*, ed. Jeremy M. Anglin, 218-38. New York: W. W. Norton.

———. 1975. Language as an instrument of thought. In *Problems of Language and Learning*, ed. Alan Davies. London: Heinemenn.

———.1986. *Actual Minds, Possible Worlds*. Cambridge: Harvard University Press.

Carr, David. 1983. Adult learning and library helping. *Library Trends* 31: 569-83.

―――. 1989. *Proceedings of the Sixteenth Annual LOEX Conference.* Ann Arbor, Mich.: Pieran Press.

Dervin, Brenda. 1983. Information as a user construct: the relevance of perceived information needs to synthesis and interpretation. In *Knowledge Structure and Use: Implications for Synthesis and Interpretation,* ed. Spencer A. Ward and Linda J. Reed, 133-53. Philadelphia: Temple University Press.

Dewey, John. 1933. *How We Think.* Lexington, Mass.: D.C. Heath and Company.

Graesser, Arthur, Kathy Lang, and Dianne Horgan. 1988. A taxonomy for question generation. *Questioning Exchange* 2: 3-15.

Kelly, George A. 1963. *A Theory of Personality: The Psychology of Personal Constructs.* New York: W. W. Norton.

Knox, Alan B. 1977. *Adult Development and Learning.* San Francisco: Jossey-Bass.

Kulthau, Carol C. 1988. Longitudinal case studies of the information search process of users in libraries. *Library and Information Science Research* (July/September).

―――. (In press) Developing a model of the library search process: investigation of cognitive and affective aspects. *RQ.*

Lindeman, Eduard. 1926. *The Meaning of Adult Education.* New York: New Republic.

Polanyi, Michael. 1958. *Personal Knowledge.* Chicago: University of Chicago Press.

Polya, G. 1957. *How to Solve It: A New Aspect of Mathematical Method.* Second ed. Princeton, N.J.: Princeton University Press.

Terkel, Studs. 1974. *Working: People Talk about What They Do All Day and How They Feel about What They Do.* New York: Avon.

Tough, Allen. 1982. *Intentional Changes.* Chicago: Follett.

Vygotsky, Lev S. 1978. *Mind in Society.* Cambridge, Mass.: Harvard University Press.

Whitehead, Alfred North. [1929] 1967. *The Aims of Education and Other Essays.* Reprint, New York: The Free Press.

Librarians as Learners, Librarians as Teachers of the Internet in Academic Libraries: A Literature Review

Laurie J. Lopatin

The past few years have witnessed the explosion of the use of the Internet as an information resource, and one of the major responsibilities of academic librarians has become that of teaching the Internet to the academic community. The Internet is very complex and constantly changing, and librarians have to learn its intricacies themselves before they can teach it to students and faculty. As both learners and teachers, it is incumbent upon academic librarians to keep up with rapidly changing technological developments. To be effective teachers, librarians also must be knowledgeable about different learning and teaching styles.

This article presents a selective review of literature on library science and education from 1993 to 1998 on issues pertaining to academic librarians learning and teaching the Internet. It begins with discussions of learning theories, such as lifelong learning. An overview of training and professional development for librarians in general is followed by articles on librarians learning the Internet. In-house professional development programs often provide training for librarians on the Internet, and several such programs are presented. Then articles focusing on librarians teaching the Internet are presented, including studies of librarians at specific academic institutions teaching the Internet to other librarians, faculty, and students. This article concludes with books and articles offering Internet training tips.

Learning the Internet Learning Theories
Learning as a Lifelong Endeavor

A theoretical framework for adult learning and the teaching of adults is presented by Jarvis (1995). He examined various adult learning styles and different teaching methods appropriate for adults. He asserted that:

> human learning is a lifelong process, one which has acquired greater significance as the speed of change in society has increased so that its members are almost compelled to keep learning in order to remain members. . . . Lifelong learning has, consequently, become a more conspicuous concept in the literature of recent years (13).

The concept of continual learning is discussed by Harris (1996) in the context of the virtual library and the library's role as a learning organization. Individuals are encouraged to take responsibility for their own learning—"such learning will form the basis upon which librarians will gain the understandings required to provide service to virtual library patrons and to meet their needs" (52).

Adult Students as Participants in Designing Their Education

Arp (1995) addressed some of the differences between training (defined as teaching practical skills) and education (defined as teaching concepts) in reference to teaching about technology and the Internet. Hert (1994) also discussed adult learning theory in the context of Internet training. Noting that adults learn differently than children, the author stated that "the basic tenet of adult learning theory is that adults need to be responsible for their learning experiences. This principle suggests that trainers need to involve trainees as much as possible throughout the process of training development" (p. 38). In a similar vein, Johnson and Thomas (1994) discussed cognitive learning theory in relation to technology education, and they stated that "the cognitive view requires a stimulating learning environment in which students are active participants in planning, implementing, and evaluating teaching and learning" (39–40).

Customized Instruction

McLellan (1996) discussed theories of mental processes and learning styles, and noted that a trend in education is toward "mass customization—adapting instruction to individual learners" (13). McLellan argued that computer-based technologies can support different types of learning—"as our electronic tools become more powerful, they can be customized to individual preferences" (13).

Training and Professional Development

A number of authors stressed the importance of librarians taking advantage of training and professional development opportunities in order to stay current with rapid changes in technology. Kreszock (1997) discussed adult learning theory and the needs of adult learners as they relate to professional development activities for librarians. She stated that "there are perhaps few other professions for which the concept of 'lifelong learning' is so important" (7). Echoing this sentiment, Woodsworth (1998, 62) asserted that "we must all commit to a lifetime of continuous education." McConkey, Carle, and Larsen (1996, 12) stated that "staff development is critical in the changing environment of today's libraries. To meet these changing demands, it is essential for the institution to provide opportunities for the library staff to learn and grow." And Woodward (1997) discussed the importance of continuing staff development for midcareer librarians who may not have the computer skills of younger librarians.

Varlejs (1996) reported on the results of a survey of a random sample of members of the American Library Association (ALA) to determine librarians' involvement in professional learning activities. The results indicate that 77 percent of the respondents participated in substantial learning projects and 83 percent participated in at least one professional activity during the preceding year. The learning activities of librarians are more fully described by Varlejs later in this book. Wilding (1995, 78) asserted that "the need to stay current with new technological tools has become one of the most crucial needs in academic libraries for training and development." He discussed the characteristics of good training programs and sources for training, such as library consortia, professional associations, and electronic discussion lists. Tennant (1995) also suggested various types of training, including in-house training, vendor training, and classes.

Monty and Warren-Wenk (1994) discussed using the Internet as a tool for professional development, including electronic discussion lists, continuing education courses over the Internet, and electronic mail. Ford (1998), president of the ALA, also advocated using the Internet for professional development. She suggested several "opportunities for lifelong learning" (33) provided by ALA, including Web-based training, discussion lists, and electronic newsletters and journals.

Besides librarians, other professionals are struggling to keep up with technology. Maddin (1997) discussed several training models for teachers integrating computer technology into classroom instruction, and she stressed the importance of a support system for maintaining skills. In addressing issues of business education, Neal (1997, 133) stated that "the constantly changing subject matter in today's technological world mandates continual updating and retraining."

Learning the Internet
The Challenge of the Internet

In addition to staff training on technology in general, librarians must learn how to use the Internet in order to use its wealth of information as part of their professional responsibilities, including teaching it to their colleagues, faculty, and staff. Learning the Internet is a very time-consuming process, not without problems. Anderson (1996) discussed some of the difficulties faced by librarians in trying to learn the Internet, such as its ever-changing nature, the problems of learning Internet vocabulary and connectivity, and the difficulties of accessing information on the Internet, due to its general lack of organization. Hults (1995) maintained that only recent graduates of library schools have had formal training on the Internet, and "most of the profession is groping its informal way, in a highly technical area" (237.) She asserted that staff training on the Internet is essential: "Librarians must get the training to use and understand the potential impact of the Internet on library services" (239).

Rosenthal and Spiegelman (1996) reported on the results of a survey of the use of the Internet by academic reference librarians in New York State. The authors noted that one of the findings of the survey indicates that in order for the Internet to be a useful part of reference service, staff training on the Internet is imperative. "Internet use will certainly increase if additional personnel and time permit librarians to pursue training" (64). The authors suggested that librarians maintain their Internet skills by attending workshops, "surfing" the net, and keeping up with professional literature. Later in this book, Rosenthal and Spiegelman present the results of an updated survey of Internet use by academic librarians.

In-house Training

As indicated above, there are quite a few avenues that academic librarians can pursue in learning the Internet. Many librarians learn on their own, by trial and error, and by spending time "surfing" the Net. Others attend workshops and seminars sponsored by professional organizations. A primary method for learning the Internet is for librarians to take advantage of training provided by their own institutions. According to Basu (1995, 12), "it is up to each institution to prepare its staff to cope with its [the Internet's] intricacies and to utilize it so that they may quickly become part of this knowledge based society." Kirkpatrick (1998) discussed the results of a survey of training practices on information technology in the libraries of the Minnesota State Colleges and Universities System. She reported that training on the Internet was available in 76.5 percent of the libraries and that the most frequently used methods of training on information technology were individualized training by a coworker (54.9%) and in-house workshops (35.3%).

Several authors reported on different approaches of academic libraries to in-house Internet training. Lippert (1994) described a staff training program on the Internet developed by a group of librarians at the Engineering and Science Libraries at the Massachusetts Institute of Technology. The curriculum consisted of approximately twenty 90-minute sessions focusing on various computer skills and the Internet. The author stated that it is a "flexible training program whose content is expected to adapt continuously to changing training requirements as the dynamic technological environment of the '90's proceeds" (19). Stephenson and Willis (1994) outlined Internet in-service workshops at the University of New Mexico Library developed primarily for reference and bibliographic instruction librarians, who then teach Internet skills to faculty and students. The personnel and facilities of the campus computer center were utilized, and hands-on training was emphasized. Basu (1995) described an Internet training program for all staff members at the Learning Resource Center of the County College of Morris, New Jersey. There were two consecutive workshops with hands-on training. Follow-up sessions covering more advanced topics were scheduled for a year later, and the author recommended that with changes in technology, reinforcement sessions be held several times a year. Foster, Etkin, Moore, Staebell, and Wright (1993) reported on an intensive all-day retreat devoted to the Internet at Western Kentucky University. Library faculty learned navigational tools and how to access information on the Internet. McConkey et al. (1996) outlined the activities of the faculty/staff development committee at the University of Colorado at Boulder. The committee offers programs and workshops on computer training at regular intervals, and the authors suggested that once basic skills are taught, more advanced courses should be offered.

Teaching the Internet

After academic librarians learn about the Internet, either on their own, through seminars, or through in-house training programs, they then teach the Internet to other librarians, faculty, staff, and students. Librarians teach the Internet in a variety of ways, including workshops and seminars, programs, on a one-to-one basis, and by the use of e-mail. Cawthorne and Bleiler (1997), reviewing the results of a survey of member libraries of the Association of Research Libraries, reported that 91 percent of the responding libraries offer, or plan to offer, Internet training to their faculty, staff, and students, usually in the form of non-credit workshops.

Learning Theories Applied to Instruction

The learning theories discussed at the beginning of this article are applied to the teaching of the Internet. Librarians bring to the challenge of teaching their knowledge of instructional techniques, learning and teaching theories, and their knowledge of the Internet. Several authors discussed general aspects of teaching the Internet. Hert (1994) presented a theoretical perspective on Internet training. She stated that Internet "training should be developed not only to provide specific Internet proficiencies but also to enable staff to participate actively in organizational strategic planning" (36). The author discussed goals and conceptual frameworks of Internet training, including adult learning theory and training for computer-based technologies. She asserted that different cognitive skills and abilities of trainees should be taken into account in designing Internet training. Stephenson and Willis (1994) also discussed adult learning styles in relation to Internet training. They stated, "it is important for the trainer to learn how to design and deliver instruction which takes into account differing learning styles, and to interact with learners in ways that facilitate the learning process" (220).

Page and Kesselman (1994) outlined various techniques that librarians employ in teaching the Internet, such as targeting particular groups, structured and free-form approaches, for-credit courses, and teaching over the Internet itself.

Instruction for Librarians
Train the Trainer Programs

As indicated above, librarians learning the Internet are often taught by other librarians. After being trained on the Internet, many librarians then train students and faculty. Senkevitch and Wolfram (1996) reported on a study of a "train the trainer" program for educating rural library professionals in the use of the Internet during an intensive seven-day institute held at the University of Wisconsin-Milwaukee School of Library and Information Science. The participants were required to disseminate the knowledge gained at the institute by presenting workshops and seminars in their own library systems. The study found that "the model was effective in empowering participants to affect change" (280), and many of the participants held talks, training sessions, and demonstrations on the Internet in their own libraries. Similarly, Yerkey (1997) described a one-week institute by the School of Information and Library Studies at the State University of New York at Buffalo to train librarians to use the Buffalo Free-Net, a community computer system. The participants were expected to "act as change agents in their libraries" (121) and to train their staff and the public on the Internet.

New Training Positions and Departments

Some libraries have created new positions or departments whose responsibilities include staff training on technology. Day and Armstrong (1996) described a new library faculty position at Illinois State University. The responsibilities of the new position—the Internet reference services librarian—include instructing librarians in the use of the Internet and coordinating the Internet into library services. A new position was also created at the Denver University Library. Grealy, Jones, Messas, Zipp, and Catalucci (1996) reported that a part-time position of staff training coordinator was created to coordinate staff development programs. The authors described the extensive training programs at Denver University, which include computer software and Internet training, and which are continually updated.

Byron (1995) described the development of the user education department in the University of North Texas Libraries. The department provides training for librarians who participate in bibliographic instruction activities, offering workshops on learning theory as well as instruction on the Internet and electronic information sources.

Instruction for Faculty

Stimson and Schiller (1996) reported on an individualized approach to teaching faculty about the Internet at the Science and Engineering Library at the State University of New York at Buffalo. The librarians offer one-on-one instruction in faculty offices, assisting faculty with their research needs. An intensive three-day workshop for faculty at Stetson University in Florida is described by Bradford, Kannon, and Ryan (1996). The workshop featured hands-on lab exercises, discussion topics such as privacy and ethics, and "customized discipline-specific handout[s] of all types of Internet sites" (238), prepared by the librarians. In a collaborative effort, computer center staff presented knowledge of hardware and software, and librarians taught how to locate Internet resources.

Instruction for Students

Academic librarians teach students Internet skills on a one-to-one basis, through workshops and regular bibliographic instruction classes. Some college and university libraries also offer undergraduate Internet classes for credit. Rockman (1993) described such a course at the California Polytechnic State University at San Luis Obispo. "This course helps students to clearly articulate research questions, recognize the type of information desired, identify appropriate locations and formats of information, evaluate the information, and apply it to a specific need at hand" (66). The course is revised as necessary to respond to new Internet resources and changes in technology. Fishel and Stevens (1994) outlined some of the challenges encountered in developing and teaching an Internet course for undergraduates offered during the January session at Macalester College in St. Paul, Minnesota. They conclude that "effective instruction requires that staff have the time to explore and learn the Internet themselves. Staff development and continuing education in particular, must be a priority" (118). Kohut and Sternberg (1995) reported that at Saint Xavier University in Chicago, a course on emerging technologies in the Department of Mass Communication included a segment on the Internet taught by a reference librarian. For the final assignment, the students used their Internet skills to find online resources for their term papers.

Instruction for the Academic Community

Librarians often design Internet instruction programs to include the entire academic community—other librarians, faculty, staff and students. Many Internet programs employ hands-on exercises, which are described by Konrad and Stemper as being "critical to the success of any Internet training session" (1996, 15). For example, in describing the Internet workshops presented by the York University Libraries in Toronto, Canada, Warren-Wenk (1994) emphasized the importance of hands-on learning activities, not only for the initial workshops, but also for the follow-up sessions.

Workshops and Seminars

Miller and Ziegler (1994) described an interactive day-long workshop, "Striking it Rich with the Internet," developed jointly by librarians and computer center staff of Lebanon Valley College in Pennsylvania. The authors stated that at the outset, "it quickly became evident . . . that we would need to improve our own Internet skills in order to train others" (169). The workshops included hands-on sessions with various Internet exercises. Konrad and Stemper (1996) described the collaboration between the library and the Division of Information Technology in developing and teaching Internet workshops for students and staff at the University of Wisconsin-Madison. The authors maintained that Internet instruction is an extension of traditional bibliographic instruction, and they discussed various teaching strategies, such as tool-based instruction and subject-based instruction. They also stressed the value of employing hands-on exercises. Kalin and Wright (1994) reported on Internet seminars developed by the University Libraries at Penn State University. The authors outlined the planning process, the objectives, and various follow-up activities. Diaz and VonVille (1994) discussed Internet workshops presented through the combined efforts of the library and the Academic Computing Services at Ohio State University. The authors emphasized the importance of trainers staying abreast of the constantly changing Internet: "A strong need exists within libraries to have personnel who can keep current with Internet changes, and who can articulate to library users and other librarians the relevance of this powerful tool in meeting research needs" (95).

Programs

Greenfield, Tellman, and Brin (1996) outlined a model instruction program at the University of Arizona Library on joining listservs. The authors stated that "building on the existing skills of the learner, understanding different learning styles, and communicating the need for sharing expertise are equally important elements in preparing to teach" (22). The learning objectives and the course design are described, and a Checklist for Preparing an Internet Instruction Session is included. Koltay, Trelease, and Davis (1996) in an innovative instructional program for faculty and students at Cornell University's Albert R. Mann Library stated: "Instructors need to be made aware of the concrete possibilities that new technologies hold for improving the effectiveness and efficiency of their teaching . . . . They also need students whose information literacy skills are high enough to be able to make the best use of the new learning tools" (83). The instructional program consists of workshops (including hands-on exercises), which are continually revised and supplemented by Web-based tutorials.

Instruction via E-mail.
Several university libraries teach the Internet using e-mail as a delivery mechanism. Burke (1996) described an Internet seminar developed by librarians at Fairmont State College in Fairmont, West Virginia, that was distributed entirely by e-mail. The author stated that the advantages of e-mail instruction include the ability to teach large groups of people on and off campus and "flexibility resulting from the elimination of time constraints" (40). Vishwanatham, Wilkins, and Jevec (1997) reported on an Internet course "Ride the eTrain: An Introduction to the Internet at UIC." The course was developed by librarians at the University of Illinois at Chicago to be delivered via e-mail to students, faculty, and staff at the various campuses of the university. The content of the sixteen-lesson course is outlined, as well as the advantages and disadvantages of e-mail instruction.

In a more subject-oriented approach, Jensen and Sih (1995) described an instruction program developed by reference librarians at the Science & Engineering Library at the University of California, San Diego, which utilizes electronic mail to teach the use of the INSPEC database to faculty and students. The authors stated:

> By providing these tutorials in addition to more traditional instructional methods, we are making a powerful statement to our patrons about the library's attentiveness to their needs

... Users continue to cite the electronic tutorials as evidence of their librarians' approachability, accessibility, and awareness of technology in the research environment. (86)

Internet Training Tips

There is no lack of help for librarians developing Internet training programs. Several authors provide guidance for Internet trainers, not only giving tips on teaching the Internet but also providing information about the Internet, sample lessons, and demonstrations. Tennant made the following suggestions: "First of all, it is important to know basic instructional techniques ... delivering the information to your audience in simple, easy-to-understand terms ... Second, it is vital that you know the topic well" (1994, 22). He also discussed the needs of the audience as determining what will be taught, and the preparation and presentation of the course materials. Makulowich (1994) listed fifteen tips on teaching the Internet, including deciding what level of training is needed, tailoring sessions to student interests, and having interactive sessions. Brandt (1995) posed the question of whether the Internet trainer should focus on teaching how to use the hardware and software or whether the trainer should focus on information-seeking skills. He recommended blending the teaching of system features and information skills as the most effective way of teaching the Internet.

There are several comprehensive handbooks for librarians engaged in Internet training. Kovacs and Kovacs (1997) gave tips for Internet training in their book *The Cybrarian's Guide to Developing Successful Internet Programs and Services.* They discussed the planning and implementation of Internet teaching and covered such topics as the availability of training facilities, the level of training required, and the content of the training course. In *The Complete Internet Companion for Librarians* (1995), Benson included tips and exercises for Internet training, including sample demonstrations. In *Crossing the Internet Threshold* (1994), Tennant, Ober, and Lipow presented small-group discussion topics and a checklist for Internet trainers. A supplement to this book is *Introducing the Internet Plus: A Trainers Workshop* (1994) by Jaffe. It assists trainers in developing introductory classes, and includes presentation slides that trainers can use in their lectures. *The Internet Trainer's Guide* (1995), by Kovacs, includes step-by-step exercises on Internet skills, such as e-mail, Telnet, and Netscape. Kovacs's *The Internet Trainer's Total Solution Guide* (1997) presented more in-depth coverage, such as training modules on "Effective Research on the Internet" and "Designing and Authoring World Wide Web Pages."

Besides using printed sources, the Internet trainer can find many online resources, such as those outlined by Hagenbruch and Pozansky later in this book. Weissinger and Edwards (1995) presented an annotated list of online resources for Internet trainers, including course materials, online tutorials, and guides to the Internet. Makulowich (1995) listed online resources to support Internet trainers. Also, in *The Internet Trainer's Guide*, Kovacs included a directory of training materials available on the Internet.

In the early 1990s, when the Internet first became available in many libraries, there were few resources to help librarians with Internet instruction. In contrast, today there is a proliferation of these resources. Thus, the growth of online information resources, which has characterized the information revolution, has been accompanied by a growth in instructional materials for librarians to help cope with that revolution.

References

Anderson, B. 1996. The Internet as career, job, and employment resource: Transition, assimilation, instruction. *Reference Librarian* 55:7–17.

Arp, L. 1995. Reflecting on reflecting: Views on teaching and the Internet. *RQ* 34(4):453–57.

Basu, G. 1995. Traveling towards the information superhighway: Training to explore cyberspace. *New Jersey Libraries* 28:10–13.

Benson, A. C. 1995. *The complete Internet companion for librarians*. New York: Neal-Schuman.

Bradford, J. T., K. E. Kannon, and S. M. Ryan. 1996. Designing and implementing a faculty Internet workshop: A collaborative effort of academic computing services and the university library. *Research Strategies* 14(4): 234–45.

Brandt, D. 1995. What does 'teaching the Internet' mean? *Computers in Libraries* 15:34–35.

Burke, J. J. 1996. Using e-mail to teach: Expanding the reach of BI. *Research Strategies* 14(1):36–43.

Byron, S. 1995. Preparing to teach in cyberspace: User education in real and virtual libraries. *Reference Librarian* 51/52:241–47.

Cawthorne, J. E., and R. Bleiler, comps. 1997. *Internet training in ARL libraries*: A SPEC kit. Washington, D.C.: Association of Research Libraries.

Day, P. A., and K. L. Armstrong. 1996. Librarians, faculty, and the Internet: Developing a new information partnership. *Computers in Libraries* 16:56–58.

Diaz, K. R., and H. M. VonVille. 1994. Internet training at the Ohio State University: The process, the product, the potential. In *The Internet library: Case studies of library Internet management and use*, ed. J. Still, 85–96. Westport, Conn.: Mecklermedia.

Fishel, T., and J. Stevens. 1994. Teaching the Internet: An undergraduate liberal arts college experience. In *The Internet library: Case studies of library Internet management and use*, ed. J. Still, 109–26. Westport, Conn.: Mecklermedia.

Ford, B. 1998. Lifelong learning: Global reach and local touch. *American Libraries* 29(3):33.

Foster, C. L., C. Etkin, E. E. Moore, S. L. Staebell, and P. Wright. 1993. The net result: Enthusiasm for exploring the Internet. *Information Technology and Libraries* 12(4):433–36.

Grealy, D., L. Jones, K. Messas, K. Zipp, and L. Catalucci. 1996. Staff development and training in college and university libraries: The Penrose perspective. *Library Administration and Management* 10(4) 204–9.

Greenfield, L. W., J. Tellman, and B. Brin. 1996. A model for teaching the Internet: Preparation and practice. *Computers in Libraries* 16:22–25.

Harris, H. 1996. Retraining librarians to meet the needs of the virtual library patron. *Information Technology and Libraries* 15(1):48–52.

Hert, C. A. 1994. A learning organization perspective on training: Critical success factors for Internet implementation. *Internet Research* 4(3):36–44.

Hults, P. 1995. Noodling down the Internet: Or, one foot in the fast lane, the other stuck in the trenches. *Reference Librarian* 51/52:235–40.

Jaffe, L. D. 1994. *Introducing the Internet plus: A trainer's workshop.* Berkeley, Calif.: Library Solutions.

Jarvis, P. 1995. *Adult and continuing education: Theory and practice*, 2d ed. London: Routledge.

Jensen, A., and J. Sih. 1995. Using e-mail and the Internet to teach users at their desktops. *Online* 19(5):82–86.

Johnson, S. D., and R. G. Thomas. 1994. Implications of cognitive science for instructional design in technology education. *Journal of Technology Studies* 20(1):33–45.

Kalin, S., and C. Wright. 1994. Internexus: A partnership for Internet instruction. *The Reference Librarian* 41/42:197–209.

Kirkpatrick, T. E. 1998. The training of academic library staff on information technology within the libraries of the Minnesota State Colleges and Universities System. *College & Research Libraries* 59(1):51–59.

Kohut, D., and J. Sternberg. 1995. Using the Internet to study the Internet: An active learning component. *Research Strategies* 13(3):176–81.

Koltay, Z., B. Trelease, and P. M. Davis. 1996. Technologies for learning: Instructional support at Cornell's Albert R. Mann Library. *Library Hi Tech* 14 (4), 83–98.

Konrad, L. G., and J. Stemper. 1996. Same game, different name: Demystifying Internet instruction. *Research Strategies* 14(1):4–21.

Kovacs, D. 1995. *The Internet trainer's guide.* New York: Van Nostrand Reinhold.
———. 1997. *The Internet trainer's total solution guide.* New York: Van Nostrand Reinhold.

Kovacs, D., and M. Kovacs. 1997. *The Cybrarian's guide to developing successful Internet programs and services.* New York: Neal-Schuman.

Kreszock, M. 1997. A holistic look at professional development. *North Carolina Libraries* 55(1):7–11.

Lippert, M. 1994. Continuing computer competence: A training program for the '90s. *Bulletin of the American Society for Information Science* 20:18–19.

Maddin, E. A. 1997. The real learning begins back in the classroom: On-the-job training and support for teachers using technology. *Educational Technology* 37(5):56–59.

Makulowich, J. S. 1994. Tips on how to teach the Internet. *Online* 18(6):27–30.
——— 1995. Meeting the demands of Internet training. *Online* 19(4):54–55.

McConkey, J. S., D. D. Carle, and S. T. Larsen. 1996. Staff development in the university libraries, University of Colorado at Boulder. *Colorado Libraries* 22:9–12.

McLellan, H. 1996. "Being digital": Implications for education. *Educational Technology* 36(6):5–20.

Miller, D. L., and M. C. Ziegler. 1994. An Internet workshop for Lebanon Valley College faculty and staff: "Striking it rich with the Internet." In *The Internet library: Case studies of library Internet management and use,* ed. J. Still, 167–79. Westport, Conn.: Mecklermedia.

Monty, V., and P. Warren-Wenk. 1994. Using the INTERNET as a professional development tool: An analysis. *Education Libraries* 18(1):7–10.

Neal, D. A. 1997. Retain, retrain, and reward business educators. In *The changing dimensions of business education,* ed. C. P. Brantley and B. J. Davis, 130–35. Reston, Va.: National Business Education Association.

Page, M., and M. Kesselman. 1994. Teaching the Internet: Challenges and opportunities. *Research Strategies* 12(3):157–67.

Rockman, I. F. 1993. Teaching about the Internet: The formal course option. *Reference Librarian* 39:65-75.

Rosenthal, M., and M. Spiegelman. 1996. Evaluating use of the Internet among academic reference librarians. *Internet Reference Services Quarterly* 1(1):53-67.

Senkevitch, J. J., and D. Wolfram. 1996. Assessing the effectiveness of a model for educating rural librarians in using Internet resources. *Journal of Education for Library and Information Science* 37(3):272–85.

Stephenson, N., and D. J. Willis. 1994. Internet in-service training at the University of New Mexico General Library. *Reference Librarian*, 41/42:211–24.

Stimson, N. F., and N. Schiller. 1996. Internet Rx office visits: Just what the Dr. ordered. *College & Research Libraries News* 57:723–25.

Tennant, R. 1994. Tips & techniques for Internet trainers. *Bulletin of the American Society for Information Science* 20:22–24.

Tennant, R. 1995. The virtual library foundation: Staff training and support. *Information Technology and Libraries*, 14(1):46–49.

Tennant, R., J. Ober, and A. G. Lipow. 1994. *Crossing the Internet threshold: An instructional handbook*. 2d ed. Berkeley, Calif: Library Solutions Pr.

Varlejs, J. 1996. The professional responsibility of continuing learning: How well is it met? *New Jersey Libraries* 29(4):7–10.

Vishwanatham, R., W. Wilkins, and T. Jevec. 1997. The Internet as a medium for online instruction. *College & Research Libraries* 58(5):433–44.

Warren-Wenk, P. 1994. Moving toward Internet literacy on the university campus. In *The Internet library: Case studies of library Internet management and use*, ed. J. Still, 127–65. Westport, Conn.: Mecklermedia.

Weissinger, N. J., and J. P. Edwards. 1995. Online resources for Internet trainers. *College & Research Libraries News* 56(8):535–39+.

Wilding, T. 1995. Training and development for library staff. In *Academic libraries: Their rationale and role in American higher education*, ed. G.B. McCabe and R.J. Person, 71–89. Westport, Conn.: Greenwood Pr.

Woodsworth, A. 1998. Learning for a lifetime. *Library Journal* 123(1):62.

Woodward, J. 1997. Retraining the profession or, over the hill at 40. *American Libraries* 28(4):32–34.

Yerkey, A. N. 1997. Librarians and community computer networks: A training institute. *Journal of Education for Library and Information Science* 38:116–28.

Profile of the Academic Librarian as Self-directed Learner

Jana Varlejs

It has been well established that librarians need to know much that is not taught in library school (Powell 1988; Shonrock and Mulder 1993). Moreover, as change continues to pervade the academic library environment, without the "capacity to learn constantly and quickly ... they [librarians] will find it difficult to do the job" (Tennant 1998). How do academic librarians cope with the pressure to keep up, especially with volatile technology? Formal training may be the best antidote to technostress (Clark and Kalin 1996), but is not always available at the place and time that it is needed (Cromer and Testi 1994). There is evidence that Internet users have learned the Net largely without the aid of courses (Lazinger, Bar-Ilan, and Peritz 1997; Ratzan 1998). One might conjecture, then, that many academic librarians also have gained their Internet skills without the benefit of formal instruction.

The primary focus of the research reported here was not on how librarians learned the Internet but, rather, on work-related learning in general (Varlejs 1996). The findings did reveal, however, that a great deal of effort was centered on technology, and much of that was informal and self-directed. This article briefly describes the study, presents the data on academic librarians, and compares them to the data on the entire sample studied.

51

Methodology

The purpose of the study was to examine work-related, self-directed learning among librarians, within the context of a model that took into account personal and situational characteristics. A sample of 849 was drawn from the estimated 39,900 personal members of the American Library Association (ALA) who were employed in libraries in 1994 (i.e., excluding students, retirees, vendors, etc.). Of the 849 to whom questionnaires were mailed, 76 either did not meet the criteria for being in the sample or could not be located. Of the remaining 773, 521 returned usable questionnaires, for a response rate of 67 percent. A comparison of the characteristics of these 521 respondents with the ALA membership profile at the time showed almost exact congruence (Varlejs, 1996 60–61).

The questionnaire was designed to elicit basic information about the work environment, professional activities, formal and informal learning, and a limited number of personal characteristics. It was expected that those librarians who worked in a more information-rich setting, had more learning opportunities, and who felt a stronger sense of autonomy as learners would report more self-directed learning. It was also hypothesized that those librarians who were most involved in self-directed learning would also exhibit the greatest evidence of professional achievement. The primary hypothesis, however, was that overall, time spent in self-directed learning would exceed time spent in formal continuing education.

The variables selected to represent the work environment were:
- resources—access to current awareness and communication aids, staff size, library literature holdings;
- administrative support—financial support and release time for research, professional and continuing education participation;
- type of library.

The learning opportunity variables were:
- memberships in professional associations;
- involvements in associations—meetings attended, presentations, committee service;
- journals read regularly;
- participation in formal continuing education.

The professional achievement variables were:
- elective office;

- publications;
- administrative position;
- size of staff managed;
- salary.

Measures of the primary dependent variable, self-directed learning (SDL), were derived from Allen Tough's concept of learning projects (1978). Respondents were asked: Please think about situations you have encountered as a librarian during the past year where you chose to learn something in an area you wanted to know more about. For example, a committee assignment, job change, new equipment, or new services might have led you to investigate a topic or acquire new skills. In responding to the questions that follow, limit your replies to those work-related learning projects on which you spent at least seven hours within a six-month period, and which you planned and carried out on your own.

Respondents were then asked whether they recalled any such projects, and if so, how many there were and how many hours they spent on them. They were also asked to think about one representative project and to answer a series of questions about that project, dealing with what triggered the learning, what skill or knowledge was sought, who else was involved in planning, and what resources were used.

Table 1
Self-Directed Learning by Type of Library, No. of Librarians

SDL Projects	Public	School	Academic	Other	Total
No SDL projects					
Observed frequency	56	19	31	15	121
Expected frequency	44	22	41	15	
Column percent	30%	20%	18%	24%	23%
One or more SDL projects					
Observed frequency	132	76	144	48	400
Expected frequency	144	73	134	48	
Column percent	70%	80%	82%	76%	77%
Column total	188	95	175	63	521
Percent of total	36%	18%	34%	12%	100%

Chi-square=8.1 at d.f.=3; significance level p=.04.

Table 2
Characteristics of Respondents

Characteristics	Public, School, Other Librarians	Academic Librarians
Sex		
Men	61 (18%)	48 (27%)
Women	285 (82%)	127 (73%)
Age		
25–34	37 (11%)	22 (13%)
35–44	10 (31%)	60 (36%)
45–54	141 (41%)	59 (35%)
55–68	48 (14%)	26 (16%)
MLS		
No	59 (17%)	7 (4%)
Yes	286 (83%)	167 (96%)
Highest degree		
None	4 (1%)	
B.A.	20 (6%)	1 (1%)
MLS or other master's	244 (70%)	105 (60%)
6th year	14 (4%)	4 (2%)
MLS + other master's	49 (14%)	48 (28%)
Ph.D. candidate	5 (1%)	5 (3%)
Ph.D.	8 (2%)	11 (6%)

Findings

Of the 521 librarians who returned usable questionnaires, 175 were academic librarians. Table 1 shows that 82 percent of them reported self-directed learning projects, a somewhat higher proportion than the other types of librarians. The difference is statistically significant.

In what ways do the academic librarians differ? Tables 2 through 6 present the data on the personal and professional characteristics of the academic librarians and of the rest of the sample. As shown in table 2, the academic librarians were slightly younger, more likely to be male, and had more education than the group as a whole. Table 3 shows that

Table 3
Respondents' Employment Data

	Public, School, Other Librarians	Academic Librarians
Size of professional staff		
Mean	33	34
Median	5	18
Employees supervised		
Mean	13	11
Median	3	5
Salary ($)		
Mean	38,895	40,028
Median	36,835	37,500
Position		
Director	156 (45%)	24 (14%)
Assoc./asst. director	20 (6%)	19 (11%)
Dept. head	75 (22%)	59 (34%)
Supervisor	31 (9%)	25 (14%)
Nonsupervisory	55 (16%)	48 (27%)
Support staff	9 (3%)	

Table 4
Distribution of Full-Time Professional Staff Size
by Type of Library

FTE Staff Size	Public	School	Academic	Other	Total
Median FTE < 9					
Observed frequency	78	82	53	40	253
Expected frequency	92	46	85	30	
Column percent	42%	86%	30%	66%	49%
Median FTE > 9					
Observed frequency	110	13	122	21	266
Expected frequency	96	49	90	31	
Column percent	58%	14%	70%	34%	51%
Column total	188	95	175	61	519
Percent of total	36%	18%	34%	12%	100%

Chi-square=88.4 at d.f.=3; significance level p=.00; missing observations, 2.

Table 5
Provision of Professional Development Support
by Employer

	Public, School, Other Librarians	Academic Librarian
Library literature current awareness system	256 (74%)	143 (82%)
Access to fax machine	287 (83%)	163 (93%)
E-mail account	195 (56%)	160 (91%)
Reports from colleagues on workshops, etc., attended	224 (65%)	134 (77%)
In-service training	249 (72%)	117 (67%)
Indexes to library literature, print or online	193 (56%)	151 (87%)
Staff meetings for updating/ information sharing	268 (77%)	148 (85%)
Release time for:		
• research	29 (8%)	74 (42%)
• professional meetings	317 (92%)	163 (93%)
• continuing education	242 (70%)	137 (78%)
• academic courses	89 (26%)	94 (54%)
Financial assistance for:		
• research	11 (3%)	43 (25%)
• professional meetings	276 (80%)	162 (93%)
• continuing education	232 (67%)	118 (67%)
• academic courses	122 (35%)	82 (47%)

	Mean	Median	Mean	Median
Lib/info sci journal subscriptions	20	8	52	20
Reimbursement for professional development expenses ($)	708	200	602	450

academic librarians' positions and staff size were more evenly distributed than those in other types of libraries. The difference in the median staff size suggests that this is one of the key variables that sets the academic librarian sample apart from the others.

Table 4 shows that 70 percent of the academic librarians worked in libraries with a full-time equivalent professional staff of nine or more, nine being the median for the entire sample. There is a statistically

Table 6
Respondents' Professional Activities

Professional Activities	Public, School, Other Librarians		Academic Librarians	
	Mean	Median	Mean	Median
Professional association memberships	2.5	2	2.6	3
Professional meetings attended	4.1	2	3.4	2
Papers, panel, poster presentation	.7	0	.5	0
Committee service	.8	0	1.3	1
Elective offices	.2	0	.2	0
Journals read regularly	4.3	4	5.1	5
Hours of formal continuing education	22.1	18	17.4	16
Contributions to the literature	12.4	0	15.3	3

Table 7
Number of Self-Directed Learning Projects and Hours Spent

	Public, School, Other Librarians	Academic Librarians
Did not report any projects	90 (26%)	31 (18%)
Did report projects	256 (74%)	144 (82%)
Number of projects:		
1–2	156 (61%)	76 (53%)
3–4	70 (27%)	47 (33%)
5–6	18 (7%)	13 (9%)
7–14	6 (2%)	6 (4%)
15–22	3 (1%)	
missing data	3 (1%)	2 (1%)
Hours spent on projects:		
7–25	58 (23%)	24 (17%)
30–50	76 (30%)	41 (28%)
55–100	57 (22%)	44 (30%)
105–1500	59 (23%)	32 (22%)
missing data	6 (2%)	3 (1%)

Table 8
Extent to Which Self-Directed Learning Criteria Were Met

	Public, School, Other Librarians	Academic Librarians
Identified project trigger	254 (99%)	144 (100%)
Planned 50% of project	194 (75%)	125 (87%)
Remembered resources used	231 (90%)	142★ (100%)
Met all three criteria	183 (72%)	116★★ (81%)

★ Data missing in two cases
★★ Data missing in one case

significant difference among the groups.

Table 5 shows that the academic librarians potentially enjoyed greater support from their institutions for professional development activities than the others, with the exception of in-service training and continuing education.

Table 6 details the professional activities that might be related to professional development. Academic librarians read somewhat more and published at a higher rate.

Returning to table 1, 144 academic librarians (82%) reported that they had undertaken one or more SDL projects during the past year, significantly higher than was the case for the other librarians. Table 7 presents a comparison

Table 9
Learning Project Triggers

	Public, School, Other Librarians	Academic Librarians
New job assignment	40 (16%)	31 (22%)
Extra library professional involvement	28 (11%)	26 (18%)
Change in procedures or operations	29 (11%)	16 (11%)
Planning or management study	31 (12%)	7 (5%)
Change in technology	141 (55%)	74 (51%)
Other	19 (7%)	16 (11%)

Note: The numbers do not add up because respondents could check multiple triggers.

of the amount of self-directed learning engaged in by the academic librarians as opposed to the rest of the sample, as measured in projects undertaken and estimated number of hours spent.

For the academic librarians, the mean number of projects was 2.8; the mean number of hours was 106.5, with a median of 50. For the remaining sample, the mean number of projects was 2.7; the mean number of hours was 104.9, with a median of 32. Because a few respondents reported very high hours, the median measure is a better indicator of effort than the mean, so that it is clear that academic librarians were more likely to spend more hours on SDL than the other librarians. In addition to asking for recall of projects falling within the definition given in the questionnaire, several additional criteria were set to ensure that a respondent could be categorized with some certainty as a self-directed learner. These criteria called for the respondent to be able to focus on one project and (1) identify what triggered it, (2) have planned at least 50 percent of the learning, and (3) remember at least some of the resources used. As shown in table 8, of the academic librarians who reported projects, 116 (81%) met all the criteria. Strictly speaking, then, 67 percent of the total academic sample of 175 can be called self-directed learners without qualification (53% of all the other librarians).

The main difference in meeting the criteria occurred in the project planning category, where more involvement by peers and bosses was indicated by the nonacademic librarians. Because the number of academic librarians who did not meet all three criteria is so small (28), no comparison of the two groups is attempted.

In addition to serving as a criterion for determining self-direction, the project triggers are of interest in themselves. Table 9 shows that technology drove the majority of learning projects. An open-ended question about the skill the learner sought to acquire elicited somewhat more detail. Of the academic librarians who answered, 27 percent specified the Internet and another 39 percent referred to other technology.

The academic librarians who conducted learning projects used print and/or online resources 85 percent of the time, and communicated with colleagues and attended workshops/courses in 83 percent of the cases. The nonacademic librarians attended far fewer workshops or courses related to their projects. In addition to the question about project-related workshop and course attendance, the survey also asked

Table 10
Participation in Formal CE Activities
and SDL Projects

Activity	Public, School, Other Librarians		Academic Librarians	
	Participants	Avg. no. of hours	Participants	Avg. no. of hours
Formal continuing education	296 (86%)	25.6	34 (77%)	22.6
Self-directed learning	256 (74%)	104.9	144 (82%)	106.9

the entire sample the following: How many hours of formal continuing education (CE) activities (job-related workshops, courses, seminars) did you attend in the past year for purposes of professional development (count the typical one-day workshop as six hours)? Table 10 shows the hours spent in both formal continuing education and self-directed learning for those who reported participation in one or both.

These data clearly confirm the expectation that more time is spent in informal than formal learning. Although the number of hours spent was similar for the two groups, more of the academic librarians than others were engaged in SDL and fewer of them participated in formal continuing education. Taking into account the entire group of 175 academic librarians and 346 others (including those who reported no SDL or CE), the ratios of self-directed to formal learning are about 5 to 1 for the academics and 3.4 to 1 for the others.

Table 11
Correlations between Self-Directed Learning Measures and
Selected Professional Development Support Variables

	Awareness	Fax	E-mail	Lit. Indexes	Staff Mtgs	Staff Size	Jrnls Held	Research Time	$
No. of Projects	-.23*	.02	.05	.08	-.04	-.07	-.02	.00	-.02
Project Hours	-.08	-.08	.06	.12	-.00	-.03	.02	.02	-.04

Note: Minimum pairwise cases, 167; 1-tailed significance, *$p<.01$

Table 12
Correlations between Participation in Formal Continuing Education and Selected Professional Development Support Variables

	Release Time for			Financial Support for		
	Meetings	CE	Acad. Courses	Meetings	CE	Acad. Courses
Hours of formal CE	.07	.06	.05	.04	.10	.15

Note: Minimum pairwise cases, 174; 1-tailed significance, *p<.01

The greater involvement of academic librarians in informal learning appears to reflect the higher levels of support for that mode generally provided by their work settings, as shown in table 5 (i.e., e-mail accounts, library/information science literature access). However, when the learning measures are correlated with data on work setting characteristics likely to be helpful for SDL, the expected relationships are not evident, as shown in table 11. In ten cases, the correlations are negative, including the only one where the correlation is significant.

Correlations between those aspects of the work setting that might be expected to encourage participation in formal learning and the number of continuing education hours reported are shown in table 12. The relationships are insignificant, but they are all in the positive direction. The same is true of the variable measuring reimbursement for professional development expenses.

In articles describing a study of Oklahoma academic librarians' professional development behavior, quite different results are reported (Havener and Stolt 1994; Havener and Worrell 1994). A direct comparison between some of the findings reported here and those of the Oklahoma study is possible because the survey sent to the ALA sample replicated a number of the questions posed in the earlier research. For example, institutional support was measured in terms of release time and financial assistance for professional meetings, continuing education, academic course work, and research in both studies. For the Oklahoma librarians, institutional support was lower than for the ALA academic librarians, but it had a significant positive impact on their participation in professional meetings and workshops, as shown in table

Table 13
Comparison of Average Participation in
Meetings and Continuing Education by
Oklahoma and ALA Academic Librarians

	Oklahoma Librarians (n=185)		ALA Librarians (n=175)	
	with support	without support	with support	without support
Meetings	3.48	1.76	3.38	3.60
Continuing education	3.72	2.04	2.99	2.41

Note: The means for the Oklahoma librarians were significant, p=.00 for meetings and p=.04 for CE (Havener and Stolt 1994, 30–31).

13. Similarly, those Oklahoma librarians who received support for research published significantly more than those who did not (Havener and Stolt 1994, 33). In the case of the ALA academic librarians, those without research support actually published more, but the difference was not statistically significant.

Discussion
The data reported above show that academic librarians who are members of ALA are not only spending a great deal of their time on self-directed learning, but they are doing so at a significantly greater rate than their colleagues in other types of libraries. They receive more support for professional development, but that support does not make any difference in whether they pursue informal or formal learning. As discussed elsewhere (Varlejs 1997), factors not included in the model that guided this study may turn out to have greater explanatory power. Organizational culture, professional roles and the nature of job responsibilities, performance requirements, career stage—these are just some examples of potential influences on work-related learning. Also, the importance of motivation should not be underestimated (Varlejs, in press).

As Havener and Worrell (1994) point out, members of ALA are not necessarily representative of the profession as a whole. They found that Oklahoma academic librarians differed in their professional development activities depending on the type of academic library in which they worked and that librarians in doctorate-granting institutions were more likely to belong to ALA. Although the study reported in this paper did not differentiate among various types of academic institutions, the fact that 70 percent of the academic librarians worked in larger libraries suggests that one should take the advice of Havener and Worrell and not make generalizations about academic librarianship as a whole on the basis of the data presented here.

At the same time, it is not inappropriate to draw conclusions about differences between the academic librarians and the others in the sample, as long as one keeps in mind that all are ALA members and therefore not necessarily an accurate reflection of the profession at large. The most noteworthy contrast that emerges from the data analysis presented here is illustrated in table 10. Although academic librarians are more likely to be involved in self-directed learning, they are less likely to participate in formal continuing education. On the other hand, the formal CE and SDL measures are significantly correlated. It may be that academic librarians conform to the findings of a recent study of workplace learning:

> Employees develop skills and knowledge through a combination of informal and formal learning opportunities. Informal learning is ubiquitous and fulfills many learning needs. However, when both informal and formal learning occur, employees have richer opportunities for development. In general, our research considers formal and informal learning as existing along a continuum rather than being two dichotomous learning processes (Education Development Center 1998, 11).

Although the report notes that workers feel that informal learning is more important in a number of ways, it stresses the synergistic interaction of the two.

Conclusion

Compared to other ALA members, academic librarians are more highly committed to self-directed learning, much of it triggered by technological change. They rely less on formal continuing education and attend fewer professional association meetings, but read professional literature and publish more than their colleagues in other libraries. It appears that their professional development activities are not influenced by the amount of release time, financial assistance, or other support provided in their work setting. Rather, they may be motivated by factors inherent in the nature of their work and by expectations of performance imposed by employers and clients. Or, perhaps, an ingrained affinity for learning may be the best explanation. The Campbell Interest and Skill survey places librarians in a category "similar to those of people who enjoy and pursue graduate study. Their CISS scores also indicated that they preferred solitary activities" (Johnson, Nilsen, and Campbell 1994, 56).

Further research is indicated to clarify aspects of organizational culture that encourage learning, to describe the process of self-directed learning, and to assess the quality of the experience. A great deal of time and effort is devoted to informal learning, and therefore it is important to understand how that learning might better be supported and facilitated.

References

Clark, K., and S. Kalin. 1996. Technostressed out? How to cope in the digital age. *Library Journal.* 121(13):30–32.

Cromer, D. E., and A. R. Testi. 1994. Integrated continuing education for reference librarians. *Reference Services Review* 22(4):51–80.

Education Development Center. 1998. *The teaching firm: Where productive work and learning converge.* Newton, Mass.: Education Development Center.

Havener, W. M., and W. A. Stolt. 1994. The professional development activities of academic librarians: Does institutional support make a difference? *College & Research Libraries* 55(1):25–36.

Havener, W. M., and P. Worrell. 1994. Environmental factors in professional development activities: Does type of academic library affiliation make a difference? *Library & Information Science Research.* 16:219–39.

Johnson, R. W., D. L. Nilsen, and D. P. Campbell. 1994. Interests and skills of librarians as measured by the Campbell Interest and Skill survey. In *Discovering librarians: Profiles of a profession,* ed. M.J. Scherdin, 52–59. Chicago: ALA.

Lazinger, S. S., J. Bar-Ilan, and B. C. Peritz. 1997. Internet use by faculty members in various disciplines: A comparative case study. *Journal of the American Society for Information Science* 48(6):508–18.

Powell, R.R. 1988. Sources of professional knowledge for academic librarians. *College & Research Libraries* 49:332–40.

Ratzan, L. 1998. Making sense of the Internet: A metaphorical approach. Unpublished doctoral dissertation, Rutgers, State Univ. of New Jersey, New Brunswick, N.J.

Shonrock, D., and C. Mulder. 1993. Instruction librarians: Acquiring the proficiencies critical to their work. *College & Research Libraries* 54:137–49.

Tennant, R. 1998. The most important management decision: Hiring staff for the new millennium. *Library Journal* 123(3):102.

Tough, A. 1978. Major learning efforts: Recent research and future directions. *Adult Education* 28(4):250–63.

Varlejs, J. 1996. Librarians' self-directed continuing professional learning. Doctoral dissertation, University of Wisconsin-Madison.

———. 1997. Facilitating workplace learning. In *Human development: Competencies for the twenty-first century,* ed. P.L. Ward and D.E. Weingand, 98–104. Munich: Saur.

———. In press. On their own: Librarians' self-directed, work-re-

Reflections of an Early Explorer

David S. Magier

discovered the Internet as a graduate student in linguistics at the University of California-Berkeley around 1978, at a time before it was called the Internet and before it was known at all beyond a narrow group of computer people. No one had a personal computer back then, and writing projects involved nothing more technologically complex than a typewriter. A fellow student introduced me to computers and later showed me how to access and remotely edit my own files (such as drafts of my thesis) on the campus mainframe. That was the only Internet training I have ever received. I picked up the other components of the early Internet—listservs, Usenet newsgroups, telnet, ftp—gradually over the next decade, as I started to explore and discover resources of interest (as well as curiosities and entertainment), and figured out for myself how to use them.

Initially, I was not drawn to the computer network. A friend in the department showed me how to get access to the computer department's network, but I failed to see any relevance for my own work, which consisted of endless typing and retyping of drafts of term papers, on a Selectric typewriter. Over the next couple of years, I came to see the value of using the campus mainframe to compose and edit my papers. (Remember, this was long before the existence of personal computers.) Then I started hanging around the computer lab to work on term papers and learned just enough about computing to get the work done.

Necessary Problem-Solving Leads to Early Network Awareness
The Problem: Going beyond the Keyboard

At some point, however, I ran into a problem. I was working on my master's thesis, which was on the Hindi language and which needed to contain example sentences in Hindi. Although I had access to an old manual Hindi typewriter and theoretically could use it to type the Hindi portions of my paper, I did not want to go back to manual retyping and decided to try to figure out a way to do this work on the mainframe. So I spent more time at the computer lab, eventually hitting on the idea of using a romanized transliteration to represent the Hindi.

However, I still had the problem of representing the diacritical marks, which were not part of the standard character set (nowadays known as ASCII). For example, the established way to represent a long "a" sound was to type the "a" with a macron over it. (The macron is a short horizontal line over a vowel, to represent vowel length.) To represent a nasalized vowel, one would type a tilde over it. (The tilde is the curly line [~] that appears over the "n" in many words in Spanish. Kids call a tilde "the Nike swoosh").

For my Hindi work, I needed to represent long nasalized vowels, which would require both a macron and a tilde to be placed over the vowel. How could I type my files onto the mainframe and get them to print out with these kinds of nonstandard diacritical marks? I solved this problem by teaching myself how to write macros (programs) to control the printer. I was using a standard text editor and printing to a daisy-wheel printer. I started to write a program to instruct the printer to carry out complex instructions to compose the diacritical marks I needed.

In effect, my program told the printer,
> print the letter 'a',
> then backspace,
> then roll the paper roller up some small amount (say 3/32 of an inch),
> then type a hyphen over the 'a' (to represent the macron),
> then backspace again,
> then roll up another small specified amount,
> then type a tilde over the hyphen,
> then roll the paper back down to starting text baseline,
> to continue typing the rest of the word . . . .

By writing a series of macros similar to the above to cover every possible letter-plus-diacritic combination I would need for Hindi, I was able to develop a "language" for the printout of my work.

Macro Knowledge Sources

How did I come to write such macros, not being a computer person and not being particularly drawn to the computer lab environment? I had to read print-driver documentation files that had to be retrieved from the mainframe and even from other computers via FTP (file transfer proto-col). This put me in touch with how the networks operated to give me access to remote files. Therefore, though I had started out just seeking a way to save time on my work, it turned out not to be a time-saver but a challenge and I started to enjoy it. I hung out late nights when I could get a terminal in the dingy computer lab just to pick up what I thought I needed to make my work easier, but I stuck around not because it really was easier but because it had become interesting.

E-mail: The Next Step

The next step came in 1979 or so, when a colleague in the linguistics department showed me e-mail. Almost no one beyond the computer science department was using it, but it was possible to send in-house e-mail to one or two students and one professor in my own depart-ment. E-mail had a unique flavor to it. It gave the computer a feeling of having a life of its own. Instead of just being an obscure (and fairly boring) tool for word processing, suddenly there was a real person at the other end interacting with you. The computer became a window onto other things that had nothing to do with computers themselves.

Going Away and Coming Back to Computers: Culture Shock

I spent a semester in Pakistan on the Berkeley Urdu Language Program in Pakistan (BULPIP). It was a time away from computers and computing. When I came back, I noticed that more people were getting involved with the campus computing environment, and some were even experimenting with early personal computers. I started to hear about people buying a Kaypro or other PCs. One anthropology professor had programmed all his papers onto his PC, just as I had done on the mainframe. I was definitely intrigued by all this new growth and attention to computers by noncomputer people, and I began to spend more time at the computer lab to learn more.

In 1981, I went on a year-long Fulbright Fellowship to India to do the fieldwork for my doctoral dissertation on the Marwari dialect of the Rajasthani language (a language of more than 35 million speakers whose grammar had never been described linguistically). I stayed in villages around the state of Rajasthan, picking up the language, recording conversation, gossip, political debates, etc. I brought back hundreds of hours of audiocassettes which I eventually analyzed to write my 400-page dissertation titled "Topics in the Grammar of Marwari."

When I arrived back in Berkeley from India, I really began to live down at the computer lab. I survived on candy and lousy tea from the vending machines set up there for the all-night maniacs like me throwing themselves at the rows of keyboards and screens. For the drafts of each chapter, I again used the daisy-wheel printers and my diacritic macros. I had to purchase my own daisy wheels (which wore out about every two weeks) and my own printer ribbons.

My work was all stored on the mainframe, and I had to trust that it would not disappear one day. At one point, I did start to worry about this and bought some reels of tape to back up my files, though few people were doing back ups. (Today, we take file backup for granted because it is so easy to do. At that time, however, making a physical copy of one's mainframe files was a major undertaking).

I could access my files from the computer lab, but the environment there was starting to wear me out. The linguistics department had a terminal with a 300-baud acoustic analog modem (you dial the phone and then place the handset into a foam-cupped cradle so it can transmit the sounds through a microphone to communicate with the main-frame). One could use the linguistics terminal for e-mail (mostly for diversions and social activity), but I could not spend the hours there that I needed for my dissertation writing.

The library also was not a solution because at that time it was totally unconnected to the computer networks and my research was based almost exclusively on fieldwork. So little had been written about Marwari, I actually did not spend a lot of time there. The solution to my problem came when the Center for South Asian Studies lent me a terminal and a 300-baud modem to take home so that I could access and edit my mainframe files over the telephone from home.

I worked on my dissertation this way for a couple of weeks, but then I had to stop. At a 300-baud transmission rate, your eyes automatically follow the cursor as it slowly displays the text and updates the screen character by character. This endless back-and-forth eye movement led to blinding headaches. Eventually, the Center for South Asian Studies got me a state-of-the-art 900-baud modem. Now my headaches went away as I was tracking line by line (instead of character by character) at this blinding speed!

As I edited from home, I went twice a week to the computer center with my daisy wheels and ribbons to print out the drafts of each chapter for review by my dissertation committee. As the committee reviewed my work and gave extensive conceptual and editorial feedback, I had to continually rewrite each section many times. The power and value of word processing over typewriters was abundantly obvious!

However, to keep on schedule, when one of my committee members went on sabbatical, I had to find a way to get my drafts to him and get his comments even while he was away. That is when I began to use e-mail extensively for my work. I found that I could not send whole chapters at once because the e-mail program would not accept such large files. I e-mailed "chunks" of my work one at a time. The committee member would print out the e-mail chunks, mark them up with corrections and comments, and mail them back to me by post.

Then, I began to get comments by e-mail itself: comments and corrections referred to my chunks by paragraphs and lines. This operation sold me on the merits of e-mail. I was also starting to use the library's computers to do a literature search for the dissertation.

In the fall of 1983, I completed my dissertation and was awarded my doctoral degree in linguistics. I went off to a year of teaching in Pakistan, followed by a second year there as field director of the Berkeley Urdu Program. When I returned in 1985, I took up another one-year teaching position in linguistics at Michigan State University. I experienced extreme culture shock upon my return. Now many people had their own PCs and few high-tech electronic typewriters and word processors. E-mail was spreading rapidly; ftp was ubiquitous, and there was a flurry of listservs and group forums. So much had changed while I was away, and I was desperate to catch up and cash in on this network bonanza.

I purchased an early MacPlus on academic discount and was the proud owner of a state-of-the-art, top-of-the-line hard drive—a mind-boggling 20 megabytes! It only cost $900 back then! Using my spiffy new 1200-baud modem, I could dial into the campus to connect to the campus network. I could search for books in the library and not only locate the record of the book I needed, but even issue an online request to have it delivered to my office.

I kept in touch with my old friends and colleagues back at Berkeley via e-mail. We circulated preprints and ideas for papers, and I found various online amusements such as great science fiction stories being posted to early newsgroups. I could store such files on my account on campus and then download them for printout. I was browsing around ftp archives around 1987 when I found a wonderful cache of science-fantasy graphic image files. Although it could take up to three hours to download such a file, it was great fun to select one, download it, print it on my Mac printer, and attach it as a "cover" to my printouts of new science fiction stories I had also found on the Net. This was living!

Becoming a Librarian and an Internet Trainer

The real explosive growth in the Internet's content during the late 1980s and early 1990s came about as a direct result of the evolution of consistent user-friendly integrative services—gopher and, eventually, the Web—and accompanied my own career jump from professor of linguistics to librarian, with daily responsibilities involving use of the Internet.

During 1987, my first child was born. After bouncing around from city to city, I started to find such one-year stints in academe tiring. I decided to make a career leap and applied for the position of South Asia Librarian at Columbia University Libraries. It sounded like interesting work, I personally knew most of the faculty as colleagues in my field, and it was in my hometown, New York. What did I have to lose? After I got that job, I found that I could satisfy my urge to be in front of a classroom by doing bibliographic instruction. During the first two years, I also taught regular for-credit courses for the Southern Asian Institute at Columbia, including an interdisciplinary course on language and society in South Asia.

Columbia University Libraries, Development of Internet Training: The Beginnings

Columbia had cutting- edge networking technology and a strong inclination to invest in development of Internet resources and services. I was elected to the Representative Committee of Librarians the year that we conducted an intensive study of the libraries' internal communication needs. One of our chief recommendations was that all librarians should be given direct access to e-mail, and this recommendation was carried out. (Nowadays, many institutions take this for granted, but it was a novel concept at that time.) As a symbol of the perceived importance of coordination, Columbia's Libraries and Academic Computing (AcIS) have been administratively joined since 1987. Campuswide cable pulling for ethernet was a major project under way, and everyone's office was set up for direct network access. In the late 1980s, individual computers were placed on most librarians' desks. The message went out that we had to "master this computer," although quite a few had no idea what it might do for them or why it would be important to the work they were already doing. Still, most welcomed the connectivity and the opportunity to see where all this was heading.

Knowing Computers, Teaching Others

Although I really did not know what I was doing, as an "old-timer" on the Internet, I became a de facto computer guru within the library. Although I did not have a library degree and was a newcomer to the field of librarianship, my close connection to the faculty and my apparent ease with the networking content brought me into close cooperation with my colleagues. People would bring their issues and puzzles to me and I helped them out as best I could.

Internet Training: Grassroots Origins at Columbia Libraries

In 1991, Internet training began to rise as an issue and a puzzle for Columbia libraries. This began at first with a small, grassroots group of Internet users. I believe we called ourselves the Library Internet Users Group, and we came together to share knowledge and ideas. This group was later officially recognized by the administration as the Internet Core Group. Catherine Thomas and Dan Caldano, whose reflections also appear in this book, were in that first exploratory group. The demand for Internet access and use also came from grassroots sources. People began to perceive their needs for training and actively sought it. Eventually, they came to this core group to get advice and hands-on help, and this, along with growing administrative recognition of the broad strategic need for well-trained librarians, ultimately moved the group into directly confronting the challenge of designing a systematic Internet training program.

Internet Training Program

In 1992, we were renamed the Internet Training Program. The consequences of that shift (from grassroots demand to formal training program) included assigned roles, formal charges to committees, mission statements, program development deadlines, formal evaluation instruments, and other organizational aspects. It meant that we had to move from reacting to expressed needs to planning what others ought to know and what we would teach. Patricia O'Brien Libutti observed the Internet Training Program in action for an entire semester in 1994. These observations are reported elsewhere in this book. The reflections of Catherine Thomas and Dan Caldano provide other perspectives of the experience. My own development with Internet training continued and is described in some detail in the second part of this book.

Part II

Enlarging the Internet-Literate: Early Training and Learning Experiences

Six Degrees of Connectedness: Assessing the Beginning of Internet Expertise

Rona L. Ostrow and Debra Randorf

ittle research focuses on the librarian who attained Internet expertise early in the diffusion of the technology. This article begins by
examining early studies of surveys examining factors involved in
the learning and teaching of the Internet. Six Degrees of Connectedness, an ACRL/NY-sponsored program held at Bobst Library, New
York University, in May 1994, was attended by many librarians wishing to explore the who, what, where, why, and how of Internet learning and teaching. Before attending, librarians were encouraged to respond to a survey questionnaire electronically distributed to listservs.
The data were qualitatively analyzed and presented. Surveys that focused on the same phenomena since 1994 conclude the article.

Background

Librarians have been admirably coping with new technologies on an
ongoing and continuing basis since the late 1970s, despite early dire
predictions about their inability to adapt to rapid technological change.
The occupational culture of professional librarians, long considered
one that emphasizes and values continuity, established practices, and
time-honored traditions (Martin 1984), has meant that librarians have
viewed themselves, and have been viewed by others, as likely to resist
change and unlikely to take technological advances in stride. Wilson
(1982), for example, cited the Maryland Manpower Project (1967–1970)

which had predicted that librarians would not be able to meet the challenges of technological change.

Similarly, Birdsall (1994) reminded us of the 1977 American Library Association (ALA) annual conference which had identified the "identity crisis" of professional librarians faced with the demands of the information society (28). Boisse and Stoffle (1978) reported that the conference was marked by: (1) ambiguity and uncertainty about the role of librarians and libraries in modern society; (2) a "continued malaise" about library education; (3) fear of the uncertainty of the future and the rapid technological advances to come; and (4) exasperation with their inability to fully participate in the path the information society of the future was likely to take. Finally, Giuliano's 1979 article "Manifesto for Librarians" warned librarians to shift their loyalty away from the "outmoded relic of the Industrial Age" (i.e., the library) and embrace the Information Age. Given this perceived high level of apprehension, it is not surprising that the extent to which libraries readily accept technological advances and incorporate and absorb them into their existing structures varies widely.

However, librarians have learned to coexist with, and even capitalize on, successive waves of technology in the past quarter century, and the profession has grown and changed accordingly. Technological issues are now taught routinely in graduate schools of library science, so that new graduates enter the profession with an unprecedented degree of technological expertise. Online catalogs and union catalogs; mediated searches on Dialog, BRS, and STN; and user-friendly CD-ROM databases have been successively and successfully mastered not only by librarians, but also by the constituencies they serve. Indeed, as Ostrow (1998) discovered, innovation in libraries has resulted in a leadership role for librarians who cast themselves in the role of advocates for and teachers of information technology. Thus, in many cases, librarians have become both consumers and teachers of technology.

Certainly not all librarians are equally willing, able, and eager to adapt to each wave of technology, but the profession has certainly spawned its share of innovators and early adopters. The diffusion of innovations has been defined and studied by Rogers (1995) and others. In marketing terms, an innovator is the "first consumer to adopt a new product, service, or idea. Innovators tend to be . . . willing to take considerable risk in adopting new trends" (Ostrow and Smith 1988,

121). Similarly, early adopters are "consumers who are among the first to purchase a new product or service. They frequently . . . occupy leadership positions, and are anxious to keep up with the latest trends . . ." (Ostrow and Smith 1988, 82). As part of the diffusion process by which a product or service is adopted in successive stages by members of a target market, many librarians may be classified as innovators and early adopters, continually experimenting with new ways of providing information to their respective constituencies.

Again in marketing terms, the concept of the diffusion process implies that other, more conservative consumers will gradually follow the lead of the innovators and early adopters. In terms of the diffusion process, members of the early and late majorities, laggards, and finally nonadopters all play their respective roles (Ostrow and Smith 1988). Use of the innovation results from emulation of the earlier groups and often word-of-mouth diffusion. In the case of librarians learning to use the Internet, training one's colleagues has also resulted in increased Internet use.

This ability to adapt, adjust, and teach has now carried over to the Internet. As we approach the close of the twentieth century, Internet use has become commonplace not only among librarians working in libraries, but also among end users working from their homes and offices. However, in the early 1990s, widespread use of the Internet was still rare and somewhat cumbersome for most users. Prior to the advent of the now-ubiquitous World Wide Web, both librarians and end users struggled to master the challenges presented by electronic mail, gophers, Archie and Veronica, Mosaic, listservs, and ftp (file transfer protocol). Training was not widely available, equipment was primitive by today's standards, and most learning was a matter of trial and error requiring time, patience, and curiosity.

This article deals with those early library adopters and innovators who were among the first in the profession to incorporate Internet use into the information arsenal provided by their libraries. Specifically, it presents the results of a survey of academic librarians conducted via several library-related listservs prior to the May 25, 1994, ACRL/NY program Six Degrees of Connectedness. The open-ended questions found at the end of this article allowed participants to comment on and describe in their own words their early Internet learning experiences, their advice to novices, the types of innovative programs they had already begun to provide for others, and their relationship with other campus departments, particularly the local academic computing center.

Although an extensive and thorough review of the literature concerning librarians as learners and teachers of the Internet is provided in another article, a brief look at the results found by similar survey instruments, particularly in the early 1990s, is in order here. The following section contains a discussion of some of the more germane survey results concerning the early adoption of the Internet by librarians.

Pre-1994 Surveys

Several surveys, similar in scope and content to the 1994 study, help us to identify some of the key issues in the relationship among the librarian, the end user, and the Internet and to clarify the issues that impact on librarians as learners and teachers. As such, these surveys contribute to our understanding of the results of the present study. Some of the issues include the availability of formal or informal training, the allocation of time for self-directed learning, the overall sense of connectedness and being part of a networked community the Internet imparts to its users, the relationship between the computer center and the library, and the relationship among academic librarians, students, and classroom faculty.

Outreach and Networking

For many early adopters of the Internet, its main attractions were the outreach and networking capabilities it represented, particularly in the form of electronic mail and listservs. Ladner and Tillman (1993) surveyed fifty-four special librarians and information specialists in the summer of 1991 to determine the ways in which they used the Internet to provide reference service to their clientele. Respondents reported an overwhelming use of the Internet for communicating with colleagues. Internet access helped to mitigate these librarians' feelings of isolation and to foster a sense of connectedness with the wider library community. Respondents also expressed satisfaction in being able to speedily communicate with external organizations. Indeed, one early reference use of the Internet was to elicit the assistance of other librarians in the search for answers to otherwise problematic reference questions. The responses showed an ongoing and participatory networking use by special librarians.

Ladner and Tillman (1993) further found that electronic mail expedites reference service as well as the delivery of materials. Participants also utilized online discussion groups (listservs or lists) such as BUSLIB-L, LIBREF-L, MEDLIB-L, and STUMPERS-L. Respondents also reported satisfaction and success in using the Internet to search the online public catalogs (OPACs) of other libraries and to access bibliographic services and databases such as OCLC, RLIN, MEDLINE, and DIALOG. Not surprisingly, because these special librarians were working in corporations, institutes, museums, hospitals, and other nonacademic venues, all of the use of the Internet was performed by the librarians themselves as they continued to serve as information intermediaries for their constituents.

Reference Work and Direct Access by Patrons

Early Internet use in academic libraries was somewhat different from its intermediary-based use in special libraries. Academic libraries were more likely to focus on end-user access and, consequently, end-user training. For example, Tenopir and Neufang (1995) compared the results of 1991 and 1994 surveys of Association of Research Libraries (ARL) members. They reported that three-quarters of the large academic library members of ARL had incorporated Internet access for library patrons into their electronic arsenal by 1994. They also found that "electronic reference had been fully integrated into reference work in most of these libraries" (67), primarily for ready reference or e-mail reference. Other uses included remote database access, research consultation, and access to other library catalogs.

Particularly relevant to the current study is the user education and training provided by these academic research libraries. Tenopir and Neufang found that instruction had become even more important in responding libraries in 1994 than it had been in 1991. They also found that instruction librarians taught access and computerized information basics in addition to sources and content. Many of the participating ARL libraries offered Internet training within the confines of the library building. The librarians provided both individual and group instruction and taught special Internet classes as well as Internet components of regular library instruction. None of the responding libraries had yet begun to utilize computer-assisted instruction or videotapes for the purpose of Internet instruction. Finally, the authors found that online remote access, including access to the Internet and commercial online systems aimed at end users, was rapidly replacing CD-ROM and tape loads as the preferred mode of electronic access to information.

In order to be able to teach Internet use to others, the librarians themselves had to learn about its capabilities and its use. For some early innovators, training involved only their own exploration, motivated by either their own curiosity or an administrative directive. The following section describes survey results concerning how librarians learned the Internet.

Training for Librarians

In 1993, Basu (1995) surveyed librarians in New Jersey and found that most of the librarians who responded were still novice users of the Internet; only 20 percent of respondents had used it for more than two years. Some of the librarians had received training in the form of lectures, workshops, and hands-on experiences, and many were self-taught; a full 30 percent reported having received no formal training. Although some respondents had received training from campus academic computing centers, most had learned to use the Internet from reading, experimenting, hands-on training, and joining user groups. Basu reported that librarians frequently mentioned lack of sufficient time to explore and practice and that Internet training was rarely done as a regular staff development activity. Although the respondents commented favorably on the availability of gophers, Archie, WAIS and Mosaic to make Internet searching more manageable, they also expressed concern about the sheer quantity of available information and the lack of uniformity, indexing, protocols, and standardization for effective use. Ultimately, this survey showed that many librarians were not using the Internet to answer reference questions and that those who did had only intermittent success.

Another early survey involved a 1993 workshop at the Western Kentucky University Libraries. The workshop focused on effective means of training librarians to use the Internet so that they might teach it to others. Participants included all Western Kentucky University Libraries faculty from public and technical services, special collections, and the Kentucky Museum (Foster et al. 1993). Although all participants reported some experience with electronic library resources, the campus had not yet been wired for the Internet. The authors of the survey concluded that the intensive workshop (which had included a variety of presentations on Gopher, Veronica, and Archie accompanied by online demonstrations and a hands-on session in the computer lab) was an effective way of introducing librarians to the Internet so that they might, in turn, empower nonlibrarian end users.

Sutton (1992) describe some of the early pitfalls encountered by librarians eager to learn the Internet. These problems include economic and technological access (merely providing access on campus), training (for the librarians), and the desire to help make the Internet more logical and accessible. As a survey by Miller (1994) demonstrates, learning the Internet has sometimes been a time-consuming and anxiety-provoking activity, depending on support librarians did or did not receive from their supervisors and administrators; yet most librarians polled considered e-mail and networking well worth the effort.

Given this backdrop of librarians' concerns regarding the Internet, the present study is intended to elucidate the experiences of some of the early Internet adopters and innovators in the academic library field to better understand their role in the overall diffusion process (i.e., spreading the word to their library colleagues, students, and faculty). As we have seen above, librarians' concerns have been manifested in a number of specific needs such as (1) training, (2) time to explore and discover, (3) cooperation from campus academic computing centers, (4) training programs for endusers, and (5) standardization and organization of Internet resources.

Methodology

The fifteen-item survey on which this reflection is based was developed by Lisa Dyckman and distributed electronically over several Internet listservs aimed at academic librarians, including BI-L and NYACRL-L. It originally targeted librarians participating in the ACRL/ NY program Six Degrees of Connectedness. Patricia Libutti tabulated the results and used them to prepare a report for the program. The program was organized by Elena Cevallos, Lisa Dyckman, and Patricia Libutti, chairs of ACRL/NY interest groups.

Although more than 60 participants actually attended the program, the survey also included librarians who did not attend but who were anxious to share their views electronically. The responses, collected via e-mail prior to the conference, provide insight into the ways these often self-described "loners" educated themselves about the Internet. Respondents represented the full range of expertise (novice to cybernaut on a self-rated scale of 1 to 10), with most librarians rating themselves at the high middle range of the scale (5 to 7). Conference attendees received preliminary summaries of the survey results. The open-ended questionnaire is provided in the appendix of this article.

The data were coded manually by Debra Randorf and content-analyzed by Rona Ostrow. Qualitative analysis was selected as a means to elicit the unique responses of participants. Wherever possible, participant's own words and comments have been incorporated into the analysis.

Results

The Internet may be traced to the development of ARPAnet by the Defense Department in the 1960s and its subsequent transformation into an information network by the National Science Foundation (Rosenthal and Spiegelman 1996, 54); the proliferation of resources available through its use and its ever-growing availability to the general public resulted in its incipient adoption by libraries in the 1990s. The respondents to the present survey were all pioneers on their respective campuses and overcame a number of obstacles to introduce Internet use to their constituencies. How they themselves learned to use the Internet, any support and encouragement they received, and the level of training available for librarians are the subjects of the following section.

Librarians as Learners

The overwhelming majority of the survey's innovators and early adopters were self-taught or learned through colleagues or family members who were involved in academic computing or programming; little, if any, formal training was available to most of them at the time. One wrote: "I have taught myself the little I know about the Internet. I read a book . . . but basically I 'surf' to find new things! It's not so easy." Several report forming teams with colleagues who helped each other learn.

All these self-taught learners reported devoting a great deal of time to practicing their Internet skills and exploring (surfing) whenever time allowed. One respondent reported learning "by bumbling around and having colleagues do informal demos." Characteristically, e-mail, listservs, or both were the first Internet capabilities to which the librarians were introduced. One participant who went from being a learner to a teacher wrote:

I was first asked to be a rover and help others during a hands-on part of a workshop in the spring of 1992 . . . . I help mostly with e-mail and ftp, logon, etc. From that time on, I learned sources and procedures by demos from other librarians as we got new and changing sources. Lots of practice and then taught classes and at reference.

Time was one of the main considerations for these early users, as little recognition was afforded Internet expertise and little consideration was given to those self-starters who were learning it on their own. Indeed, most reported having to work Internet exploring into their already-crowded schedules and workloads, and some honed their skills at home. One self-taught librarian wrote: "I first connected through NJIN [NJ Intercampus Network] and used the start-up information they provided. I worked at home on my PC and learned mostly by trial and error and help from Ed Krol's book." Only one respondent reported having the Internet introduced by a library director who supported the librarians' devotion of time to mastering it.

Those who were already computer literate found Internet use a natural outgrowth of their other activities. One wrote: "I learned it on my own, an outgrowth of using VM for the past 10 years." Another explained: "[I am] self-taught while beginning as a reference librarian at Princeton University. Also, my husband is a computer programmer, and he helped me learn UNIX."

Several respondents worked at campuses at which the academic computing center was already using the Internet and providing training for students and faculty as well as librarians. Others reported learning the fundamentals at a local workshop and then pursuing additional Internet knowledge on their own. For example, one respondent wrote: "About two years ago I went to a LACUNY workshop on electronic mail. This gave me an overview; then I just basically taught myself."

The handful of recent library school graduates who responded to the survey had all received some introduction to the Internet as part of their course work. One recent graduate, who had been exposed to the Internet in library school, experienced a degree of frustration in trying to learn more from experienced Internet users. She explained:

Started with library school in '92. Then began to explore on my own. Found that those who know "do." It's hard to tear them away to teach others. That's how they become experts. However, if you take some initiative, try things, then ask specific questions, expert users will be more helpful.

Of course, it should not be surprising that librarians turned to books to help them learn about the Internet and several participants mentioned particular print resources they had consulted. A few even joined training workshops presented on the Internet itself and gleaned tips from various listservs and teleconferences. Several reported participating in online Internet "hunts" designed to guide exploration.

Still others utilized a variety of strategies to improve their Internet skills. One respondent, who exemplifies the resourcefulness that early adopters characteristically demonstrate, explained her personal odyssey as follows:

> I read several periodical articles including "Surfing the Internet" by Jean Armour Polly. Also, I had seen at least one demonstration of the Internet. One occasion which comes to mind was at an MPALS Search Instructors Group meeting, which was held at Manhattan College a year or year and a half ago. A librarian at Manhattan College gave us a brief demonstration, focusing, as I recall, on Telnet. I have also read through parts of a number of books on the Internet. Most recently, since our computer labs now have full Internet access, I have explored the Internet on my own, primarily by using the NYSERNET gopher based in Albany, NY. I had heard from computer center staff that one of our psychology professors was showing his students how to use the Internet. I asked if I could attend one of his classes. He showed how to access Internet services in the computer labs and introduced us to the NYSERNET gopher. I realize, of course, that there . . . is a lot more to the Internet than gopher.

In this early period of library adoption of the Internet, very few librarians were using the Web; they cited, instead, listservs and gophers as their favorite Internet resources. Some reported using the Internet for commercial document delivery services, and several mentioned accessing the catalogs of other libraries. However, the popularity of gophers, in particular, indicates the subject/keyword approach of the library community and suggests the kinds of uses librarians hoped to make of the Internet.

Librarians as Teachers

Academic librarians also reported leading the way in teaching the Internet to others on their campuses, providing programs for other librarians, faculty, and students in approximately equal numbers (with only a slightly smaller number providing training for staff).

Not surprisingly, the librarians tended to train their constituents in all aspects of Internet use, even those that have little direct relationship to library research. Thus, gopher, e-mail, and listservs are all widely taught; Telnet, ftp, Usenet, and Mosaic rank close seconds.

For the most part, this training took the form of one-shot presentations, though a few librarians reported providing a sequence of sessions. Almost universally, the goals of these early sessions were to introduce beginners to the Internet and give them enough exposure to enable them to explore on their own. Follow-up was often limited to consultation in person, by telephone, or by e-mail. Most respondents had begun these programs on their own initiative, often filling a recognized void on their campuses; a few of the respondents, however, had initiated training programs at the request of their directors.

Hands-on instruction, preferably in an electronic classroom, was almost universally advocated by responding librarians. Whereas a few librarians reported having electronic classrooms of their own, several utilized the facilities of the campus academic computing lab. However, this was not a problem-free solution. One librarian wrote:

> The sessions I have done, I did in the computer center. They have an IBM lab with 30 networked PCs. Problem is, I can only use it on Monday and Wednesdays from 12–2. I think hands-on training is absolutely necessary. I have done both and when you just present material, people get a kind of glazed-over look. I know I would! The classroom planned for the library will have 16 PCs which I think is a manageable number. Maybe we'll have it in the fall. Maybe not.

Programs tended to center on Internet function (e.g., Veronica, gophers, and e-mail) rather than on subject area or discipline (e.g., psychology, literature, or history). Most librarians considered it the library's responsibility to train Internet users, though some suggested a joint responsibility shared by the library and academic computing. For example, one respondent indicated the dual nature of the Internet when she wrote: "The librarians should be able to help users with research/reference-related Internet use, but I think the computer center should offer generic courses in computer/Internet use."

Another responded:

> I have no idea whose job it is. It appears to be the job of anybody who will do it, in addition to their already-full plate. We have a crying need for somebody to help faculty and students technically—setting up modems, etc.—and I do believe that there should be a designated responsibility. Because I like to do it, and because it gives the library some panache, I think the library might be designated to teach content. I do believe that the Internet is going to be part of the reference librarian's panoply of skills.

Research Conclusions

The librarians who responded to this survey were quite obviously self-selected and leaders of the pack. They did, after all, already know their way around e-mail and listservs—or they would not have been able to either receive or respond to this survey. The results, therefore, help us to understand a group of pioneering librarians who had to scramble to learn what they could about the Internet, teach themselves much of it, and quickly turn around and transfer that information to others in the diffusion chain—other librarians, students, faculty, and staff. In so doing, they showed a determination not to be left behind on the Information Superhighway of the early 1990s and an unwillingness to let go unchallenged predictions that the widespread use of the Internet would mean an end to the library profession. Indeed, by becoming the pioneer users and teachers of Internet skills, these librarians carved out a new role for libraries and librarians and in the information future.

Post-1994 Surveys
Increased Instructional Role

Subsequent studies have confirmed many of the findings of our survey. Condic (1995), for example, surveyed 150 academic libraries to determine Internet teaching methods, promotion, the use of librarians' time and service, and maintenance of search skills. The results showed that training programs aimed at library staff and the wider academic community frequently took the form of workshops and presentations and that libraries and computer centers often collaborated to provide instruction.

Rosenthal and Spiegelman (1996) reported the results of a survey of New York State academic reference librarians. Their results confirm our own findings of an increased instructional role for librarians. Rosenthal and Spiegelman argued that the Internet has cast librarians increasingly in the role of conduit of Internet knowledge for the entire campus" (64). The researchers found that the Internet was rarely used at the reference desk for ready reference or general reference purposes. Even sophisticated respondents, experienced users of electronic technology, sometimes thought the Internet overrated. Rosenthal and Spiegelman further found that formal training contributed significantly to the actual use of the Internet by academic reference librarians. The authors recommended that librarians play a role in the organization and management of the sometimes-unwieldy Internet resources and take an aggressive approach to its implementation on their home campuses (65). The results of a follow-up survey (Rosenthal and Spiegelman 1998) are discussed elsewhere in this volume.

Cawthorne and Bleiler (1997) surveyed 119 ARL academic libraries to determine which ones were offering workshops and classes on use of the Internet and the Web. Most respondents reported that they provide Internet training for faculty, staff, and students in the form of workshops. Whereas most of the responding libraries had access to at least one electronic classroom for Internet training, many used the facilities of the campus computing center for hands-on instruction. Although librarians taught most of the courses, library administrators, support staff, and classroom faculty also taught Internet use. This trend toward cooperation between academic libraries and computing centers in response to campus demands for Internet training was further confirmed by Schiller (1994).

Training the Trainers
Training for librarians, particularly in academic libraries, is often geared to training the trainers, the hope being to diffuse knowledge from the librarians to the students and faculty members they serve. Surveys

conducted by Zipkowitz (1995) and St. Lifer (1996) have shown that Internet knowledge and use is having an impact on librarians' career paths as well.

On a related note, Market Data Retrieval, Inc. (1997), conducted a national survey of schools and educators who use the Internet/Web. The survey included 6,000 teachers, computer coordinators, and school librarians. Their results indicated four important themes delineating what educators want from the Internet: "(1) greater access to the Internet, especially in the classroom; (2) materials supporting 'real' curriculum areas and actual textbooks used in the classrooms; (3) more organization and content evaluation by subject and grade levels; and (4) more training for teachers."

Hults (1995) explained that although recent library school graduates may have received some formal Internet training, most librarians currently in the field have not. She also argued that librarians experience the same resistance to change as everyone else. She wrote: "Librarians fear the unknown, and the Internet and how it will change the future of libraries is one big unknown" (237). She further argued that although it is still unsure as to whether the library or the academic computing center will eventually assume responsibility for teaching the Internet, librarians will need to incorporate Internet training into their bibliographic instruction sessions, along with the critical thinking skills needed to help students distinguish between the reputable and the questionable information they will certainly find there. Consequently, she maintained that academic librarians must learn to use the Internet and that library administrators must make the time and money available for staff training (239).

Senkevitch and Wolfram (1996) evaluated a model for educating rural library professionals in the promotion and use of Internet resources. Their focus was on rural librarians because this group was judged to be more isolated from formal training opportunities than their urban counterparts. The authors identified "a pressing need, not only for programs to increase librarians' awareness and understanding of the Internet, but also for a massive effort to provide Internet-related educational opportunities for pubic librarians" (274). The train the trainers model they adopted identified and targeted librarians who would be likely change agents (i.e., those who could be expected to continue to diffuse the innovation to others). These librarians were gathered together for an intensive and highly structured institute that came to be termed

Internet Boot Camp by participants (281). Results showed that although the postinstitute success in implementing Internet technology in one's home library was dependent on a large number of outside variables (such as community support and availability of funding for technology), the librarians themselves had largely become vocal advocates for Internet technology in their home communities.

All of these Internet-related themes have been picked up in professional commentaries. Saunders (1996), for example, discussed new roles for librarians emerging from the increased use of information technology and, particularly, the Internet. She recommended updating job descriptions to include responsibilities that relate to Internet use and training, including outreach and training of classroom faculty. She also argued that the lines between librarians and computing professionals are continuing to blur.

Day and Armstrong (1996), maintaining that the Internet is transforming the relationship between librarians and classroom faculty, further developed this argument. The authors saw an important role for librarians in helping university faculty identify information resources related to their disciplines, for both their own research and their classroom assignments. The authors recommended teamwork between the librarians and the computer systems staff to help faculty develop Web pages for their departments, citing their own cooperative pilot Internet project with one such academic department in 1994.

Finally, Woodsworth (1998) argued continuing education for librarians, enabling them to master information technology and lead and manage change. Although noting that many "hack" their way to technological competency (62), Woodsworth suggested a more systematic approach may be considered. She particularly recommended that an advanced certificate program in information technology be made available to librarians whose skills are more than five years old. To that end, she recommended that academic libraries devote more of their budgets to staff training and development.

References

Basu, G. 1995. Using Internet for reference: Myths vs. realities. *Computers in Libraries* 15(2). [Online journal]. Available at: http://www.umi.com/pqdweb and/or http://web4.searchbank.com/infotrac.

Birdsall, W. F. 1994. *The myth of the electronic library: Librarianship and social change in America.* Westport, Conn.: Greenwood Pr.

Boisse, J., and C. Stoffle. 1978. Epilogue: Issues and answers: The participants' views. In *The information society: Issues and answers*, ed. E. J. Josey, 115–21. Phoenix, Ariz.: Oryx.

Cawthorne, J. E., and R. Bleiler, comps. 1997. *Internet training in ARL libraries.* SPEC Kit 220. Washington, D.C.: Association of Research Libraries.

Condic, K. S. 1995. *Internet and academic librarians: Training, promotion and time.* ERIC ED 387 136.

Crawford, W., and M. Gorman. 1995. *Future libraries: Dreams, madness and reality.* Chicago: ALA.

Day, P. A., and K. L. Armstrong. 1996. Librarians, faculty, and the Internet: Developing a new information partnership. *Computers in Libraries* 16 (5). [Online journal]. Available at: http://web4.searchbank.com/infotrac.

Foster, C. L., C. Etkin, E. E. Moore, S. L. Staebell, and P. Wright. 1993. The net result: Enthusiasm for exploring the Internet. *Information Technology and Libraries* 12(4). [Online journal]. Available at http:www.umi.com/pqdweb.

Giuliano, V. E. 1979. A manifesto for librarians. *Library Journal* 104 (Sept. 15):1837–42.

Hults, P. 1995. Noodling down the Internet: Or, one foot in the fast lane, the other stuck in the trenches. *Reference Librarian* 51/52:235–40.

Ladner, S. J., and H. N. Tillman. 1993. Using the Internet for reference. *Online* 17. [Online journal]. Available at: http://www.umi.com/pqdweb.

Market Data Retrieval, Inc. 1997. National survey of Internet usage: Teachers, computer coordinators, and school librarians, grades 3–12. ERIC ED 412 894.

Martin, L. A. 1984. *Organizational structure of libraries.* Metuchen, N.J.: Scarecrow.

Miller, J. P. 1994. Should you get wired? *Library Journal* 119(2). [Online journal.] Available at: http://umi.com/pqdweb.

Ostrow, R. 1998. "Library culture in the electronic age: A case study of organizational change." Unpublished doctoral dissertation. Rutgers, State University of New Jersey, New Brunswick.

Ostrow, R., and S. R. Smith. 1988. *The dictionary of marketing.* New York: Fairchild.

Rogers, E. M. 1995. *Diffusion of innovations*, 4th ed. New York: Free Press/ Simon & Schuster.

Rosenthal, M., and M. Spiegelman. 1996. Evaluating use of the Internet among academic reference librarians. *Internet Reference Services Quarterly* 1(1):53–67.

———. 1999. The Internet and workflow: Impact and inferences. In *Librarians as learners, librarians as teachers: The diffusion of Internet expertise in academic libraries*, ed. P. O. Libutti, 181–201. Chicago: ACRL.

Saunders, L. 1996. Changing technology transforms library roles. *Computers in Libraries* 16 (5). [Online journal]. Available at: http:// web4.searchbank.com/infotrac.

Schiller, N. 1994. Internet training and support. Academic libraries and computer centers: Who's doing what? *Internet Research* 4(2):35– 47.

Senkevitch, J. J., and D. Wolfram. 1996. Assessing the effectiveness of a model for educating rural librarians in using Internet resources. *Journal of Education for Library and Information Science* 37(3):272–85.

St. Lifer, E. 1996. Net work: New roles, same mission. *Library Journal* 121(19). [Online journal]. Available at: http://web4.searchbank.com/ infotrac.

Sutton, B. 1992. The networked future of academic libraries. *Illinois Libraries* 74(6):500–6.

Tenopir, C., and R. Neufang. 1995. Electronic reference options: Tracking the changes. *Online* 19(4). [Online journal]. Available at: http:/ /www.umi.com/pqdweb.

Wilson, P. 1982. *Stereotype and status: Librarians in the United States*. Westport, Conn.: Greenwood Pr.

Woodsworth, A. 1998. Learning for a lifetime. *Library Journal* 123(1). [Online journal]. Available at: http://web4.searchbank.com/infotrac.

Zipkowitz, F. 1995. New directions for recent grads. *Library Journal* 120(17). [Online journal]. Available at: http://web4.searchbank.com.

Appendix

Survey Questionnaire for
Six Degrees of Connectedness Meeting
May 25, 1994, New York University, Bobst Library

First: About your Internet learning/experience.

1. How did you learn Internet? Possibly give sources or stories re: learning Internet.

2. What print/online resources would you recommend for a novice?

3. What are your favorite Internet resources?

4. Rate your expertise with Internet on a 1–10 scale.

Second: A brief review of your institution's/your implementation of Internet

1. Who is your intended audience (librarians, faculty, graduate students, students in a particular class or department, etc.)?

2. Which aspects of the Internet and its resources do you cover in your programs (i.e., electronic mail, listserv discussion lists, UseNet, telnetting to library catalogs, using gophers, WAIS, WWW, Mosaic, ftp, Archie, etc.)?

3. Who presents your program? (Is it a one-person endeavor, a collaboration, a shared responsibility, or . . .?)

4. What is your format—one-shot presentation, a sequence of sessions, a multisession class, or . . .?

5. What are the goals and objectives of your program?

6. What is the genesis of your program? Were you breaking new ground or filling a gap? To what extent was this on your initiative and to what extent responding to your constituents' needs?

7. Where do you teach or present your program?

8. How much follow-up support do you offer (can you offer) the audience for your programs?

9. How do you structure your programs—is the material organized by type of resource, Internet function, or scholarly function? Or according to another framework?

10. Briefly describe the training that has been provided for librarians in your institution.

11. [The controversial one]. Whose job is it, in your opinion, to teach Internet resources on campus?

Please return to libutti@mary.fordham.edu BEFORE May 21, 1994, for use during the meeting on May 25.

Code Book For Six Degrees of Connectedness
Questionnaire Responses

1.Librarians learning Internet
   1.1 Teachers
      1.1.1 Librarian colleagues
      1.1.2 Computer center
      1.1.3 Self-taught
      1.1.4 Friends/family members
   1.2 Venues of instruction
      1.2.1 Library school
      1.2.2 Workshops
      1.2.3 Library systems office
      1.2.4 Computer center courses
      1.2.5 Other courses
   1.3 Aids to instruction
      1.3.1 Books
      1.3.2 Articles
      1.3.3 Listservs
      1.3.4 Browsing gophers
      1.3.5 Surfing/exploration
      1.3.6 Internet "hunt"
      1.3.7 Demonstrations

2. Print and online resources for novices
   2.1 Particular Books
      2.1.1 Whole Internet Guide
      2.1.2 Zen and the Art of the Internet
      2.1.3 Internet for Dummies
      2.1.4 Other books
   2.2 Online resources
      2.2.1 Listservs
      2.2.2 Mosaic
      2.2.3 Lynx
      2.2.4 gophers
      2.2.5 Nysernet

3. Favorite Internet resources
   3.1 Library catalogs
   3.2 Gophers
   3.3 Veronica
   3.4 UseNet
   3.5 Listservs
   3.6 E-mail
   3.7 Mosaic
   3.8 CARL Uncover
   3.9 OCLC FirstSearch

4. Levels of expertise (self-rated 1-10)
   4.1 Novice (1)
   4.2 Novice + (2)
   4.3 Novice ++ (3)
   4.4 Some experience (4)
   4.5 More Experience (5)
   4.6 Experienced (6)
   4.7 Almost expert (7)
   4.8 Fairly expert (8)
   4.9 Cybernaut (9-10)

5. Intended audience of training programs
   5.1 Librarians
   5.2 Other staff
   5.3 Faculty
   5.4 Students
      5.4.1 undergraduate students
      5.4.2 graduate students
      5.4.2.1 library school students
   5.5 Alumni and other community stakeholders
   5.6 Administration
   5.7 Multiple constituencies

6. Resources covered in training programs presented by librarians
   6.1 World Wide Web
   6.2 Mosaic
   6.3 FTP (file transfer protocol)
   6.4 Listservs

6.5 Gophers
6.6 Archie and Veronica
6.7 Lynx
6.8 E-mail
6.9 local network information

7. Presenters/trainers
   7.1 One-person endeavor
   7.2 Collaborative effort
   7.3 Both

8. Format of presentations
   8.1 One-shot presentations
   8.2 Sequence of several sessions
   8.3 Private instruction/tutorial (individualized)

9. Goals and objectives of program
   9.1 To bring librarians up to speed quickly
   9.2 To bring understanding of and competency in Internet to campus
   9.3 To equip public services staff and students with basics
   9.4 To acquaint faculty with Internet\
   9.5 Job security

10. Genesis of programs
   10.1 Breaking new ground
   10.2 Filling Gaps
   10.3 Acting on own initiative
   10.4 Initiative from director or administrator
   10.5 Filling expressed need (requests)

11. Venue and style for library-sponsored presentations
   11.1 Electronic classroom
      11.1.1 in library
      11.1.2 in computer center
   11.2 Format
      11.2.1 Hands-on
      11.2.2 Demonstration/lecture

12. Follow-up support
    12.1 Minimal
    12.2 Consultations
    12.3 E-mail
    12.4 Help Desk
    12.5 Telephone help (help line)
    12.6 Handouts

13. Organization of programs:
    13.1 By type of resource
    13.2 By Internet function
    13.3 By scholarly function
    13.4 By academic discipline

14. Training available for librarians
    14.1 None
    14.2 Teaching each other
    14.3 Self-taught (reading, exploration, surfing, etc.)
    14.4 Training by computer center
    14.5 Workshops/conferences
    14.6 Online tutorials
    14.7 Continuing education classes (non-credit)
    14.8 Certificate programs (for credit)

15. Whose job is it?
    15.1 Library
    15.2 Computer Center
    15.3 Joint effort
    15.4 Other departments/faculty

The Teaching and Learning Process in the Internet Training Program at Columbia University Libraries: A Qualitative Exploration

Patricia O'Brien Libutti

Introduction: Teaching and Learning in a High-Technology Library Environment

Librarians face the necessity of lifelong upgrading of their technology skills. The work environment is technology rich and constantly changing. Librarians in a midcareer stage have experienced the replacement of the card catalog by online public access catalogs (OPACs) and using the Internet for reference questions. These major changes in task methodologies have involved institutional and personal adjustment. The presence of the Internet has been a catalyst for the occupational disequilibrium seen in the early 1990s. This disequilibrium is illustrated in the proliferation of terms in titles of national conference programs, such as "retooling," "re-ngineering," and "redefining our roles" (http://www.ala.org/events/dc98/programs/satpm.html).

Although librarians have applied technology to identify, analyze, manage, and acquire information resources for more than a decade, the presence of the Internet put librarians at a disadvantage in the early 1990s because they were learners and teachers simultaneously, usually in a rushed, frantic pace (Grassian 1998). The librarian has been forced to face educational issues that depart in significant ways from prior technology experience. Viewing the Internet as both a subject to be taught and an instructional medium to be used departs from the use of prior educational technologies, in which the medium was not a subject in itself (Kozma, 1991). These dual capacities (librarian as learner and teacher, Internet as subject and medium) are likely to continue. The methods that were used in the early 1990s to cope with these changes in one library environment are the components of this article. The Internet Training Program (ITP) at Columbia University Libraries was observed and qualitatively analyzed to explore the teaching and learning experiences of librarians in an Internet course.

Internet Education: Issues for Trainers and Learners

The Internet was seen early in this decade as an educational subject that had both technological and contextual aspects for trainers to consider (Connell and Franklin 1994). Initially, trainers using the Internet regarded it as an extension of earlier media and explored the location, accession, and use of information available through the Internet. The difficulties in this initial use of the Internet are summarized in Connell and Franklin's article, reflecting the context for this retrospective examination of an Internet course.

The difficulties of locating, accessing, and using information resources on the Internet are well documented. Many librarians have expressed frustration at having so much information available but not quite being able to get at it. Other commonly perceived difficulties in identifying information, keeping track of information after it is found, sharing information about what is available or maintaining accurate, up-to-date information, and needing different mechanisms to access different types of files. Another difficulty, less frequently addressed, is the problem of knowing when one is done searching the Internet. When nothing new is discovered, is it because the searcher has found all that is to be found or that the searcher did not try all options? Organization and standardization have become major issues (Connell and Franklin, 1994 620).

The example cited above illustrates the stage of Internet technology and the educational issues inherent in Internet training in the early 1990s. The emphasis on use of tools for information location and developing formats for use of the information may be seen in the literature of the period. Some of these tools (e.g., gopher, Veronica, Usenet, and WAIS) have disappeared from the vocabulary of current Internet trainers due to the World Wide Web application; others (e.g., ftp, telnet) remain important to trainers and students.

In-house Librarian Education Programs

At the time that the study reported in this article was in progress (1994–1995), few library staff education programs were documented in the library science literature. An inspection of the Library Literature database (1994–1995) indicated that students and faculty were the constituencies for instruction about Internet in higher education. The articles that did examine staff training and resources for training (Dillon 1994, Glogoff 1995; Raish 1994; Weissinger and Edwards 1995) reported workshops, online resources, and all-day immersion learning as the training formats. Columbia University Libraries' Internet Training Program appeared to be unique in that it devoted a large block of time to librarian training, with strong administrative support.

Qualitative Analytical Methodology and Librarian Education on the Internet

Gregory (1995) did the closest study to that reported in this article at approximately the same time as the data for the ITP study were being collected. The report delivered at the ACRL conference (Pittsburgh, Pa, Jan. 1995). The qualitative methodology was based on "freewrites," questionnaires, and diary excerpts by MLS students during a course on "library networks and systems" at the University of Soutern Florida. The data on librarians' problems with the Internet included the "pack rat syndrome" (difficulty discarding electronic communication), protocol problems with the many forms of Internet access, and disenchantment with listservs over time. This study, performed at roughly the same time as the reported analysis in this article, has comparable aspects, which are examined later in the discussion section.

Other relevant qualitative studies done prior to the ITP study included research examining the impact of the computer on learning patterns in electronic classrooms (Levine 1988). The Levine qualitative study of Apple classrooms continues to be relevant to the design of instruction in an electronic setting. Kulthau's series of qualitative studies on user behavior (1991) informed this examination of teaching and learning behaviors because the search process outlined in her article focused on the processes users employed. Such processes, whether used for print or online searching, need to be anticipated by trainers planning Internet education.

Methodology: Qualitative Analysis of the Internet Training Program

ACRL/NY received an ACRL Initiative Fund for the term 1994–1995 to develop a research project directed at explorating the ways librarians learned and taught the Internet. The project was to be qualitative in nature, with data from a variety of sources that related to librarians' understanding of the Internet. The project proposal, prepared by the author, outlined a case study (Yin 1994) of an Internet course. The data (observations, interviews, and evaluations from trainers and students) were to be qualitatively analyzed using NUDIST (**N**on-**N**umerical **U**nstructured **D**ata **I**ndexing **S**earching and **T**heorizing), a computer program for textual analysis. The research setting was Columbia University Libraries' ITP, which had been presented four times before the time of the research. This article explores librarians' approaches to the new technology that presented them with linear and nonlinear structural components (Spiro and Jehng 1990).

Questions Guiding the Investigation

A survey (Libutti 1994) for the program Six Degrees of Connectedness, sponsored by the ACRL/NY chapter provided direction for this project. The characteristics of the attendees and respondents to the electronic survey were termed *innovators* or *early explorers* with Internet, as reported by Ostrow and Randorf. These Internet enthusiasts were self-directed, learning the Internet on their own, often out of innate curiosity. Several aspects of the responses to the Six Degrees of Connectedness Questionnaire were extended into questions to examine the training program in progress at Columbia University Libraries:

• What aspects of the training would emerge as most relevant for students' reported learning?

• What online demonstration behaviors would be seen as effective by trainers and students?

• What work-related factors enhanced or strained reported teaching or learning?

• What expectations accompanied trainers' and students' participation in the course?

• What outcomes were reported as significant by trainers and students?

Description of the Research Setting

The ITP at Columbia University Libraries during the fall 1994 semester consisted of fifteen two-hour sessions held in a computer laboratory, with an independent terminal for each student. The course was divided into class sessions and laboratory sessions. The purposes of the program included developing librarians' proficiencies on the Internet, developing a core of Internet trainers, and enabling librarians to utilize Internet resources in their subject areas and to assist end users to do the same. Graduates of the ITP were expected "to create and maintain Internet pathfinders and to continue to use the Internet in their work" (Thomas 1994). The prerequisites for the course were basic computer literacy, e-mail competency, and Kermit file transfer competency. Each student had to apply for participation in the course and was provided the time to take the course. Each student was expected to attend an overview session. All students had the support of one-on-one training in the basic computer operations needed to start the course.

Trainers were librarians who had graduated from the program and had prepared for individual topics. The trainer–student ratio was approximately 4 to 1, including the helper who accompanied each trainer. The laboratory sessions had a trainer and a helper to guide students when needed. The classroom was equipped with projection equipment for online demonstrations. The course materials included an "ITP notebook", a loose-leaf binder that contained all the documentation for each topic taught, as well as exercises, readings, and resource listings. *Crossing the Internet Threshold*, (second edition) by Tennant Ober, and Lipow was used as an adjunct text. Practice exercises were provided for each topic taught. The course syllabus used in fall 1994 was tool oriented and included:

- Columbia's Internet Host The basics of CUNIX, the operating system for Columbia University Libraries;
- File Transfers from Remote Computers;
- Logging on to Remote Computers:Telnet/TN3270;
- Special Interest Groups and news groups;
- Discovering Resources (Archie, ColumbiaNet, Gopher, Veronica, WAIS, World Wide Web, others);
- Tips and Review: Strategies for compiling pathfinders, general review, Internet etiquette, keeping current (Internet Training Program, 1994, 110).

Sources of Data for the Study of the Internet Training Program Course

The data were derived from interviews, with observations of, and evaluations by trainers and students, as well as the investigator, who was a participant-observer. All the trainers participated in a focus group interview immediately following the December session of the fall 1994 course. Individual interviews with the three major planners were done in January 1995, and student interviews were done during January and February. The interviews usually lasted one-half hour. A tape recorder was used to capture the interviews. A semistructured question set was used, with open-ended questions on motivation to take the ITP course, past experience as a librarian, prior experience with Internet, and learning in the ITP sessions. The open-ended questions included opportunities to discuss the student's perception of learning from the course, impressions of significant factors affecting the learning, and plans to use the training. The Guiding Questions for the ITP Interview are appended at the end of this chapter in Appendix A.

The primary sources for the observational data were two logs kept over the fifteen-week period by two participants. The first log, a Participant Observer Log, was done during the class by the investigator. Field notes were done using a laptop computer each week from September through December 1994. A student volunteered to do the second log (Student Log) after each class. Students completed course evaluations, which were included in the data coded in this study.

Analysis of Data
Code Development for the ITP Qualitative Analysis

Analysis of data was continuous, as required for a qualitative analysis. Initially, raw field notes were categorized each week following sessions by the investigator. Some categories changed over the course in response to new information seen in different classes. The second stage of code development occurred after the focus group with the trainers and after each interview with a student. Following each interview, the investigator listened to the tapes to note aspects of the vocal quality that indicated shades of meaning for coding (Rubin 1995). Typed course evaluation summaries were scanned with an optical character recognition (OCR) scanner and entered as documents for coding. Codes were developed from the collapsed categories after the interviews and evaluations had been examined.

A skilled textual transcriber, funded by the ACRL Initiative Fund, transcribed all audio-recorded interviews. The field notes made by the participant-observer were part of the textual material used for analysis. An initial exploratory code assignment for several documents using the NUDIST computer program resulted in code simplification, with memos appended to each document noting examples or variations from the code that needed attention (Weitzman and Miles 1995). NUDIST was then used across all sources of data for analysis. The final codebook is reproduced as Appendix B.

Application of NUDIST Program to Coded Documents

The NUDIST program was used to code the properties of text in the documents with a numerical system indicating a particular property of the text as a specific code. In the ITP case study, all transcripts, field notes, evaluations, and logs were entered into the program as documents. Codes were assigned to the text units, defined as lines of text, which amounted to 11,623 across all sources of data. Four broad categories contained 226 codes. These code categories (or nodes) were Behavioral, Experiential, Valence (positive, neutral, and negative effect), and Source of the data. Source data were coded according to the origin of the data (trainer, student, participant-observer, student-observer, and evaluation). Two broad categories (Behavioral and Experiential) had categorical subsets. The Behavioral category had Teaching Behaviors and Learning Behaviors as sub-sets. The Experiential code category had Factors Affecting the Processes and Expectations and Outcomes as subsets.

Observations were the basis for actual teaching behaviors, with supporting data from trainer and student recall. Aspects of teacher behavior (preparation, talk, action, support, and role) were the major code subsets of behavioral teaching codes.

Student interviews and evaluations provided most of their learning experiences. Following the coding of each document, NUDIST was employed to collect specific examples across all sources of data for each code. Specific examples reported in this article were drawn from the pool of collected data for each code.

Results of the ITP Study

In most cases, recall of specific behaviors was difficult for both trainers and students. Because the course was in a laboratory setting, it was expected that there would be considerably more demonstration and practice behavior than in a traditional university lecture class. In fact, the kind of preparation focused on the specifics needed for thorough demonstrations.

Online Demonstration Behaviors Seen as Effective by Trainers

Two of the trainer behaviors seen as important for online instruction emerged: preparation for a demonstration and explanatory steps for an online demonstration. Trainers focused primarily on the extensive preparation they had put into their sessions. The preparation included examining documentation, as well as trying out all the connections (both physical and the Internet addresses). One trainer noted an effect when some addresses did not work:

> In looking at the documentation, the examples, and mak-
> ing sure everything works, I don't want to be able to get
> into all this stuff. That also serves as a handy crutch for not
> going and looking at all the examples, and changing them
> all every time you do it, but I want people to try to ftp to
> sites and find out that their subdirectory is no longer there,
> or to telnet to a location and find that it doesn't exist any-
> more and there may be a message that it is no longer there.

Backing up the slow Internet connection time, or the conditions when the Internet condition was not working at the time, was part of preparation for most of the trainers. Both trainers and students found this frustrating. One trainer commented:

> I sense that one thing one needs to be ready for is the
> Internet being much slower than one would like it to be
> and the likelihood that you can't get into resources, so that
> this time I did what others have done in the past, which is
> prepare a virtual Internet in the form of overheads that
> one can show to try to walk people through things. The
> choices of examples I had were based pretty much on sites
> that I had a sense would work.

Trainers concurred on reading the documentation carefully, because the syllabus planners "scripted" sessions to ensure coverage of

essential points. However, there was still a major amount of variance in the choices for presentation:

> I actually do a rehearsal, a run-through, of the whole session for the purposes of timing the session because worse is trying to do too much, which we have found we have tried to do. And not having enough time, so the rehearsal to me is important really to see, "Well, I can't spend more than five minutes on this, I'm sorry, you might raise an interesting point, but on to the next topic. We don't have enough time." And also being sure I hit all the main points.

Demonstration explanatory steps. A trainer had an overhead that graphically represented the order of an interaction path to get to a site from one's computer, which, when shown, was accompanied by talking it through, step-by-step. The overhead illustrated the path from the computer (at the bottom) to the resource (at the top):

Search gopherspace by title words via uinett/U. of Bergen
Search titles in gopherspace using Veronica
Other gopher and information servers
(including U. of Minnesota)
Off-campus services outside Columbia
Connections to computers and Internet Main menu

A trainer tried another aspect of visual demonstration in combination with "talking aloud" the particular protocol. The screen display was changed to black print, white background, instead of the reverse. Then, the trainer pointed to each part of the screen that was relevant to the protocol before proceeding with the interaction path. Each step was explained, and the screen was kept stationary for longer than other trainers had kept screens stable. During each step of the demonstration, the trainer pointed to the results of the previous interaction.

Expectations That Accompanied Trainers' Participation in ITP
"Crowd control" with access to sites. Trainers were heard preparing students for the way to participate in a demonstration:

Watch me, listen to me now, this is my demo. And keep your hands off that keyboard. Then we will have a hands-on together.

Another trainer noted that:

People are tempted to follow along sometimes, and there are those moments when you can tell, that's tipping the critical balance. And I know in my presentation, at least once, I couldn't get into what I was showing because... [Another trainer interrupted with the comment: "because everyone else was!"]

Student cues for trainer behaviors. A trainer focused on the students who were in the class as the final determining factor in delivery methods for the session, which was repeated in various ways by the other trainers:

I also tried to really focus on the individuals that were in the classes, and I do know most of them fairly well at this point, so that I was able to pick up, I think, fairly quickly if someone had a puzzled look on his or her face or seemed not to be following along appropriately. Then I could make an attempt to herd them back into line or find out what the problem was, and the practice sessions then were a whole different thing. I found them just as useful from a training point of view as the training sessions themselves.

Trainers recognized the difficulty students were having following the displays and drew attention to the behavior needed. One called attention to a particular aspect that was crucial to the success of the protocol: "They literally mean to do it like this: use quotation marks around it." The trainer then illustrated what happened when the protocol was followed and what happened when quotation marks were not used appropriately.

Motivating or demoralizing aspects of class interactions. Trainers during the focus group discussed their own coping styles. One trainer who used overheads to illustrate interactive pathways was disappointed in student reactions:

> I think people think it's the kind of work going back to the...some low tech, and, my impression is that they didn't like it that much. Overall, I thought it could have conveyed more essential information....Somebody commented, a couple of people commented in their evaluation sheet.

Another trainer faced his perceptions of student dislike of a topic by "playing it up" differently:

> It's not so much the difficulty of the software and how you run it, but that people are not necessarily thoroughly convinced that they should want to do that. So I play up the opposite angle. I don't say, "This is a lot of fun." I start, I try to win them over and say, "We're allies in this. This is a horrible mess, but there's something here that I need, that's worth getting, that's worth the effort."

Positive factors that trainers observed included recognition, as well as seeing the students succeed:

> Some of the positive stuff is the light of recognition or delight that sometimes you get. All too rarely, but occasionally, it will happen where someone really gets it, and that's not always easy [with a difficult topic]....

Another motivating factor was a way of thinking about the material for one trainer:

> One of the things that I think when you consider who we're training and how people learn, it's we're training more than the technical things. It's almost we're trying to...it's a different game, we are almost teaching new attitudes.... Teaching people a new way of looking at, approaching things.

Work-related factors that enhanced or strained teaching. The fact that the librarians were teaching their colleagues had both positive and negative effects on trainers. One stated:

> I think the one thing that really surprises me about this program, and this is the fifth time now that I've been involved in it, is that we're all colleagues. None of us are paid as consultants or specialists....We're just colleagues, and none of us have been allocated any special time for this. I mean, like, somehow we have taken on the challenge, which I think is absolutely appropriate as librarians. It's just totally inappropriate for us to say, "Well, there's nothing of relevance for me; therefore, I'm not going to learn this." As librarians, we're information specialists. This is a new, exciting way of getting information, it's our responsibility to learn everything there is about it. But some of these people, I get the feeling, are thinking, "I shouldn't have to learn this until it's perfect, until the whole Internet has been somehow perfected to the point where it's just like a book on a reference shelf. And when it becomes that straightforward, then maybe I'll find out about it, but until then, don't bother me."

Although the research questions guiding the analysis could be examined, they did not appear to be the most important questions that could be asked about the teaching experience. The major aspect of the teaching process, that of teacher preparation for all parts of the class, was most important for the trainers. Less spoken about, but observed often, were the explanatory steps taken by the trainer about a protocol. At the beginning of this investigation, was the effect of working as a trainer with one's peers was not considered, but it did emerge as important in this study for the trainers.

Aspects of ITP Most Relevant for Students' Learning

The complexity of the ITP course from the trainers' points of view was matched by the students. Factors that appeared to be most related to the students learning as they reported such were time, utility of the program, concurrent work experiences, and their motivation(s) for taking the course.

Expectations that accompanied students' participation in ITP. The utility of the course itself had several dimensions. One was the immediacy of the need for knowledge the course would provide.

> I felt that I needed to have more knowledge…a knowledge base to do in-depth training of other library users, whether they were other staff or other library users, so that' what I was looking to get out of the course and what I brought into it.

> I feel like, "Relax! It's going to change and it's just not that important to me at this time."

Many of the students referred to their expectations to keep abreast of developments in the field.

> There is some sense that, everyone is talking about this, you'd better have at least some idea in general what it is, even if it isn't in general pertinent to what you're doing at the moment.

The learning styles of the students varied across the class, with a mixture being reported by all depending on the quality of the activity. Most students expected to "know how to navigate the Internet" or "the component parts and how they worked." Some had other reasons to take the course.

> I wanted to see what was involved in a librarian sitting down and selecting resources for information on workstations in libraries.

Student learning behaviors. Students focused in their class work on activity: the predominant observed activities included following demonstrations or exercises, downloading materials, and examining the documentation for exercise. Little verbal behavior was observed during class sessions. The verbal behavior observed consisted of either questions to the trainer (and occasionally to a peer) or reports of difficulty (with the exercise or the connections). Informal peer interaction occurred most often during a laboratory and was one of the observed methods of resolving problems. The ITP Notebook was a companion for each student, and was used in and out of class extensively, according to student interviews.

Online demonstration behaviors seen as effective by students. Students reacted to the presence or absence of explanatory steps of an online demonstration:

> [The trainer] would make it amusing as well as lead you through the steps. I mean, often when you're doing this, people type in things, and they don't say what they are doing...if you don't look at the screen, you don't see what you're doing. They don't say, "I'm doing this now, I'm doing this...."

Exercise extensions were a common occurrence. Students reported bringing in questions for a search or ideas for a project for development. Others voiced the opinion that the documented exercises were enough for the session and did not prepare beyond that.

Outcomes seen by the students. The students were interviewed within six weeks after the completion of the class. As seen in their reports on postclass activity, outcomes were evident shortly after the last class session. However, both students and teachers were unsure that producing and learning could (or should) occur concurrently. Some expressed the feeling that learning would take sufficient time without the added pressure to produce a product. As seen above, however, this expectation about outcomes was not held uniformly by either students or teachers. Some students reported activity in progress (projects or library activity); other students reported plans for the near future.

> I don't know if I would have everything under my belt, but in terms of using the existing resources on the Internet and creating my own organization, I can certainly do that. I know enough about using gophers and using bookmarks and checking addresses and figuring that out, and my own sense of organization in terms of an outline and how I would cluster things. How I would sit down in front of a terminal and make it all happen, I still don't know.

Several students referred to expectations from their supervisors to acquire Internet competencies and to use these skills in the job setting.

> That's what I've been doing since about mid–November [preparing a pathfinder]. I have been using mostly gophers trying to find text and addresses and all kinds of listservs and sites where there's information on Africa. And just piling up the list, but it takes a lot of time to see what the quality of these things are and still we're doing that.

Student attitudes about the Internet. Students reported their emerging attitudes about the Internet during the course, which included their judgments on the quality of the information, the changing nature of the Internet, the difficulty in evaluating resources, and other problem areas. Information and useless data seemed to be intermingled on the Internet for some.

> It's tricky, though. At this point, we feel we have to evaluate any source before we make a recommendation, or even just give directions to its availability, because we don't feel that the students here and the faculty here have the time to wade through things that are unnecessary...and it's our job to help them to find and get to expeditiously the good things that are out there.

Participants noticed how the Internet "is constantly changing" (malleability). Two issues that were important for the students were the organization of the Internet and copyright problems.

> I'm hoping that it's organized better, eventually. I mean, it's still a growing thing. I think it'll become so much that people will have to organize it in certain ways so you'll have gateways to this or that. I'm a little concerned now from what I read and what I hear that it's just too much, people can't navigate through it unless you've been told in advance: "take these steps to what you're looking for."

Students had mixed reactions about the immediate utility of the Internet, most seeing it as being useful "in the future." One was concerned about both the technology and users' skills:

> I don't think most users in our primary clientele are at that
> point yet.... And that is two things: is the technology there
> yet, and are the users there yet. And we don't feel confident
> that both of those are.

Several students spoke about the inevitable issue of copyright infringe-
ment:

> I looked mostly at the Library of Congress online exhibi-
> tions because at the time we were lending...we now cur-
> rently have something at the Library of Congress on exhi-
> bition, and I guess that they do that online exhibition all
> the time, and we were asked to allow them to do this. And
> the thing is that they do have people sort of allow them to
> upload them and that was something that we didn't want....
> Also copyright questions: some of it is proprietary interest
> and so on. And so I think we didn't allow them, but I think
> it's an inevitable situation.

Influence of the ITP course. The course itself left strong positive impressions on most students, as seen in the following array of comments from evaluations and interviews:

> Oh, I would urge them to take it [the ITP course].

> I certainly thought the opportunity to get a nice introduc-
> tion to Web-related resources and a compare and contrast
> was useful 'cause otherwise, it's all kind of, like, black box
> magic stuff was good. And I think for me, the built-in time
> that was provided was the biggest advantage.

Work-related Factors that enhanced or strained learning. Time and work-
related factors were often reflected as barriers to learning or teaching in the ITP course. The students' ideas for change, based on
the aspect of length of the course and workload (in some cases)
matched those of the trainers. Recommendations included short-
ening the course (compressing the course, having shorter time

slots, and having a two-tiered course for novices and intermediate skill levels).

Another aspect of the recommendations was the reflection of "doing work" at these sessions. Providing mandated evaluation (pretests and posttests, assignments, and a product expectation that would be evaluated), rearrangement of sequence, and reduction of laboratories were strong suggestions. The expectation of putting the learning to work was reflected in a modification of class structure, in which a segment of each class was turned over to each person to report on his or her use of what had been learned the previous week.

> I suggest online tutorials so you don't have to give up all that time for classes.

> I think they need to do canned searches so you're not so dependent on the Internet.

> I think that if maybe people go in there with a theme or something like that and concentrate on that, that's much better; but I think you need to do that and plan for it in advance.

Learner as teacher and teacher as learner. In the ITP study, the source of the data was coded because many of the codes could, theoretically, have emerged from either trainers or students and indeed did so. This is highly likely to continue because librarians and end users face continuing evolutions and permutations of technology in information access, acquisition, and use. The Internet will continue to evoke and provoke attitudes in its users and developers.

Discussion of Results Relevant to Aspects of Training for Learning
Qualitative Research on Internet Training after 1994

Gregory's (1995) study focused on several factors not explicitly seen in the ITP study. The disenchantment with listservs over a period of time reported by Gregory was systematically recorded through diaries and "freewrites," in which the listservs the students subscribed to and described were seen to be less interesting over the course, which covered the same amount of time as the ITP course. One distinction that needs to be examined is the difference in topics over time in the ITP course, whereas the topics in Gregory's course were revisited often. Also appearing in Gregory's analysis is the role of the librarian as an active agent, which was seen in the trainers' comments. Baseline measures on Internet experience were part of Gregory's methodology (as was the case in the ITP study in the interviews), which included questions about Internet experience. As in Gregory's data, the majority of the ITP course members had not used the Internet except for e-mail.

Studies that involved qualitative analysis of technology in a classroom done after 1995 were examined for comparison to the ITP study. Yang's (1997) study used verbal protocols (think-aloud) and observations of the learner's information-seeking processes. The study resulted in observations of coping mechanisms used by students, as well as the establishment of the information-seeking classification models developed by Marchionni (1992) and Dreher and Guthrie (1993). The description of the students' coping mechanisms while exploring a complex database (the Perseus hypermedia system) included self-regulating behaviors, such as selective attention, to keep track of exploration and avoid the feeling of being overwhelmed. Students still have difficulty with navigating complex systems, as did the ITP students who reported such in 1994. The deliberate teaching of such cognitive strategies for keeping "place" in a complex database is helpful to the trust a person has in his or her ability to use databases effectively.

In current classes, the kinds of preparation may differ in content, resulting in a shift from tool-based Internet training to subject access and collection-building issues, as well as development of resources by librarians. However, the specific trainer behaviors associated with effective training are likely to be present in current settings: explanatory online demonstration steps and online demonstration preparation. Therefore, the kinds of issues involved in current training are likely to contain remnants of the past as well as new areas for development. The Association for Training and Development has online anecdotes of successful trainers who conduct many kinds of training (http://www.astd.org). Although not investigated empirically, the anecdotes echo those of the trainers in the ITP course. The American Society for Training and Development maintains a bibliography list and *Training & Development* online. Issues reported recently (April 1999) include the ASTD state of the industry report, *Point, Counterpoint.* The amount of technology-based training is projected to rise to 27 percent by the year 2000, indicating there will be many opportunities for trainers to work with live classes for the near future. The skills of presentation and preparation seen in this study will need to be part of a trainer's repertoire.

Another current development to is certify Web trainers, specifying areas of expertise (Kovacs 1999). One example of such a program is Diane Kovacs's proposed curriculum for Web trainers. The components of the curriculum, which would be presented by subscription to a part of the listserv NETTRAIN called Net-CERT, include instructional design. The first skill in that area is "the ability to judge how to present information to effectively train learners on a given level" (http://www.kovacs.com/trainer.html#idreqs), which was the area most developed in the focus group with the trainers in the ITP course.

Effective online demonstration behaviors. It is not surprising that there are more discrete codes for teaching behavior than learning behavior because teaching behavior dominates the classroom in the case. This follows the findings for several decades that teacher behavior (specifically, "talk") dominates a classroom activity observation (Amidon and Hough 1963). It is also noted that teaching behavior is usually the result of specific decisions about behaviors to use, noted in the scripts prepared for this course, whereas learning behaviors may happen with less predetermination by the student.

Studies have been prepared on the qualities of human tutors that needed to be incorporated in computer tutorials (Lepper 1993). The aspects seen in attending, inquiring into the state of the student, and extending the student's questions by a human tutor were cited as those very traits needed in a computer tutorial. The trainers in the ITP study were seen exhibiting these behaviors, and students recalled the presence or absence of them. If these traits are important to examine for emulation in a computer tutorial, they are at least equally important for trainer development.

Summary and Recommendations for Further Research
From 1994 to 1999: Major Changes in Technology, Teaching, and Training Needs

The ITP study demonstrated that many factors beyond individual trainer and student competence are important for Internet education. The factors that emerged in trainer demonstration behavior are likely to remain important in the classroom. Student preparation, purpose, and selected action upon learned subject matter will also remain as important as seen in 1994. Despite the major changes in the technology and the increased sophistication of the librarian (Grassian 1998), the aspects of teacher presentation and preparation that will most likely remain important in a live class are those of explanatory steps and preparation for online demonstration seen in the ITP course and described in several current articles (e.g., Kirk 1998).

Research recommendations: "electronic literacy." As librarians advanced in training users with Internet, their teaching approaches advanced beyond the extensions of older media seen in the early 1990s (Connell and Franklin 1994). It will be important to pay attention to the literacy factors in "reading" a Web page. Kerr (1990) reflected the characteristics of computer screen reading that were significantly different from prior reading experience. Nonlinear reading ("hot spots" and cursors could be anywhere on a screen), the disappearance of the text when one advances to a new screen, and the malleability of the text by the user were seen as important areas for literacy research.

These factors have extended into the late 1990s, with advanced malleability of text, images, and transfer of information, seen by Costanzo in 1989. The area of literacy using the Internet is central to the main issues of information literacy (Libutti 1998). These aspects of literacy need research to understand the processes involved in navigating the Internet. At this time, these areas are most likely in the domain of literacy and reading, which has been changed with the infusion of the Internet and other electronic media. Studies such as Yang's (1997) examination of students working with a hypermedia system need to be extended beyond the information-seeking models and reported coping style into the area of literacy and its components.

Training recommendations: Explanatory steps and online demonstrations. Current awareness of advanced teaching skills for electronic resource education is emerging (Basile 1998). Developing teaching behaviors is the verbal equivalent of preparing an excellent training manual for Internet searching. Integrating the explanatory steps with the array of behavioral possibilities available for Internet operation takes considerable skill. Research on optimal combinations of explanatory steps and choices in search patterns prepared as exercises for an Internet class would be needed to confirm the initial observations emerging from this study. Neither teaching skill is easily acquired. Understanding what constitutes excellent explanatory steps is an area for future research. Some of these behaviors may be sequencing of steps, physical dexterity of talking and typing simultaneously, and methods of scanning the class for comprehension before proceeding to the next stage of a demonstration. The interaction of trainer and student behaviors will always be important in a class. They need to be defined and taught to trainers for effective teaching about the Internet. The factors seen in excellent trainers could be case studies for emulation, taught to other trainers as an aspect of Internet teaching methodology.

Although the Internet training program reported above was a snapshot in time, the importance of the commitment, continuity of the program, and teamwork of the trainers has carried Columbia University Libraries into their present programming. Columbia University Libraries modified the program approach from one of a lengthy course to one that is a "build-your-own" training program, as described by Catherine Thomas, Director of the Internet Training Program. The Web resources and schedule of current librarian training opportunities are collated at: http://www.columbia.edu/cu/libraries/inside/internet/. Further details on the experiences following the 1994 semester form the larger parts of the articles prepared by Catherine Thomas, Daniel Caldano, and David Magier in this volume. These transitions are reported by the trainers themselves in the following two articles. The last article in this volume, by this author, was developed for the changes in preparation patterns for Internet training, in which options for Internet training expertise is offered online through many options.

References

Amidon, E. J., and J. B. Hough, eds. 1963. *Interaction analysis: Theory, research, and application.* Reading, Mass.: Addison-Wesley.

Basile, A. J. 1998. Extending a virtual hand: Promises and problems of electronic instruction. *Finding common ground: Creating the library of the future without diminishing the library of the past.* New York: Neil-Schuman, 111–15.

Connell T. H., and C. Franklin. 1994. The internet: Educational issues. *Library Trends* 42 (4), 608–25.

Costanzo, W.V. 1989. *The electronic text: Learning to write, read, and reason with computers.* Englewood Cliffs, N.J.: Educational Technology Publications.

Dillon, D. 1994. An Internet experience at the University of Texas. *Library Issues* 14(5):1+.

Dreher, M. J., and J. T. Guthrie. 1993. Searching for information. *Contemporary Educational Psychology* 18(2):127–279.

Gregory, V. L. 1995. Electronic networks: The role of the librarian/ information specialist. Views from an LIS classroom. *Proceedings of the ACRL 7th Annual Conference, Pittsburgh, PA: March 29–April 2, 1995*. Chicago: ALA/ACRL, 373–80.

Glogoff, S. 1995. Library instruction in the electronic library: The University of Arizona's electronic library education centers. *Reference Service Review*, 7(12),:39+.

Grassian, E. 1998. Alt.help.I.can't.keep.up! Support for the electronically challenged. *Finding common ground: Creating the library of the future without diminishing the library of the past.* ed. C. LaGuardia and B.A. Mitchell, 136–39. New York: Neil-Schuman.

"Internet Training Program." 1994. Unpublished manuscript: Columbia University Libraries.

Kerr, S. 1990. Pale screens: Teachers and electronic texts. In P. Jackson, ed., From Socrates to software: The teacher as text and the text as teacher. Yearbook of the National Society for the Study of Education 88(2):202–20.

Kirk, E. 1998. Exploiting technology to teach new and old skills: Novice researchers and Milton's Web. *Finding common ground: Creating the library of the future without diminishing the library of the past.* ed. C. LaGuardia and B.A. Mitchell, 152–60. New York: Neil-Schuman.

Kozma, R. 1991. Learning with media. *Review of Educational Research,* 62(2):179–211.

Kulthau, C. 1991. Inside the search process: Information seeking from the user's perspective. *Journal of the American Society for Information Science* 42(50):361–71.

Lepper, M.1993. Motivational techniques of expert tutors. *Computers as cognitive tools.* ed. S. P. Lajoie and S. J. Derry, Hillside, 75–105. N.J.: L. Erlbaum.

Levine, H. G. 1988. *Computer-intensive school environments and the reorganization of knowledge and learning: A qualitative assessment for Apple Computer Classroom of Tomorrow. Annual Meeting of the American Educational Research Association. New Orleans, LA: April 4–9, 1988.* Education Document Reproduction Service No. ED 301154.

Libutti. P.O. 1994, May 25. "Six Degrees of Connectedness: Responses to an electronic survey." Paper presented at ACRL/NY program: "Six Degrees of Connectedness: The Who, What, Where, and When of

Internet Training in Academia." New York University, Bobst Library.
————. 1998. Expertise in electronic scholarship: Psychological factors in individual inquiry development. *Finding common ground: Creating the library of the future without diminishing the library of the past.* ed. C. LaGuardia and B.A. Mitchell, 219–24. New York: Neil-Schuman.

Marchionni, G.1992. Information retrieval interfaces for end users. *Journal of the American Society for Information Science* 43:156–63.

Raish, M. 1994. "Network knowledge for the neophyte. Stuff you need to know in order to navigate the electronic village." Unpublished workshop handout, SUNY Binghamton University Libraries.

Rubin, H. J. 1995. *Qualitative interviewing: The art of hearing data.* Thousand Oaks, Calif.: Sage.

Spiro, R. J., and J. N. Jehng. 1990. Cognitive flexibility and hypertext: Theory and technology for the nonlinear and multidimensional traversal of complex subject matter. In *Cognition, education, and multimedia.* ed. D. Nix and R. Spiro, 1990, 163–206. Hillsdale, N.J.: L. Earlbaum.

Tennant, R. J. Ober, and A.G. Lipow. 1994. *Crossing the Internet Threshold: An instructional handbook,* 2d ed. Berkeley, Calif.: Library Solutions Pr.

Thomas, C. 1994, August. "Memo to Trainers, ITP." Personal correspondence.

Weissinger, N. J., and J. P. Edwards. 1995. Online resources for Internet trainers. *College & Research Libraries News* 56(8):535–39.

Weitzman, E. A., and M. B. Miles. 1995. *Computer programs for qualitative data analysis.* Thousand Oaks, Calif.: Sage.

Yang, S. C. 1997. Brief communication: Qualitative exploration of learners' information seeking processes using Perseus hypermedia system. *Journal of the American Society for Information Science,* 48(7):667–69.

Yin, R. Y. 1994. Case study research: Design and methods. *Applied Social Research Methods Series.* Thousand Oaks, Calif.: Sage.

Appendix A

Guiding Questions for the
Internet Training Program Interviews

Trainers: Focus Group

Investigator: Introduction and explanation of the purpose for the focus group: "to discuss the factors the trainers thought were important in the ITP course."

Orienting Questions:

1. Would you please introduce yourself, and tell a bit about the role you played in this semester's Internet training program?
2. How did you prepare for your part in the course?
3. What did you see students do or hear them say that seems important now?
4. What thoughts do you have about the outcomes of the course?
5. What else would you want to say about the course as you experienced it?

Student Interviews

Orientation: The investigator introduced herself and explained that the purpose of the interview was to give the student an opportunity to examine the experience in the ITP course. The student then selected an assumed name, which was to be used in transcriptions of the interviews.

1. Would you tell me a bit about your experience in library work?
2. What was your experience with the Internet before the course?
3. Why did you take the ITP course?
4. What was important for you in the ITP course?
5. What plans do you have to use what you have learned in the ITP course?
6. Is there anything you would want to add to what you have said?

Appendix B

CODEBOOK: Internet Training Project

1. BEHAVIORAL: Teaching
1.1 Teaching:Talk(Observed)
1.1.1 Focuses class on topic
1.1.2 Explanation
1.1.3 Question to class or to student
1.1.4 Response to student question or statement
1.1.5 *Explanatory steps* used in demonstration
1.1.6 Reference to documentation
1.1.7 Humor, diversion
1.1.8 Reassurance to student
1.1.9 Rationale for decision for teaching process
1. 1.10 Persuasion to try activity
1.2. Teaching Process: Action:
1.2.1 Roving, looking at terminal screens
1.2.2 *Demonstration online*, chalk board, overhead, visual aid
1.2.3 Troubleshooting (online connection or protocol trouble)
1.2.4 Pointing, drawing attention visually to aspect of demonstration
1.3. Teaching Process: Preparation
1.3.1 Preparation: Materials (print, for distribution; overheads)
1.3.2 Preparation: Exercises (rehearsal of online demonstration)
1.3.3 Preparation: Syllabus
1.3.4 Preparation: Individual class

2. BEHAVIORAL: Learning Processes
2.1 Activity (Observed)
2.1.1. Does exercise from notebook (or brought-in materials)
2.1.2 Performs tangent search
2.1.3 Tries to replicate demonstration
2.1.4 Examines documentation in notebook
2.1.5 Downloads materials, captures screen, records data
2.1.6 Difficulties: Makes protocol errors, experiences mechanical difficulties
2.1.7 (Whole class) involved in different activities
2.1.8 Diversionary action: (nontask related)

PERIENTIAL: Expectations and Outcomes
EXPERIENTIAL: Expectations
4.1.1 Individual characteristics that might affect learning
4.1.2 Information load
4.1.3 Content and operation
4.1.3 Utility
2 EXPERIENTIAL: Outcomes
4.2.1 Projects
4.2.2.Library activity
4.2.3 Indefinite
3 Attitudes (combine with valence)
4.3.1 Specific value of ITP
4.3.2 Need for library in future
4.3.3 Internet material: Attitude
4.3.3.1 Quality
4.3.3.2 Malleability of Internet:
4.3.3.3 Utility
4.3.3.4 Problem areas
4 Modifications (from either/both students/trainers)
4.4.1 Mandatory evaluative components
4.4.2 Structure of course
4.4.3 Content of course
5 Utility of laboratory
6 Utility of notebook

ALENCE (combine with prior codes only if reported or
rved)
1 Positive
2 Neutral
3 Negative

ource of data
1 Trainer (interviews)
2 Student (interviews)
3 Participant-observer (log)
4 Student-observer (log)
5 Evaluations of ITP class and/or course

Perspectives on the Internet Training Program at Columbia University Libraries

Catherine M. Thomas
Daniel J. Caldano

Internet Trainers Are Students, Teachers, and Practitioners
Catherine M. Thomas

arly in 1992, librarians and administrators at Columbia University Libraries recognized that the Internet possessed enormous potential to increase the ways in which libraries could provide services to end users. To become familiar with the new options for selecting, acquiring, cataloging, storing, and disseminating information, an Internet Tools Group was formed. This group consisted of administrators from the libraries and from academic computing, as well as selected members of the library systems office and a handful of librarians who were both subject specialists and technologically sophisticated.

The Internet Tools Group served three main functions: it enumerated and discussed the existing Internet "tools" or applications, and it stated unequivocally that it was essential for librarians to learn how to use the Internet. Moreover, it served as the parent body of the libraries' Internet training program for staff.

The target audience of the Internet training program was approximately 130 librarians at Columbia University Libraries. The purpose of the program was to enable the participants to become proficient on the Internet, to develop a core group of Internet trainers, and to enable reference librarians and bibliographers to utilize Internet resources in their subject areas and to assist end users to do the same.

A team of staff members worked together for six months to simultaneously learn the Internet and design a series of formal training sessions, which would be presented during the spring 1993 semester. We quickly realized that gaining Internet proficiency would be a gradual process: it could not be easily accomplished in a half-day or one-day workshop, except possibly by exceptionally computer-literate trainees. For most of us, it took quite a bit longer to begin to master the skills necessary to discover and use Internet resources.

The pilot Internet training program was unveiled in January 1993. The first incarnation was a semester-long program that required trainees to commit two hours per week for twenty weeks; by fall 1993, it was shortened to sixteen weeks. The Internet training program has existed continuously since 1993, in various, evolving forms.

From Internet Pathfinders to Web Pages

Early on, even before the development and proliferation of the Web, we recognized that one of the biggest weaknesses of the Internet was in the area of subject-oriented access. We could see that there were many different types of resources, such as various kinds of files, directories, and databases; and electronic journals, electronic mail, Usenet newsgroups, and mailing lists. Especially when the Web was in its infancy, the Internet lacked organizing principles or devices, which would have facilitated uniform subject access to all of these different types of resources at one time. Each type of resource required a different access method. For example, it was necessary to know how to use mail and news reader clients, listserv software, Archie and ftp, Veronica and gopher, Telnet, WAIS, and Lynx in a thorough search of the Internet and retrieval of information from it.

The goal of the Internet training program was to empower properly trained librarians to help overcome the weaknesses of the Internet by creating handy guides for end users approaching the Internet with subject-specific information needs. We called this type of guide an Internet pathfinder: a list of Internet resources (Telnet addresses, ftp sites, gopher services, names of listserv mailing lists and Usenet newsgroups, etc.) relevant to a particular subject area. Because the Web was so new when our training program got under way, we envisioned that these so-called pathfinders would be available in paper form as handouts available at reference desks and perhaps on ColumbiaNet (our gopher-based campuswide information system). Thus, the purpose of our Internet training program was essentially to teach all the skills necessary for compiling such subject-specific Internet pathfinders, long before Web pages were commonplace devices for listing links to various resources on a particular subject.

Evolution of the Internet Training Program

Amazingly, the syllabus for the first round of Internet training (spring 1993 semester) did not include the Web as a topic. By the fall 1993 semester, approximately one hour was devoted to the Web, although, as I recall, the first presentation relied on the text-based Lynx browser and did not include the early graphical browser Mosaic.

The sixteen-week program syllabus initiated in fall 1993 is listed below. It was used to train librarians at Columbia University through 1995. Two weeks were spent covering each of the eight topics. For each topic, the first week was devoted to a formal classroom presentation with some hands-on exercises, and the second week consisted of a supervised hands-on practice lab. The class met once a week for two hours.

The curriculum had some prerequisites: basic computer literacy, electronic-mail competency, Kermit uploading and downloading competency, and attendance at a two-hour introductory Internet overview session.

Topic 1. Columbia University's Internet Host. What is our Internet host; Internet applications available on our host; comparison of our Internet host machine and microcomputers; comparison of Unix and DOS; essential Unix commands; space management; searching text files stored on our Internet host machine; getting online help.

Topic 2. File Transfers from Remote Computers: FTP. Space considerations; using temporary directories; interpreting citations; connecting; anonymous log-ins; navigating directories; displaying files; getting files; file formats; compression types.

Topic 3. Logging on to Remote Computers: Telnet and TN3270. Finding out about Telnet-accessible resources; interpreting citations; connecting and disconnecting; troubleshooting; session logging; Hytelnet.

Topic 4. Special Interest Groups and Newsgroups. Finding out about groups; notes files available on our Internet host; participating in Usenet newsgroups and listserv mailing lists; searching mailing list archives; nonlistserv mailing lists.

Topic 5. Discovering Resources, Part A. Using directory services to find Internet addresses, using Archie.

Topic 6. Discovering Resources, Part B. ColumbiaNet (Columbia University's campuswide information system), gopher, Veronica.

Topic 7. Discovering Resources, Part C. WAIS, World Wide Web (WWW).

Topic 8. Tips and Review. Strategies for compiling Internet pathfinders, general review, Internet etiquette, keeping current.

In 1996, the Internet training program was substantially redesigned to (1) increase the amount of time spent covering Web-related topics, (2) eliminate some of the non-Web topics, and (3) convert the program from a monolithic sixteen-week sequence to a modular, topical, build-your-own, mix-and-match series of one-hour sessions. The following topics are now offered on a regularly scheduled basis: *Internet Overview* (two one-hour sessions), *Web Overview, Netscape, Web Searching, Unix* (three one-hour sessions), and *Creating a Web Page.* Many other topics are available on demand as one-on-one tutorials or group sessions, as needed.

The Results of Internet Training

Librarians at Columbia University have created and are maintaining more than thirty subject-specific Internet pathfinders in the form of Web pages on a growing list of numerous diverse topics such as African studies resources, African-American studies, American history, ancient and medieval Studies, architecture and fine arts, archives and manuscript collections outside Columbia, biology, business and economics, earth Sciences, East Asian studies, government information, electronic data resources, electronic text resources, engineering, health sciences, history of science, Jewish studies, journalism, mathematics, Middle East studies, music, New York history, oral history, physics and astronomy, psychology, social sciences, social work, South Asian studies, and women's studies.

More than forty individuals are designated as Web masters. Each Web master is responsible for a portion of the Columbia University Library Website; each portion consists of a series of pages providing access to descriptions of services related to a particular branch library, administrative department, area of study, or type of electronic resource. Due to the size and complexity of LibraryWeb, this collaborative approach, with distributed, decentralized responsibility is indispensable. The overall effort is guided by a LibraryWeb steering committee.

Internet Training Tips

Internet training, even under the best possible conditions, is usually challenging and often frustrating. The following tips are based on the experience of doing Internet training for six years and on feedback from trainees.

We have found that it is best to limit sessions to one hour on a narrowly defined topic with reasonable and practical learning objectives. We like to limit attendance to make sure each trainee has his or her own microcomputer to use during the session. We usually distribute evaluation forms at the conclusion of each session.

Trainees complain that lectures and demonstrations can be boring and tedious, so we try to keep the amount of time spent on them to a minimum. Well-designed, hands-on exercises are usually more effective. If the lecture portion is at all lengthy, we distribute handouts as a record of the points being made.

Experience has proven that it is a good idea to get to the training facility at least thirty minutes before the session is scheduled to begin and test the equipment. We expect equipment, access problems, and try to be prepared with transparencies and alternatives such as multiple methods for demonstrating points.

The documentation should be as clear and concise as possible, with a lot of white space, limited, if feasible, to one page per topic. The best documentation is not generic, but tailored to the peculiarities of our local Internet host. We make most of the documentation available both online and in paper form. We try to encourage awareness and use of online help, tutorials, and documentation.

Trainees like it when we prepare hands-on exercises for each topic. It is strongly advised that trainers offer a structured laboratory setting in which trainees may do their practice exercises. If there will be more than six trainees, schedule a training helper to supplement the roving assistance the trainer provides during the hands-on exercises.

Ongoing Support for Internet Learning

In addition to our Internet training program, we have developed many mechanisms for continuing to develop ourselves as students, teachers, and practitioners. For example:

- We have set up local electronic notes files and e-mail aliases to facilitate the sharing of information.
- We have formed a Web users group that meets once a month to discuss activities, developments, problems, training needs, etc., associated with our use of the Web.
- Every Friday afternoon, the library systems office hosts a two-hour open house in the training center lab to allow libraries staff to drop in for practice and tutorials on Ethernet-connected Windows workstations.
- We have created a staff Web service that describes the Internet training program and provides for online sign-ups; this service also contains an enormous amount of locally maintained documentation as well as links to useful external resources.

Conclusion

At Columbia University Libraries, the Internet in general and the Web in particular have become integral to everyday information services activities. It is clear that learning to use the Internet has become a way of life for librarians, an exciting process that continues to unfold and never seems to end. As any librarian who is a Web master or who is creating or maintaining a subject-specific Internet pathfinder can attest, we are simultaneously students, teachers, and practitioners of the Internet. We are constantly learning to use new tools in order to integrate the Internet into traditional services in new ways, to provide more effective access to resources, and to search for resources more efficiently. Engaged in a self-perpetuating cycle, we are eagerly working together to learn, improve services based on what we learn, share what we have learned with our colleagues, and provide timely, effective teaching and guidance to our end users.

Learning/Teaching the Net
Daniel J. Caldano

One of the disconcerting factors in setting up a program for teaching the Internet is that for a time there were no training models. No one taught me the Internet; I learned it on the job, as it evolved and as the technology became available. For a long time, I thought of the Internet as something hidden, not apparent to most librarians. Although technology was exploding in the 1980s, most users experienced it as a desktop computer that could write things and do calculations or that could connect to a mainframe to access a database or an OPAC. The Internet itself, that vast and evolving means of communication and information interchange, was still the province of systems staff and other arcane types. Somewhat like the kabala, it needed to be interpreted by experts and was not available to just anyone. Even e-mail, that most obvious element of the Internet, was not readily available to most staff until the late 1980s, and even then, usually because of technological limitations and finances, only from the top down.

The gradual emergence of the graphical user interface (first introduced commercially by the Macintosh in 1984, then evolving into Windows) and then browsers later in the decade, along with the increasing availability and affordability of extraordinarily powerful desktops (well, in comparison with the original IBM PCs and Macs), really placed the Internet in its foremost position as an information resource and made it something no librarian could ignore.

Not that they did not try. Although many of us were thrilled in the early days of the computer revolution, there were almost as many who were skeptical and wary, unwilling to chance yet another learning curve for a dubious product (the favorite term of denigration for a new Mac in 1984, its debut year, was "toy"). But inevitably, technology prevailed, and librarians had to move aside their typewriters and stacks of cards to make room for the gray box and its screen. I remember almost having to persuade some early users of the utility of word processing and spreadsheets, and encountering a scowl of resistance or, worse, that glazed look of indifference.

The increasing availability of e-mail during the 1980s changed many users' attitude and jump-started the in-house training programs many of us became involved with in those early years. As systems staff, we always had ready access to many of the Internet features now taken for granted, but we had to learn them, sometimes painstakingly (does any-one remember rn or trn?).

As we got further into e-mail, librarians started hearing about other things available through the Internet, such as accessing other OPACs and information resources. Terms such as WAIS, gopher, and Archie (Archie?) started floating about, and staff wanted to know more. This is how the Columbia University Internet Training Program (ITP) first started. As more and more OPACs became available worldwide, librarians had to know how to access them using telnet or tn3270. Our program originally developed out of a series of ad hoc sessions for small groups (three or four at the most) of librarians eager to learn these techniques.

I evolved a syllabus and some examples of OPAC access, as well as recovery tips for emergencies. It soon became apparent that things were exploding at such a rate that some more formalized series of training sessions, covering a much broader spectrum of the Internet, were necessary. Hence our initial Internet Training Program, starting in 1993.

Our first programs were highly structured, with much documen-tation provided and with regularized schedules of classes and lab prac-tice. Librarians "volunteered" (some were instructed to attend) and were given in-depth immersion in all aspects of the Internet, from Unix, e-mail and rn, to the lofty reaches of WAIS, gopher, Archie and now Veronica. The Web (which was to change everything) was just emerging and not yet readily available to most staff in 1993, so it was not even included (other than in demo mode) in these training ses-sions. Windows was not generally available as well, and most were still using old DOS-based PCs, so there was much grueling information to slog through. That old resistance that I had encountered earlier in the 1980s, when computer technology was first introduced, reappeared again.

Some staff felt overwhelmed by the sheer amount they were ex-pected to master. Our program was essentially an intensive crash course, with much study time expected, even homework. Many were dis-mayed, and there was some valid resentment in the fact that they were expected to maintain their current workload while studying and learn-ing these increasingly more complex technologies. Most trainers sym-pathized, because we soon realized that there was no one Net guru who knew all. We each had our own specific areas of expertise, some more than others, and worked within those confines. In fact, this proved most fruitful for the trainers because they could spend more time preparing their expert presentations than having to learn yet another aspect of the Internet. We set up a system of "coaches" or mentors, whereby an expert on one facet of the Internet (say, trn) would tutor other trainers and fill in their gaps, even acting as a backup if necessary. All this took quite a commitment of time and energy on the part of both trainers and trainees.

This approach was not without shortcomings: some assigned trainees (i.e., those told by their supervisors that they needed to attend the ITP), were unhappy and woefully unprepared. A lot of the concentrated information we were throwing at them simply went over their heads, and many of them felt left behind from the start. I never came so close to throttling a colleague as I did during a session in which one librarian obdurately wanted every term and every procedure explained in the simplest terms until understood by her. She questioned everything and threatened to bring the class to a screeching halt (there is nothing like staring out and seeing half your trainees rolling their eyes, the other half fast asleep). Counting to ten, I realized she had been one of the assigned librarians and was simply not happy to be there. So, instead of throttling, I sat with her after the class and had a frank discussion on how we could help her and why these arcana might eventually prove to be of some use. She eventually softened and started cooperating (or at least not stonewalling). I cannot say how much she got out of the program, but the experience crystallized one of the most important considerations we all had to face with our trainees—their level of competence and interest.

This was impossible to judge—and came in all varieties—from younger staff who had their own computers and were eager to learn more, to older staff still connected to their typewriters and their catalog cards who were skeptical and resistant. Putting them all together in one session sometimes presented a volatile mix. We would distribute forms for the trainees to evaluate the trainers, and although much useful information was gleaned, there were also bizarre results that made one wonder how the same trainer could appear to be so expert and so incompetent at the same time to the same class.

Many of these difficulties were resolved when we altered our method of presenting classes. From a programmed schedule of classes and study time, we evolved to a series of topically defined, one-hour sessions, given with periodic regularity, so staff could pick and choose what topics to study and pursue. This made for a much happier trainee population and a lighter load for trainers (especially when no one signed up for your class). All were invited to attend, but at their own pace, so no one would feel pressured. There was no homework and no defined study sessions, although we made a point of making our training room available every Friday afternoon for staff to practice and enlarge their skills on their own. We have a defined syllabus and suggested course of progress, but staff can now pick and choose as they please. The one-hour format is also a boon: no information overload for the trainees, no concentrated prep time needed for trainers. Topics were broken down into digestible sections (e.g., one session devoted to the concepts behind the Web, another to the specifics of using Netscape, other classes in learning HTML, etc.).

This method works far better for us; we now are getting committed and interested trainees (most of the time) and less burdened trainers. With the advent of the Web, many aspects of the training agenda have changed. Instead of forcing staff to know about gopher, Archie, and WAIS, we now offer these topics only on demand (which is low), with increasing emphasis on the Web and its ramifications, which are many. In many ways, the evolution of the Web has made for extraordinary changes in all aspects of how we work, even how we live, and has galvanized training procedures. Most of our staff now have Windows (and Web access) on their desktops, and the "coolness" of the Web in society at large, with all its attendant publicity, have actually put some of us trainers in the curious position of offering material that the customers are actually clamoring to learn. (This situation is contrary to the situation years ago, in which I more often felt like a doctor giving a dose of medicine to "patients" who looked as if they were dreading it.)

It is fascinating to capture the enthusiasm of a trainee who is keen on setting up his own home page and set him on his course of learning how (oh, you don't know HTML? Well, some would be helpful. What about Unix? Do you know about chmod?). The trick, of course, is to keep students interested and to demonstrate the possible results. The Web is good at this, often offering instant gratification, or at least placation.

In teaching various aspects of the Net, from e-mail and ftp to file formats and Web concepts, I have always tried to remember how foreign some of these concepts might appear to the neophyte trainee, recalling my own cloud of unknowing from years ago. Analogies are essential in Net instruction, and I have employed them shamelessly— brandishing an abacus and calling it the first calculator (which it was) and a prototype of our current desktops, and likening the impact of the Web on society to that of television. Although teaching the nuts and bolts of any Net procedure is important, it is also imperative to make sure the user understands what is going on and why the particular procedure operates the way it does. Most trainees will meet you halfway if you are patient and pitch things at their own pace. Besides, we all know that lots of what we are all learning today will be outmoded in a few years. Now if only we knew what . . . .

The METRO Experience: Four Views

Eleanor R. Kulleseid

David S. Magier

Dottie R. Hiebing

Roger T. Harris

METRO In-service Internet Preparation Programs
Eleanor R. Kulleseid

The Metropolitan New York Library Council is a not-for-profit multi-type library system, the largest of nine reference and research library resources (3Rs) systems originally chartered by the New York State Board of Regents on behalf of the State Education Department. Since 1964, METRO has supported the collaborative efforts of academic, public, school, and all kinds of special libraries in New York City and Westchester County. Over the years, METRO has grown from 25 to 276 member library and library systems, of which more than a hundred are academic. There are 1,200 individual library sites run by some 9,000 librarians and support personnel. Funded by the state library and membership dues, Metro's mission is to provide a vehicle "through which its members can coordinate and relate their diverse activities to create a more effective information service Network for the region" (METRO 1997).

Programs and services are guided by broad goals and objectives related to resource sharing, professional development, member services, advocacy and partnership with state government, and appropriate governance functions. This is a daunting task, given the fact that the region is one of the most information rich in the nation with a large and highly diverse member population. If the expectations and perceived needs of a librarian in a major university library system may differ somewhat from those of a middle school librarian, those of their administrators are often more divergent. METRO must find the common ground to establish major priorities, then distribute resources equitably across an extremely wide range of user needs while observing state library guidelines associated with funded programs.

The metaphor of "electronic doorway libraries" linked by an Information Superhighway has provided that common ground for METRO and other 3Rs agencies. Librarians in all settings need to learn how to read the road map, work the controls for various vehicles, drive carefully, and even to develop new roadways on the Internet. In 1993, the author became a member of METRO's Board of Trustees, a group consisting of 25 representatives from all types of libraries and from the lay research community. The board was in the final stages of a strategic planning process that was completed in 1994. The first three of twenty-six program goals were to:

> Improve communication to and among METRO members through the use of the Internet and its successor. Provide education, technical information, training, hands-on workshops, basic technology support, on-site instruction, and the electronic communication Network path for members to link to the Internet and its successor. Have all METRO members connected to the Internet and its successor by 1997 (METRO 1994).

In 1993, the New York State Library's Regional Bibliographic Databases and Interlibrary Resources Sharing Program (RBDB) funded implementation of an automation plan developed by METRO's Automation Systems Advisory Council and Technical Services Committee. New equipment, telecommunications lines, and technical support staff provided a modest foundation for Internet training efforts. That same year, METRO received a Federal Library Services and Construction Act (LSCA), Title III grant to fund two conferences, as well as sessions on Internet basics for small- and medium-size libraries. In the fall, a Higher Education Act (HEA) Title IIA grant was awarded to provide Internet training for academic librarians in both small and large-group settings. Some training was carried on in member libraries' facilities, and by the fall of 1994, the HEA IIA program had provided basic training to more than 250 academic librarians from thirty member libraries.

The METRO board, guided by the goals approved in the 1994 strategic plan, supported implementation efforts recommended by the board's Automation Systems Advisory Council and by the new executive director and her staff. During 1995 and 1996, there was steady progress marked by: improvements in METRO's training facility; in METgate Internet services; in the number and content of Internet training sessions conducted by METRO consultant Dr. David Magier and other outside trainers; and in customer demand for all the above.

Largely, training was in classroom lecture and demonstration mode, with some discussion. Attendees represented a cross section of library types, institutions, specialties, and career stages typified in two 1996 sessions attended by the author. Among the forty or so participants were a retired library school professor, a music librarian, a number of midcareer academic and school library people in both program and administrative leadership positions, and a few younger newcomers to the field. Some people brought a good deal of expertise to the session; others were mere novices. Interests ranged from archival preservation to current financial market trends. The sessions themselves were both fascinating and frustrating. On the upside, an expert instructor presented a good deal of stimulating information in a logical and lively manner. On the downside, there was no concrete, hands-on activity to reinforce the abstract concepts and complex procedures being demonstrated.

In a 1996 meeting with the board, Dr. Magier summarized three years of work in which more than 3,000 library staff had received various levels of Internet training. He made a strong case for the provision of computer lab workstations so that passive "eyes-on" training could be enhanced and even replaced by an active "hands-on" approach. His impressions of his role as a trainer and the needs of librarians follow this reflection.

The Rationale for Continued Internet Training: How Much and for How Long?

In May 1996, the author was appointed to a new Strategic Planning Committee charged with review and update of the 1994 document. This involved scrutiny of all current programs and services, along with a certain amount of crystal ball gazing. It was clear that the pattern of resource distribution had shifted from an earlier focus on physical resource-sharing activities, (e.g., conspectus-based collection evaluation projects for coordinated collection development [CCD]) to electronic resource-sharing and training initiatives.

The basic question for this board member, a past conspectus project advocate, was not whether to continue the pattern but, rather, to what extent. In the long view, could this be seen as "robbing Peter to pay Paul"? In addition, how long would the need to provide Internet training be urgent? There were already special funded programs with targeted user populations (e.g., the Hospital Library Services Program). Large academic and public libraries were providing their own on-site training. The program could run out of steam after providing introductory training to staff from smaller and needier libraries such as the author's. There would be competition from other continuing education providers (e.g., professional library associations, local library schools, and commercial organizations). Finally, there was the expectation that many of those "needier" institutions would finally have to catch up and train their own people in order to stay competitive.

The Strategic Planning Committee completed its environmental scan late in 1996. Surveys of members' needs and interests in a number of areas made it clear that the demand for Internet training was a continuing high priority. For one thing, the Internet itself is a moving target, subject to continuous change. For another, as access becomes ubiquitous in homes and libraries, one could expect a developmental shift in training from navigation basics to assessment, organization, and creation of Internet content.

The learning curve continues to be steep, with no plateaus in sight. On a practical level, the majority of the METRO Internet workshops have been oversubscribed; even with the introduction of fees; demand continues to exceed supply. Apparently, even larger library systems cannot always meet the individual training needs of every librarian in every location in a timely manner.

Armed with this evidence of need, the board approved a METRO headquarters upgrade to a new Hands-on Technology Training Center, funded in part by the state library's Electronic Doorway Library Initiative. The new facility hosted 49 Internet training sessions for 460 member library staffers in 1997. Lecture was combined with hands-on activities in a small-group lab setting with twenty laptop computers. Of this number, 181 registrants were from a large public library system, 106 from academic libraries, and the rest from school and special libraries. Internet workshop offerings included an introductory overview, advanced search strategies, introduction to the World Wide Web, home page design, and subject-specific sessions on consumer health, medical, legal, music, art, and archives information.

Academic librarian registration was highest for sessions on advanced search strategies. A smaller, but significant, number accounted for half of the Internet overview registrants, nearly half of the Web registrants, and more than a third of the home page design registrants. The registrant profile described earlier is still valid. The preponderance of participants were midcareer librarians trying to keep up, but there were also a number of new librarians who may have had adequate training for their MLS but found themselves in professional settings that had Internet access but no training or that provided neither access nor training.

Participants in the 1997 workshops confirmed the impressions or assumptions upon which the board of trustees and METRO administrative staff had based strategic planning training initiatives. A scan of evaluations and follow-up interviews with five Mercy College academic librarians who participated in fourteen workshops yielded remarkably common responses. All remarked on the expertise of the instructor and the high quality of the handouts. Regardless of their previous experience, all came away from the sessions with a greater understanding of Internet concepts and vocabulary, information on specific Web sites, and a sense of increased confidence in their own ability to deal with the Internet. Some were able to use parts of the METRO presentations in their own information literacy instruction sessions with students.

On the other hand, some workshop participants wondered how they would ever be able to translate complex concepts and procedures so that their students would be able to understand the Internet. There was unanimous agreement that participants in every session, regardless of topic or level of complexity, represented a wide range of Internet experience from novice to intermediate or advanced. This led to considerable overlap and repetition between different sessions. This may also account, to some extent, for participants' sense that there was a great deal of information crammed into a tight period. There was also remarkable unanimity in response to a query about additional training needs, which included discipline-related advanced search strategies and identification of good Web sites, along with strategies for teaching Internet to faculty and students.

Next Steps and New Training Paradigms
Demand for Internet training as part of METRO's continuing education

program will continue to be high. The content of and context for that training should be adapted to changes in participants' needs, in organizational and regional environments, and in the Internet itself. Five years of Internet workshops have provided a foundation for development of adult training models based on sound educational principles and practices.

Step 1 is to expand discipline-related Internet training activities. There has already been some discipline-based Internet training offered by METRO, notably in medical, legal, music, and art resources. This subject approach is likely to increase in scope and popularity with Internet users, regardless of their levels of expertise.

Step 2 is to develop a method for participant screening and placement according to objective, rather than self-assessed levels of background and experience. This would involve more METRO administrative oversight and effort, but it would allow Internet workshop instructors to focus content and presentation on specific subject matter at the appropriate level of complexity and thereby minimize duplication of content. The effort to provide a sequence from beginning to advanced pursuit of an Internet topic would be supported by adherence to prerequisites and/or some other demonstration of competency level.

Step 3 is to continue development of a replicable train the trainer workshop model that can be implemented in local settings for instructional sessions involving librarians and other faculty colleagues, as well as students. Teaching and learning issues have been evident on recent continuing education agenda of METRO. For example, one-day workshops on training staff and clients to use the Internet were held in February 1998. Content focused on assessment, learning theories, instructional strategies and resources, planning, facilities, and other relevant factors. A METRO/LAMA Institute on Managing Educational Services offered an administrative perspective titled: "Teaching and Learning in Libraries," presented in July 1998.

Dr. David Magier has recently added new train the trainer workshops to METRO's ongoing Internet training series. Stress is on needs assessment, planning, syllabus design and implementation, identification and creation of training materials, overall project management, and outcomes assessment. This approach encourages frontline academic librarians to take what they have learned in the workshop setting and develop their own continuing education sessions for faculty, course-related information literacy sessions for students, or both. These could range from individual or small-group tutorials to classroom lab sessions. METRO might extend this approach by developing its own cadre of member librarian Internet trainers who, once trained by Dr. Magier and his associates, could set up shop at various institutions around the region and repeat the process with colleagues.

Step 4 is to incorporate a more refined formal assessment process into Internet training sessions. Each workshop participant should have the opportunity to determine whether the immediate session has achieved specific learning goals and objectives. Each session ought to address evaluation, and participants should be given some tools to assess outcomes over time.

An editorial in a recent issue of *American Libraries* offers "Twenty-seven excuses for not taking that computer class." Though amusing, they are only somewhat tongue-in-cheek, directed as they are at struggling midcareer librarians who can appreciate both the humor and the editor's final exhortation: "You can't escape it. Go ahead and take the class" (Kniffel 1998, 36). Academic librarians will continue taking the METRO classes for some time, and this will serve as a springboard for them to take responsibility for giving classes: to plan, organize, design, and implement Internet instruction for faculty and students in their own settings. That is one of the most vital aspects of resource sharing in any library consortium.

References

METRO Board of Trustees. 1997. *METRO Mission and Strategic Plan.* New York: METRO, 3.

METRO Board of Trustees. 1994. *For Reference from METRO.* New York: METRO, 244. 1f.

Kniffel, L. 1998. Twenty-seven excuses for not taking that computer class. *American Libraries* 29 (3):36.

Learning from the Learner:
Reflections on Training of Librarians for Internet Use
David S. Magier

As a librarian at a research library in the late 1980s, it was obvious to experienced Internet users that the culture of the Net was rapidly changing. The "how to" of the Net began to get easier for its users. Institutional and individual creation of new content began to make the Net useful as an information resource. As Columbia's South Asia librarian, I uncovered many useful sources on the Net, such as annotated bibliographies, directories, demographic information, government documents, and even a smattering of electronic texts in Sanskrit. These resources proved to be as central to South Asian studies as many of the print books and journals I was acquiring in my "traditional" collection development role.

Recognition of the Internet as a Major Resource
It was clear to some of us that the library's mission to connect patrons with the information they need would require an overt recognition of the Internet as a major and growing source of such information. Therefore, provision of services such as collection development, reference consultation, and bibliographic instruction would need reorganization to incorporate the Internet's useful content.

Changing Librarian's Roles with Internet as a Resource
Some of us rewrote job descriptions to specify the activities of Internet collection development and reference. However, we realized that the legislation of a dramatic shift in the concept of the librarian's role would not make it happen. Even at Columbia, where high-speed Internet access was ubiquitous, easy, and institutionally well supported, many librarians were not equipped with the requisite skills and knowledge to make such changes.

Development of the Internet Training Program
Like their counterparts among the faculty (but unlike each year's incoming class of new students), many librarians were unfamiliar with the Internet beyond e-mail and perhaps a couple of listservs. Those who had dabbled with telnet, ftp, or gopher (or even the newly emerging World Wide Web) had figured out some of the how, but they did not grasp the what and can be forgiven for wondering why.

A small group of librarians realized that extensive Internet training, for both conceptual underpinnings and practical application, was necessary before most library staff could begin to implement the high-minded service goals we wished to establish. This realization led us (self-appointed as the Internet Users Group among the Columbia librarians) to conceive and propose an ambitious Internet training program.

This program with the acronym "ITP" is described elsewhere in this volume in several articles. ITP would eventually receive approval from library administration, and it has been an ongoing (and evolving!) component of life in Columbia University Libraries ever since.

Awareness of Internet Structure

My own involvement in the design, implementation, and evolution of Columbia's ITP program was a revelation for me. Conducting actual courses led me to the awareness that "what the Internet is" and "how the parts fit together" were not universally known by the trainees. Many had no idea what the Internet was—let alone how to locate subject-specific resources for a patron—even though they might have discovered which keys to press to "telnet" to the Library of Congress or how to bring up the Columbia gopher menu. A number of trainees had never been exposed even to that much.

I realized that I had taken for granted these basic concepts because I had been using the Internet on my own for so long. Therefore, we had to create a comprehensive training program that assumed no prior exposure and covered the concepts of the Internet as well as all the information formats it had to offer.

The Recognition of Training Needs outside Columbia University Libraries

From the start, other libraries were beginning to recognize these same training needs. As Columbia could not accommodate trainees from other institutions in its ITP program, some of these libraries approached me on an individual basis to conduct their own in-house training sessions.

Other Libraries' Needs

It appeared to me that many library administrators knew that they wanted Internet training but were not at all clear what that would entail or even why they wanted it in the first place. A significant factor in the explosion of demand for Internet training seemed to be simply the fear of being left behind. This same trend seemed to motivate the large investments by many colleges and universities in equipment and network infrastructure. This development happened before anyone was clear on exactly what the Internet was going to be used for or by whom.

METRO Program Development for Metropolitan New York Libraries

In the fall of 1993, METRO (now the New York Metropolitan Library Council) sought trainers to develop and conduct a new state-funded Internet training program for its member libraries. During the spring and summer of 1994, I was hired by METRO as an Internet consultant for this program. I was to conduct needs assessments and customized training sessions for librarians at seventeen member institutions throughout New York City and Westchester County.

The work plan that first year consisted of an initial interview with each library's director, other librarians and systems people, or all of them together to determine the local goals and needs for Internet training. This was followed by two four-hour training sessions on-site at each library, usually spaced about a month apart.

Needs Assessment Questions

What kinds of institutions were involved? What were the needs we uncovered? Who were the trainees? What were the training facilities like? How were the sessions organized? Looking back over the needs assessments and training logs now, it is incredible to see how much has changed in just four years.

Institutional Characteristics and Syllabus Decisions

The trainees' institutions ranged from tiny one-person libraries in small, specialized institutes (e.g., the New York College of Podiatric Medicine) to large libraries with thirty or more staff members per training session, serving major university communities (e.g., Fordham University). Despite this variety in size and breadth of subject coverage, the needs of the libraries were remarkably similar.

In virtually every case, the needs assessments indicated that no one had any substantial experience with the Internet beyond ordinary e-mail. They did not understand what the Internet was, so they could not say what they needed to learn or what they hoped to do with it.

Therefore, it was my responsibility to decide what to include in the syllabus. I thought that I needed to contravene the expectation of instant gratification of a practical how-to program in favor of a structured elaboration and demonstration of what the Internet is. Before the librarians and their administrators could decide on the Internet's potential role in the services their library would provide, they would need to understand what it is, where it came from, how it had evolved without content organization or control, and its different parts and protocols.

Syllabus Used in the Early Program

A typical syllabus for the two four-hour sessions, based on the needs assessment of a particular library (name deleted to protect the innocent), looked like this in 1994:

> *What is the Internet?* Conceptual overview. Network architecture. Varieties of connection paths. Internet address conventions. Domain names and IP addresses. Gateways between Internet and other networks.

> *Internet as a communication tool:* Using e-mail for point-to-point communication, finding e-mail addresses (finger, who is, postmaster), Internet for group communications and forums (listservs).

> *Remote log-in and telnet.* Connection to remote sites (library catalogs, databases, and specialized online services available through telnet connection).

> *File transfer using ftp.* Transferring files from remote archives to one's own host. Downloading files from the host to PC using communication software. Using Archie to explore the Internet to locate accessible files for transfer. Filenames and file types.

> *Exploring the services provided by NYSERNet* (through the NYSERNet gopher), by ColumbiaNet, and by LifeNet (NASA).

> *Structured information resources:* What is gopher? Using someone else's gopher (via telnet) when you do not have access to a gopher client of your own.

Trainees' expectations

Many trainees brought to their task a vague notion that the Internet was a structured publishing medium. This became obvious when they asked questions that began with "Why don't they . . ." Why don't *they* just make an alphabetical listing of all these FTP files? Why don't *they* set up all these telnet library catalogs to just use "library" as the log-in password? Why don't *they* give the files and directories more descriptive names?

I challenged the trainees to tell me which "they" were intended! An important goal of this early training was to make explicit what the Internet IS NOT. I demonstrated repeatedly that the Internet is not a library and lacks any kind of inherent organizational principles for its content.

Four years later the same is still true; however, now the underlying chaos is masked behind powerful integrative services such as the Web, with a user-friendly and consistent user interface. The main service that "they" are not doing now is providing subject access to the Internet's content.

Factors leading to differences in training experience

The look and feel of my demonstrations of Internet at different libraries varied. These differences were determined by a number of factors, including:

• the networking system available (terminals connected to a UNIX host on the Internet, terminals connected to an IBM mainframe on Bitnet, VAX systems, PCs using modems to dial-up shell accounts on NYSERNET, etc.),

• the available client software, all differing radically from library to library

These situations were less of a handicap than it might seem; because the primary goal was to have the trainees understand the Internet rather than teach them how to use it. The conceptual basis of the training remained constant.

Introductory Presentation Content

I devised a basic introductory presentation for the first four-hour session. The follow-up session had some practical hands-on exercises (where facilities permitted). That first year, the programs presented at the libraries were similar. Customization and variation occurred only in the choice of example sites and searches, tailored to the fields most important to each institution.

The available training facilities did shape the structure of the presentations. In 1994, at very few colleges, elaborate networked training rooms were made available for the librarians, with separate hands-on workstations for each trainee besides an instructor's workstation with LCD panel overhead projection. In such cases, I was able to alternate between *explanation* (house lights up), *demonstration* (lights down), and *hands-on practice* (lights up again). Besides reinforcing the concepts with the "tactile memory" of the operation, this sequencing served another purpose. The light switch at the METRO facility was down the hall from the classroom. "O. K., I am now running down the aisle again to turn up the lights for the demonstration to keep you all from falling asleep!"

At the other extreme were libraries with no training facilities at all. Five to as many as fifteen librarians would gather around the one available library PC that was "connected" to the Internet (often by a 9600 baud modem, and in one case, 1200 baud!). In such cases, I used blackboards, flipcharts, and handouts to try to convey what the Internet was, and was able to provide "live" demonstration of only a small portion of it.

A typical entry in the training log, for a library with no training facilities and bottom-end Internet access, will give some flavor of the challenges involved:

> Very limited Internet access is provided at this library. The director's PC is on a LAN that contains his Networking software. He uses the LAN modem to dial a local telecom access provider (Telenet), and then uses their connection to log-in to NASA, where they have a LifeNet account. Both the LAN modem and the modem directly connected to his PC are 1200 baud.
>
> All Internet access is through LifeNet itself, which is a separate network and seems to be discouraging users from accessing the Internet: all interfaces with Internet are very limited and difficult to use. For example, while they do support telnet, they have no gopher client (so one must telnet to one of the TELNET-ACCESSIBLE public gopher clients—a disappearing service).
>
> Their e-mail system is simple enough, but only if you intend to correspond with other LifeNet users. To pass messages across their gateway to the Internet, the LifeNet mail system requires you to go through a whole procedural loop to define a LifeNet nickname that points to the external (Internet) address, save the nickname in a separate file, and

then establish a link to that file within the mail program to send your message. This is necessary even if you are using the particular Internet address only once (as when subscribing to a listserv).

FTP is even worse. While one can transfer files from a remote FTP archive to the LifeNet account, the software does not allow you to have direct live interaction with the remote host. Instead, you have to specify the host name, the directory path, and the filename, with no feedback for errors, within LifeNet's own file-transfer window, and then the system attempts to go out and transfer the wanted file back, without interaction with the user. This means that browsing is virtually impossible and one is navigating blindly.

The second-stage procedure for downloading transferred files is likewise very complex and user-hostile, and was made even worse by the fact that the director's PC was connecting to LifeNet over a networked modem and using a networked software log-in script.

We did eventually succeed in getting a proper configuration of the ProComm software and the Network connection to enable the Kermit protocol to start downloading a file, but then the telnet link to NASA went down. It turns out that the NASA link drops connections roughly every 20 minutes, right in the middle of a session, on a regular basis. Although I succeeded in explaining the major Internet services and resources listed above, the demonstration of them and the "look and feel" of the Internet are obviously much less attractive when squeezed through the arcane interface of the LifeNet system, and it is a wonder that this library director is able to carry on any Internet activity at all. But he does, and is now inspired to try to do more.

Situational Comparison of Early and Present Training Programs

In 1998, real Internet access is ubiquitous and all considerations of variation in the user interface have begun to fade away. Everyone uses Netscape or Internet Explorer, and even telnet, platforms. The challenge for training has moved, appropriately, to a focus on the techniques for creating subject access to the Internet's scattered resources for the patrons of the libraries.

Variation in Trainees

The trainees in 1994 were exclusively the professional staff of the libraries. They ranged from a lone library director (as above) to the reference staff of a public library system to the entire professional staff of a large academic library. They wanted to be ahead of the curve (or at least, they did not want to be left behind) in planning for library involvement in the Internet, but they did not know what it was or how they would incorporate it into their work.

Four years later, the trainees are a much more diverse group. They are:

• catalogers who are being asked to provide cataloging for electronic journals;

• subject specialist bibliographers seeking to broaden their bibliographic instruction repertoire;

• circulation desk staff who just want to be Internet literate,

• faculty members who wish to develop Internet-based components to their class syllabi and reading lists;

• corporate library research staff wishing to hone their searching skills;

• newspaper reporters who need to use the Internet to develop background information for their stories;

• library systems staff who wish to predict how their institution (and its patrons) will be utilizing the Net from within their libraries;

• library development officers and grant writers who use the Internet to track down potential sources of funding;

• midlevel managers who wish to develop departmental homepages;

• human resources staff who want to plan substantial in-house training programs of their own.

Motivation for Training

Today's library trainees have focused motivation for Internet training. This may be because Internet exposure is much more widespread outside the training environment itself. On the other hand, my experience includes the awareness that many of these librarians feel quite at home with the Internet only because they have used their Web browser extensively and see how easy it is.

Variation in Interfaces and Consistency of Conceptual Needs

Today's interfaces are designed to be obvious and transparent. They are so user-friendly they do not even require the ability to read! (Notice that the designers of the navigation buttons in the browsers put both icons [a picture of a house] and text ["home"] on the buttons). Because this navigation is so easy, many trainees today do not believe they need any conceptual grounding on the Internet. They have become "good at it," yet I find they still operate with unclear or even false assumptions about what the Internet is and how it really works. They are still looking for a "they" behind the entire easy interface.

Changes in METRO Program: 1994–1998
Training Facilities

To meet the variety of emergent Internet training goals, I worked with METRO to refine their training offerings in the following years. In 1995, we shifted to having most of the training sessions at the training facility of METRO. At that time, it consisted of a meeting room with a capacity of about twenty (though we occasionally managed to squeeze in as many as forty people for heavily overbooked sessions).

Session Characteristics

There was only one computer in the room (a PC on METRO's ethernet Network) which functioned as the trainer's workstation. It was connected to an LCD panel with an overhead projector.

No hands-on practice was available, and the trainees could drink coffee and eat cookies at their seats. The sessions were five hours long (with lunch breaks). Sessions consisted of alternating explanation (lights up) and demonstration (lights down), with handouts of exercises for the trainees to try out back at their own libraries.

Content of Program

We offered three different sessions: "Basic Internet," "Advanced Internet," and "The World Wide Web." In addition, METRO began to offer some subject-specific Internet courses, in areas such as health, law, and art. The METRO training program was very popular, and more than twenty-five sessions were held that year, mostly filled to capacity.

1996: Laptop Computer Use and Topic Expansion

In 1996, METRO upgraded the training facility by providing networked laptop computers at each trainee's desk so that the sessions could include hands-on practice and exercises. The offerings were further expanded and refined: the sessions were reduced to four hours in length and covered less content per session, to allow time for guided hands-on work.

I began to offer an experimental new course titled "Introduction to HTML" for librarians ready to start developing home pages for their institutions. Again, the METRO sessions were filled to capacity, and several other libraries and library systems began to seek me out to give more customized and in-depth programs at their own sites.

1997: Multimedia and Syllabus Modification

In 1997, METRO added a high-power multimedia projection system to their training facility. Again, the syllabus was further refined, with more specialized courses at different levels. The course "Basic Internet Overview for Librarians" showed a gradual decline in enrollment. Therefore, it was offered less often each year. The advanced courses, which were heavily overbooked, were broken out to include "Advanced Research Strategies for the Internet." I redesigned the HTML course to include the creation of an actual home page for a "typical" mythical library (South Podunk Community College Library).

During the year, I also began to offer a train the trainer course for libraries that wished to develop in-house training programs of their own.

The Present: New Needs, New Topics

In 1998, we decided to split the HTML course into two separate sections: "Designing Library Home Pages" (Introduction to HTML), and "Refining Library Home Pages" (advanced Web site design). Additional types of material (such as collection development for the library Web) are now being considered.

Foresight: Common Threads, Critical Awareness

Across all training sessions, I have found common threads. As user interfaces became easier, and high-speed Net access became ubiquitous, insecurity became less of a motivation for librarians to seek Internet training. In fact, I see a strong desire among some librarians to leap ahead and tackle the cutting-edge aspects of Internet development.

Consistent Critical Attention to Specific Issues

I believe that the fundamental questions are still inadequately addressed:

• How does this Internet activity relate to the library's mission as a whole?

• Is the Internet just an add-on to the lives of librarians or is it part of an adjustment or redefinition of the profession itself?

• How does the role of a library change in light of the sociological phenomenon of a widespread and popular Internet with easy navigation and no information structure? (As I tell the beginners, "It is easy to go wherever you want, but hard to know where to go.")

I believe that these questions are natural extensions of the traditional role of libraries. Libraries add value to the raw universe of printed words by:

• evaluating and selecting the subset of the best publications (collection development);

• organizing them for easy subject access (cataloging);

• weeding and updating the collection (collection maintenance);

• providing assistance to help users locate what they need and use the collection effectively (reference).

These same functions constitute the librarian's tasks for Internet-based information. My focus in Internet training is always on the particular role that librarians have to play in making the best Internet information accessible and usable for library patrons.

Role of the Librarian in 1998

Although access mechanisms for the Internet have become increasingly user-friendly, the actual content of the Net is still scattered and lacking in standards for quality, subject organization, and consistent presentation. This trend (ease of access coupled with unorganized content) compels librarians to develop a critical awareness of their roles. Though the software and the commercial "search engines" are deceptively easy to use, the research and informational value of the Internet depends upon the ability of librarians. They need to direct patrons to well-organized, but hard-to-find corners, of the Net containing selective, focused subject collections. By its decentralized nature, the Internet is incapable of organizing itself into a virtual library and will always be more like a flea market.

However, scattered across the chaos of content are important sources and collections of information that come close to the organizational structure and added value of a library. Indeed, it increasingly falls to librarians themselves (individually, institutionally, and in coordinated collaborations) to create such collections on the Internet.

Past and Future Training Agenda

A major goal of my Internet training is thus to bring this perspective to librarians, to engage them intellectually in this important long-term agenda, and to give them the conceptual and practical tools to extract the most value from the Internet for their own libraries and students. To do this, they must learn to:

• find, evaluate, and select resources for their home pages (collection development);

• organize them for subject access (cataloging, classification,

and creation of browsable hierarchically organized subject collections);

• eliminate dead-end and outdated links (collection maintenance);

• provide patrons with useful online annotations;

• provide patrons bibliographic instruction in the use of these resources (reference and instruction).

Using this perspective, I believe that the mission of librarian Internet training is not different from "traditional" librarian preparation.

Internet Training of Library Support Staff
Dottie R. Hiebing

Who Are Library Support Staff?

Library support staff, or library paraprofessionals, are involved in all library operations at all levels. They may manage libraries or they may contribute very specialized expertise in some specific field. The range and complexity of their duties vary with each position, the size and type of the library in which they work, and each library's specific needs, goals, or mission. For an excellent overview of library support staff, including information on those states that offer certification of support staff, see the University of Rochester's site: URL: http://www.lib.rochester.edu/ssp/overview/overview.html.

Another relevant electronic discussion recommended by David Magier is Web4Lib. (URL: http://sunsite.berkeley.edu/Web4Lib/), which focuses on issues related to the creation and management of library-based Web servers and clients. This site includes discussions of resource selection, acquisition, and collection development procedures; cataloging and metadata issues regarding Web information; and training staff to use the Web.

Internet Training Needs of Library Support Staff

The Internet training program at the Metropolitan New York Library Council (METRO) focuses on the professional librarian. However, our Library Assistants Special Interest Group has offered Internet training for support staff. David Magier, who teaches most of METRO's Internet training classes, believes that support staff need much the same types of training that libraries offer to the public. In addition, he states that they need to know how to use the Internet for researching in the area of the library where they work.

Examples of this need for training are seen in the kinds of activities support staff routinely need to perform that are connected with the Internet. Support staff who work in the cataloging department need to understand how to log into the catalogs of other libraries. Support staff working in acquisitions may need to know where to buy books online and how to find vendors' catalogs.

A different view of support staff training needs was offered by Barbara A. Carroll, Program Director, Highlands Regional Consortium, New Jersey (URL: http://www.highlandsnj.org). She noted that the consortium, which has 940 libraries as members, is offering reference training for paraprofessionals " because they are doing reference, too. We hope the librarians got this in library school." Furthermore, she assessed the attendance of paraprofessionals at the technical courses: "more paraprofessionals and clerical staff show up for the technical courses than anyone else. They are the ones who are doing the work, and need the training" (Carroll 1998).

A Glimpse of Training Programs for Support Staff across the United States

Some states offer programs that any library staff member can attend, including support staff. In New Jersey, for example, the four regional library cooperatives train librarians and support staff, and support staff outnumber professionals in the training programs of at least one of the cooperatives. (See Barbara Carroll's comments above).

Other states that offer training, including Internet training, for library staff include:

• The Illinois State Library: The Institute for Introductory Librarianship, is intended for those who have had "limited formal library education" http://www.sos.state.il.us/depts/library/programs/trianing.html).

• Nebraska provides minicourses for library staff (http://www.nlc.state.ne.us/libdev/miniintor.html).

• The state library and State Library Association cooperate to provide opportunities for support staff at California's annual conference (http://www.cla-Net.org/conf98/highlite.html)

• A library paraprofessional interest group meets at Florida's state conferences (http://www. Flalib.org/library/fla98sched.html).

Metropolitan New York In-house Training: An Example

Large public libraries such as the Queens Borough Public Library include support staff training with training offered to professionals. Some libraries provide training in special programs. Queens, for example, also provides special training manuals for its Teen Net Mentors; the manuals explain the basics of Netscape and the library's OPAC and provides instructions on how to best train customers in the use of the Internet and the OPAC and its resources.

Training and Inclusiveness: Issues to Examine

Though some information is available on the training of support staff on the Internet, there are only glimpses of what is occurring in libraries. It is highly likely that support staff are trained with in-house programs, rarely documented.

An important question to consider is the nature of work by paraprofessionals in academic and public libraries. Is the situation of helping users different in the two library environments? Or, is it possible that currently, both academic and public library users turn to whomever is at hand for help with Internet, regardless of professional status? Knowing the situations that occurred in 1998 would help formulate policy and opportunities that are inclusive, if so needed. The topic deserves more attention than it has received here and in other materials. It is my hope that librarians, libraries, and consortia will share information and begin to document the Internet training of this group that has such importance for the library world.

References

Carroll, B. A. 1998, Oct. 23. Personal communication with P. Libutti. In P. O. Libutti, "Community and Digital Librarianship Distance Education Program: A Feasibility Study." New York: Libraries for the Future. Unpublished in-house paper, Nov. 1998, 23–24.

Navigating the Storm: Librarians on the High Seas of the World Wide Web
Roger T. Harris

It Was Another Fad, I Told Myself

When I entered library school in the summer of 1993, I had just begun to hear about e-mail. Despite my clear intentions to stay far away from all institutional computers and to lay my gentle hands only on the university's most cherished archival materials, I remember so well the thrill of being given my first magical Net address, of slipping immediately onto appealing listservs, and of flinging my first electronic messages out into the great void that we have come to revere as Cyberspace.

I was amused, but I was not convinced. It was another fad, I told myself. E-mail would go the way of eight-track tapes and other extraneous curiosities of these last decades of the twentieth century. Web sites would fall too. Sensible people would realize that "virtual library" was simply a phrase that had found its way into highly susceptible library literature. They would understand that, ultimately, patrons would never trade in their borrowers' cards for high-speed modems and the "click-on" realm of hypertext.

More Electronic Resources in the Libraries

However, even before I left library school, I saw interesting things happening at the university. More electronic resources were seeping into the libraries. Indeed, large areas of the traditional library buildings were being turned over to computer workstations, and CD-ROMS seemed to be reproducing themselves overnight.

Students were starting to create Web pages as class assignments, and many were finding jobs around the campus that allowed them to be "logged on" for hours at a time. When they were not uploading and downloading files, classmates were dodging in and out of "chat rooms" (where some found mates and others simply dates) or "scanning in" images of themselves that would be seen on computer screens around the world. All the while, I continued to arrange and file my brittle papers in university archives. I was waiting for the storm to subside.

Traditional Resources and Resources via the Internet: Impact and Inquiry

Little did I know that only a few years later I would be accepting a permanent position as a reference librarian in a fast-paced university library located in the middle of New York City. In this environment, for better or worse, I would be forced to confront on a constant basis the nuances of "Net-iquette," the reality of the "Webliography," and the frustration triggered by "dead links" scattered across the mystical terrain of the World Wide Web.

Students, faculty, alumni, and staff would be coming to me with questions prickly enough to make even the most seasoned librarian fumble for just the right approach, for just the right response. I would be torn to a greater and greater degree between the use of traditional resources and those that were coming to us via the Internet.

At this writing, although my board might be made more of paper and glue (still) than of fiber-optic cable and megabytes, I would like to acknowledge the fact that I have embraced the life of a devoted "surfer." Granted, I still have serious reservations about the way in which electronic information is revolutionizing not only the world of education, but also the world as a whole. Nevertheless, it is clear to me now that the frontiers of Cyberspace are as limitless and as seductive as the darkest corners of our own celestial universe. Moreover, interest in exploring the electronic information sphere is clearly gaining momentum by the nanosecond. There is simply no slowing this mode of "space travel."

As increasing numbers of card catalogs are retired and removed from the reach of patrons who far less than a generation ago would have considered such an idea outrageous, librarians are forced to consider again and again the impact that the Internet has had—and is having each and every day—on us and our library users. In much the same way that the conventional literary canon is periodically reevaluated amidst varying shades of political upheaval and the need for new approaches to critical theory ("Who needs Poe?" they ask), the way in which libraries gather, store, and disseminate their information is being called into question with practically every decision that we make in our daily professional lives.

Is what was appropriate last year (or last month) still appropriate today? Should certain subscriptions be canceled, although we are not sure that our online services will continue to maintain archives large enough to compensate for what we will no longer be buying and storing on paper or film? How much of our budgets should we continue to devote to books, when electronic services are in such tremendous demand? Are users fully conscious of their shift away from traditional sources of information, or have they simply been conditioned (unconsciously) to believe everything that they need will be available (if not today, certainly by tomorrow) via the Internet? And the questions go on.

In truth, no one can fully assess the extent to which the nature of librarianship is changing or the effect that this change will have on us over the years ahead. However, we do know that electronic information is something undeniably bigger than the difference between having a card catalog or not. Simply put, it is the difference between culture as a whole before and after the exodus brought about by visual information being made accessible via telephone cable.

Reflections on the Library after the METRO Workshop

At the METRO workshop that I attended last winter in Manhattan, which was led by Jane Pearlmutter, the dynamic and highly informative professor from the University of Wisconsin, I found myself wondering what I would do in her place with such a mixed group of participants as the one that sat before her. There were special librarians, school librarians, and academic librarians.

Some were quite experienced in using the Internet; others were less capable. Several seemed particularly curious about helpful sites and issues raised through discussion; others seemed anxious to get outside for fresh air and a cigarette.

In reflecting on the METRO seminar, I realized that, in many ways, I face a similar performance each time I go to work at the reference desk. Indeed, the range of experience on the part of patrons of my library is as varied as the languages they speak, the questions they have, and the number of minutes they are willing to invest in their searches.

When a student comes to me and says, "I want to get something off of the Net about Freud," I am still inclined to lead that person to the shelf on which the standard Freud texts rest. However, as the students get younger, the eyes glaze over increasingly frequently as I walk them toward the stacks. Can it be the speed with which that information is delivered via the Internet that is so convincing, or is there an invisible imprimatur on that laser-printed page that appears to their eyes and not to mine?

Obviously, much pertinent, substantial, and highly credible information is available electronically, yet it is the increasing acceptance of the Internet's complete authority on the part of growing numbers of patrons that works in direct opposition to my own skepticism. The random hits that many a search on the Web will reveal on the end user's screen seem indicative of the way in which patrons are shaped into information consumers whose ability to discriminate between poor, mediocre, good, and excellent resources withers under the forces of the electronic universe.

Evolving Role of Librarian as Navigator

As an academic, I am convinced that the role of the librarian will become increasingly the role of "navigator." The best navigators will be those who steer with the most caution, who accept the greatest responsibility for leading patrons through an increasingly complex hierarchy of information, and who are willing to use their personal, cumulative reasoning powers to weigh the various factors that might influence optimal satisfaction (and quality) for library users. When the patrons come with information needs on which they would like advice, the librarian will be the chief guide who will maneuver those individuals on the course that seems the most appropriate under the circumstances. If the patron is looking for information on the Back Street Boys, for example, the Internet will be the place to go first. If, on the other hand, the patron is looking for an illustrated collection of essays on the Holocaust, the librarian will probably prefer the more conventionally "scholarly" referrals to published volumes issued by university presses, museums, and respected commercial publishing houses.

Having said all of this, though, as time passes, and as scholarship is redefined by the electronic currents pulsating about the library, I realize that librarians will have to question ourselves habitually about the degree of confidence that we have in all available resources. In truth, who is to say that standards cannot be reinvented to such an extent that certain studies (conducted and published electronically) of popular music and the ways in which it mirrors societal trends might eventually carry more weight in the eyes of the academy and the public than anything ever undertaken by a scholarly press?

It is this reality that reminds the librarian of the need to consider all sources in light of the demand being made at the particular moment in time—and of the critical need to understand that the electrical storm enveloping all of us is nothing short of a new vehicle through which we must reconsider our places in the world.

LIB 111 Information Literacy: From Elective to Requisite Course
The Collaborative Information Literacy Project at Ulster County Community College

Patricia M. Carroll-Mathes

Little did I realize seven years ago how the Internet would change my professional life. Yes, I had found ways to update my skills and invigorate myself over the past thirty years. A sabbatical in 1981 was spent with the Federal Library Network at the Library of Congress. This experience allowed me to see networking in action and to understand the impact and use of electronic information systems at the Library of Congress, the National Library of Medicine, the National Agricultural Library, and other government libraries. However, these experiences had little impact on my actual working life when I returned to my small, rural, very traditional, unconnected college library in upstate New York. The experience did, however, prepare me to take an active role in the ongoing development of New York State regional library networks for the next decade. It motivated me to push relentlessly for the implementation of OCLC and other automation at my own library.

Initial Internet Contact: An Initiation to Confusion
I was introduced to the Internet ten years later, while again on sabbatical

visiting college libraries on a quest to find better ways to teach students needed research skills. My first exposure to the Internet was purely theoretical as Martin Raisch tried unsuccessfully to do a live presentation on his BI-List. The second contact was with a librarian from the University of Wisconsin-Madison, who shared her printed faculty training materials with me because the system was down. The third contact was with a computer systems analyst at the University of Windsor, who led a session of the Canadian Workshop in Library User Education. This first hands-on experience in a computer lab was totally confusing and frustrating. I had difficulty following the esoteric directions and had no clue as to their purpose. This experience gave me little hint of the universe of possibilities that would unfold, and though I listened to Patricia Senn Breivik speak on information literacy at the same conference, I did not recognize that the proactive leadership role she championed would encompass understanding and using that computer gibberish.

Fast Forward: Learning the Internet, One Step Ahead

When I began teaching our first "Electronic Access to Information" credit course, I was myself, struggling to understand and use gopher and ftp commands, as well as to make the whole process meaningful to students. The presence of IBM programmers, a math teacher, a regular CompuServe data user, and other librarians only increased exponentially the apprehension I already felt about my technological adequacy. The resources evolve: databases delivered over the Internet, online catalogs, end-user access to FirstSearch, bibliographic databases through the Web, student e-mail, and endless Internet resources; but the pattern is the same: install or subscribe, learn what you can to teach as soon as you can. I have long given up expecting a resource to look the same as it did the day or even week before I demonstrate it to an individual or a class.

Accepting Change: Stages of My Connection to the Internet

I've been through the stage where I subscribed to *Internet World* and *Wired* and read them cover to cover. *Wired* lost my support first, a result of its typography as much as its hype. *Internet World* became much too focused on Web developers before the print version folded. I watched *The New York Times*, the "newspaper of record," go from including a single personal computing column to publishing "Information Industries" and then "Circuits" sections. These changes are a clear acknowledgment of how networking technology has become a commonplace factor in contemporary lives.

I continue to scan my e-mail and read Edupage, CNet, and NUA Internet Surveys, as they appear to feel connected to the big picture. And I take great comfort in a statement I discovered in *Internet World*: "No one fully understands the Internet today, and no one will ever understand it fully again" (Gruener 1994). It helped me then, and it helps me now, to accept the dizzying pace of change as the only constant.

The single most important resource for my own professional growth and maintenance of sanity has been the existence of BI-List. I cannot thank Martin Raisch enough for developing, nurturing, and sustaining this electronic lifeline for librarians. I purposely say librarians, as I think all librarians, not just instruction librarians, need to be learners and teachers if this profession is to maintain a significant role in the Information Age.

The Best Way to Learn to Use the Internet Is to Teach It
The goal is to teach the staff, the students, and, more important, the faculty to understand and effectively use the multiplying resources and to comprehend the differences between using Internet resources and using the Internet to deliver resources. The Internet can be used as a tool to implement change and as a means of fostering the type of critical evaluation and engagement with the research process that all the bibliographic instruction of the past has failed to accomplish—that is, as long as the instruction is conceptually based and developmental in nature. If people do not understand the basic structure of a database, for example, it is unrealistic to expect them to grasp the finer points of advanced searching techniques. If information literacy concepts are not integrated into the fabric of teaching across the institution, librarians cannot hope to be influential. Integration requires a commitment to focus on faculty engagement, development, and collaboration, a teach the teachers or train the trainers approach to the task.

The Faculty–Librarian Partnership: Beginnings
Engagement of Faculty.
Librarians at every educational level need to acknowledge that they cannot teach in isolation. They cannot bring change to the learning experience of students without engaging the faculty. My library director Larry Berk and I recognized that fifty minutes would never be adequate and decided that credit instruction was the only way to achieve legitimacy within

the institution. To bring about the desired results, the need to enlist the faculty as partners and collaborators in the information literacy effort became clear. The need to persuade important administrators, trustees, and faculty leaders of the vital role of information literacy for students, faculty, and staff at the college also became paramount.

This was not a small agenda, and there was no thought of waiting for more time, staff, or money as Larry Berk and I both felt that the only way to initiate change was to begin. The READY, FIRE, AIM approach is to begin, to implement, and then to refine and refine and refine the process. The technology will continue to evolve, expand, and affect our collective lives. The information literacy program we initiated will also continue to evolve to incorporate changes in the Internet—changes we can anticipate and changes we cannot foresee.

Recruitment of the Faculty

Training the Faculty. Learning is a process and becoming a teacher is a process, so it follows that developing a teaching/learning focus is also a process, but one in which librarians can only effectively lead if they recognize that they cannot control the organic nature of both the medium and the message. We began the program by developing a training session for faculty and staff that incorporated the LIB 111 course material modeled (somewhat imperfectly in those early days of 1994) teaching techniques. We asked the faculty to read the text we had adopted—*Introduction to Library Research* (List 1993). Three librarians team-taught, and we enrolled 36 percent of our full time faculty, 20 percent of the staff, and 5 percent of the part-time faculty. This was an astonishing response given that faculty were volunteering, there were no financial incentives, very few were computer literate or connected to the Internet, and they committed to eight hours of instruction over four days. I cringe to think of how rudimentary these efforts were, but we did begin.

Ongoing Development of the Information Literacy (LIB 111) Program

Effectiveness Signals.

I know it is working when I pause outside the library classroom door and hear one faculty member after another talk persuasively to students about the importance of reference resources, reliability of information sources, and using the Internet with skepticism. I know it is working when a business professor teaching sections of our course for the sixth time tells me he is beginning to see the results of requiring information literacy in his marketing students who are better informed and are bringing more appropriate resources into class. I know it is working when a student constructs a successful search strategy, evaluates results, and then asks what other databases or Internet resources she might try.

Role of the Librarian in the Faculty–Librarian Collaboration

My role, and that of the other librarians, has expanded to include not only helping endless numbers of students understand and complete course assignments, but also supporting the teachers so they feel comfortable with new resources, changes in systems and interfaces, and their abilities to keep up with and teach information literacy. Some faculty have felt more comfortable team teaching until they have more experience with technology, the Internet, and the "library" material. A business professor, for example, did not have time for adequate preparation, so we first taught together and I handled much of the content, then we team-taught, then he taught the class solo with consultation before and after. Although I still help occasionally with examples for demonstrations or ideas, his skill level is such that he does not need help, even though we still collaborate. Others have taken the course with another faculty member as well as online before attempting to teach LIB 111 themselves. We also have a teaching team that meets at intervals, but not as frequently as would be ideal, to discuss problems, changes, and student difficulties and to share frustrations as well as successes. These sessions of collaboration, give-and-take, and support are essential.

Key Librarian–Faculty Partnerships

Dennis Swauger, Professor of Chemistry (early skeptic, convinced adopter, key supporter, and master teacher), who always had good research skills, credits the information literacy training with helping lead him into the Electronic Age. He has subsequently taught both classroom and Internet versions of the course, and champions the great need for developing conceptual understanding of and critical thinking about information in all students. He participated with me in offering a refined learning opportunity for faculty and staff in the summer of 1998 using our Web course as a basis for content and practice combined with classroom sessions for demonstration, amplification, and questions.

Another essential partnership was formed with Honey Fein, Professor of Nursing Emerita, who encouraged us from the outset, took the training, taught the course, and went on to chair the team that developed the online version of the course. She accompanied me to LOEX in Charleston in 1997 and inspired participating librarians with her testimony about the value of involving the faculty as teachers. After recruiting another nursing faculty member for the cause, she retired and returned to school where she excelled using the skills she developed in teaching Library 111 and continues to be an enthusiastic supporter of information literacy. I hope she will be able to return, as promised, as a part-time instructor in the near future.

Kathleen Bruegging, Chair of Interdisciplinary Studies and Professor of Foreign Languages, who has taught Library 111 regularly, helped to make this course a graduation requirement for all degree-program students, including those in the honors program. Her support went so far as to include developing and teaching Library 111 as an immersion course over winter break.

Enlarging the Pool of Faculty Collaborators

My role in nurturing the information literacy program is not only teaching, but also enlisting the participation of key faculty members as classroom and online teachers of LIB 111. The "department" has grown from one or two class sections per semester to twenty-two this fall and thirty for the spring of 1999. We have enlisted faculty from business, chemistry, English, foreign languages, physical education, psychology and developmental skills, as well as librarians from other organizations, high schools, colleges, and systems to augment our teaching staff. I have tentative commitments from biologists for the summer and fall and several new recruits for the spring. An engineering professor will begin teaching this spring after first attending a section taught by a career counselor, who debuted as a teacher this fall with excellent student evaluations and results.

From Elective Program to Course Requirement

We approached the English department initially in 1992, but not finding support, we altered our strategy and worked with faculty members in other departments, initially business, chemistry, and nursing. The business and nursing programs adopted our course as a requirement first, a direct result of faculty involvement followed by human services, chemical dependency, and criminal justice. This is where the key partnerships played an important role, as did my long-time participation as a member of the Curriculum Committee. The committee chair just happens to be that business professor who was one of the early supporters and teachers. Another committee member is the physical education/recreation leadership professor who supported the course concept from the beginning but has become an active teacher-participant. The role of information literacy in general education receives support, but consensus has not yet been reached on general education requirements. In the meantime, the English department reassessed its instructional goals and student research skill levels and proposed that LIB 111 be made a prerequisite, or corequisite, for second semester or sophomore-level writing classes. This ensures that most students will take it before graduating or transferring. The requirement was only possible with full support of the faculty from all disciplines.

The course has been a requirement for some programs for a while, initially business and nursing (a direct result of faculty involvement) and later human services, chemical dependency, and criminal justice. A new prerequisite/corequisite for sophomore English classes ensures that most students will take it before graduating. The reference area is busier than ever this fall.

Program Maintenance

Ongoing support of faculty. Constant efforts are required to enlarge the pool of full- and part-time faculty and staff who risk becoming learners themselves in order to teach. These risk-taking individuals also need support with course materials, ongoing mentoring, and a collaborative, open environment in which they may actively participate. The Internet allows me to select excerpts from Edupage, BI-List, and NUA Surveys, as well as to communicate with this teaching team through a distribution list.

Changing course content. Changing from an elective to a required course introduced new problems and new opportunities: student resistance, many multiple sections to staff and support, complaints by English students to teachers and teachers to the chair. We met individually, collectively, and with the English department and reviewed results of a student writing project, which made suggestions based on student interviews. We revised assignments, incorporating more group work and hands-on exercises, reassessed our goals and our constraints. During January intersession a writing tutor, the chair of Interdisciplinary Studies, and I collaborated to refine the course content and materials into a four-day immersion experience for sixty students. We will know soon how it works. This course will always be a work in progress.

Although I initiated the course, it has a life of its own. The course content and the teaching have benefited from evaluation and implementation by a range of teachers with different styles, experiences, and backgrounds. Experienced teachers have contributed substantially by keeping the focus on concepts and reducing the library lingo. My biggest lesson was to learn to let go. I can influence but not control the faculty or the course evolution. We evaluate regularly by collecting student evaluations at the end of each section and discussing the results and our collective experience. We continue to debate the role of the text. Initially, the lack of Internet material was a serious drawback, but the revised edition (List 1998) integrated the Internet into every chapter, which supports our conceptual presentation of the Internet as an access tool as well as a resource.

Ongoing course development. We identify concepts and use application examples, but we stress the concepts not the details, which may change and, given the nature of the Internet, frequently do. We continue to benefit from the wealth of teaching materials found on the Internet. Important resources include material from the *Internet Public Library*, the *Berkeley Digital Library* SunSITE, the *Librarians Index to the Internet* by Carole Leita, *Internet Tutorials* by Laura Cohen at SUNY Albany, and resources developed by other academic libraries throughout the country. Librarians and nonlibrarian faculty alike share Internet resources, course materials, individual expertise, and teaching strategies.

Web-based course evolution. Because of the Internet, we are able to locate the best resources available, keep up with developments, and bring them to the attention of teachers and students as well as link to many of them in our Web course. The WWW version, which debuted in the fall of 1997, is the result of a collaborative effort between librarians and two faculty members. The course designers were Ed Peifer (a math professor who taught himself what he needed to design the course) and Honey Fein (who chaired the content development team and edited the material). Peifer continues to work with me to revise the course and keep the content and links current. Although the course itself is offered through the State University of New York Learning Network, anyone can view the content and assignments on the Web at <http://itec.suny.edu/ucclib111/home.htm>.

The access of students to e-mail and full Internet access was an important factor in the development of the online course. I now respond individually to students' assignments that are submitted through the Web version of our now-required-for-graduation, one-credit information literacy course. The classroom-based version of the course begins with understanding how the *Britannica On-line* differs from the traditional print encyclopedia format. Some online course material is used in classroom sections, and the two versions have a synergistic, interlinked relationship. Both versions are continually in development, reflecting the changes in the Internet as well as our access to it.

Current Opportunities and Developments

Currently, there is another level of opportunity. The early adopters of technology (on our campus, that means the librarians and a few key faculty members) are in a position to mentor the rest of the faculty, who have just received desktops or laptops and are being connected to the new campus network with e-mail, scheduling software, access to library information resources, and full Internet access. Though our institution is late in getting everyone connected, we will be able to use our instructional materials and adapt our information literacy course to train faculty and staff as we have adapted it in the past.

Expansion of Training outside Ulster

We partnered with the regional, New York State library system in writing a grant, which was funded by LSCA in 1996. We adapted our faculty training experience to a train the trainers program for school public and academic librarians in our region. We again adapted that training to a course for teachers and librarians from a local school district in 1997. One of the school librarians is using the course as an ongoing in-service training model with teachers. We are exploring the feasibility of offering a version of our course to BOCES students in a talented and gifted program as well as to advanced placement students in area high schools.

Train the trainers. We conducted a train the trainers program in 1996 for school public and academic librarians in our region and again adapted that training to a course for teachers and librarians from a local school district in 1997. One of the school librarians is using the course as an ongoing in-service training model with teachers.

Reflections on My Present Internet Connection

I still prefer to read in the bath or bed and have no interest in spending $500 for a Rocket e-book so I can download the latest best-seller from AOL or Barnes & Noble. I suspect this "exciting" new technology will go the way of the overly hyped push technology whose declining fortunes I was only too happy to see chronicled in a recent *New Yorker.* I agree with a comment by C. L. Lynch (1998) that "the best library is the smallest library that has everything you want." The Internet allows even my small library to come close to that ideal. I see the role of librarians to be that of skeptics of the latest new thing, champions of the best of the heritage of the past, and debunkers of the hype surrounding the Internet and the techno-commerce of the wired world.

Still essential is the role of helping and, I hope leading students, faculty, and the public to make sense of the torrents of information that threaten to overwhelm anyone who does not have a sense of organization, structure, and perspective.

References

Gruener, G. 1994, September. Go on-line young man. *Internet World* 5, 50.

List, C. 1993. *Introduction to library research.* New York: McGraw-Hill.

———. 1998. *Introduction to information research.* Dubuque, Ia.: Kendall-Hunt.

Lynch, C. A. 1998, April 24. "Digital libraries and the new modes of communication." Presentation delivered at Westchester Community College, Valhalla, N.Y.

**List of Participants (Librarians and Faculty) in LIB 111
Collaborative Information Literacy Project, 1995–1999**

Lawrence Berk, teacher and Director of Library and Information
    Services, UCCC
Patricia Carroll-Mathes, teacher and Coordinator of Information Lit-
    eracy, UCCC
Dennis Swauger, teacher and Professor of Chemistry, UCCC
Honey Fein, teacher and Professor of Nursing, UCCC,
Richard J. Gelston, teacher and Professor of Business, UCCC
Kathleen Bruegging, teacher and Professor of Foreign Languages,
    UCCC
Kay Olbeter, teacher and Assistant Professor of Nursing, UCCC
Mark Anderson, teacher and Instructor of Communications, UCCC
Barbara Sartorius, teacher and Professor, College Skills, UCCC
Kari Mack, teacher and Coordinator of Library Services, UCCC
Edward Peifer, Internet course designer and Professor of Mathemat-
    ics, UCCC
Cheri Gerstung, Internet course content, Reference Librarian, UCCC
Karen Robinson, teacher and Coordinator of Career Services, UCCC
Michelle Rawl, teacher and librarian
Marti Robinson, teacher and Instructor of English, UCCC
Sheryl Chisamore, teacher and Writing Tutor, UCCC
Anita Estes, teacher and Tutor, Learning Assistance Center, UCCC
Vivien Cadbury, teacher and Instructor, College Skills, UCCC
Stephen Plumb, teacher and Assistant Professor, Engineering, UCCC
Evelyn Rosenthal, teacher and librarian, Dutchess CCC
Sue Ben-Dor, teacher and librarian, Southeastern NY Regional Li-
    brary Council
Tamm Sissac, teacher and Systems Librarian, SUNY New Paltz
Tamara Katzowitz, teacher and Librarian, Kingston High School
Ruth Boetcker, teacher and librarian

COURSE OUTLINE TITLE: INFORMATION LITERACY

DEPT/COURSE LIBRARY LIB 111 Section: 11 DEW 110
SEMESTER: spring 1999 Tuesday & Thursday: 1:10–2:30
INSTRUCTOR: Patricia Carroll-Mathes, Professor/Coordinator of Information Literacy
OFFICE HOURS: Available during most library hours, appointments can be scheduled
PHONE: 687-5208, 5218 (will be available before and after class)
E-MAIL: carrollp@sunyulster.edu

TEXT: List, Carla. *Introduction to Information Research.* Dubuque, Ia.: Kendall-Hunt, 1997.
REQUIRED READINGS: Various handouts and articles.
Jordan, Mark. "Ten Internet Myths," 1997.

COURSE DESCRIPTION
This course will introduce students to the organization, retrieval and evaluation of electronic and print information. Students will be provided with an overview of college library systems, networked information systems, traditional scholarly resources, evolving delivery systems, and the concepts underlying the research process. Students will gain an understanding of the importance of the Internet as a research tool and the changing nature of information resources. Students will utilize electronic databases, the World Wide Web, and print resources. Students will be able to apply principles learned in this course to research assigned in other courses. Students will practice thinking critically when formulating research queries and evaluating information resources.

GENERAL COURSE GOALS
To learn how to use a specific tool that is bound to change (quickly) is obviously not as useful as learning the concepts that are fundamental to information literacy such as:
1) How to ask a research question
2) How information is structured and accessed
3) How to develop a successful search strategy
4) How to evaluate the quality of information
5) How to be informed consumers of information

6) How to begin thinking about the educational, economic, social and political implications of life in the Information Age.

COURSE OBJECTIVES
At the completion of LIB 111, students will be able to:

1. Discuss the information environment and the impact of the computer in accessing and retrieving information.

2. Define basic library, information, and networking terms.

3. Choose and narrow a topic and formulate a research query.

4. Describe techniques that can be utilized to broaden and limit searches.

5. Develop and implement an effective search strategy, and appreciate the complex, dynamic process of information seeking.

6. Use basic reference sources, online catalogs, periodical indexes and the Internet to locate and retrieve information for a selected topic.

7. Describe the differences among the numerous information sources, identifying which types of resources are most appropriate for selected topics.

8. Critically analyze resources for validity and suitability for a given research project.

COURSE CONTENT AND ASSIGNMENTS
Week 1: COURSE INTRODUCTION
1/19 The Information Age Student Survey

1/21 Overview of electronic information technology
    What is a database? Examples.
    Reading: Chapter 6 and 2

    Access tools: Internet overview and Netscape basics
    Research Process
    Hands on *Netscape* and *Encyclopedia Britannica Online*
    Information Technology

    THE RESEARCH PROCESS
    Starting points: Encyclopedias and subject specific sources Periodicals
    and their role in research
    Review: Terminology
    Handout: *Primary vs. secondary information*
    Review: *Netscape Navigator*

The Disciplines: Humanities, Social Science, and Science
Information Basics Exercise
Information need analysis and search strategy

Week 2: REFERENCE SOURCES/ PRINT & ELECTRONIC
1/26 Types and examples/
Internet Reference Sources
Basic Reference Sources/Internet
1/28 Dewey Decimal System, Reference Exercise
Reading: Chapter 3 & 4 p. 39–70
Search Process Exercise, *Information Presentation*
Evaluation tools in the Reference collection

Analyzing Research Topics
Access tools: *SearchBank* databases and *Catalist*
How to Critically Analyze Information
Hands on *Catalist*, Reference Sources, *SearchBank*
MLA Style

PERIODICALS/ EVALUATION/ LIBRARY SYSTEMS
http://www.mla.org/main_stl.htm
Indexing Exercise
Periodical databases: Choices and strategies Distinguishing **Scholarly Journals**
Periodical types & formats,
Periodicals on the Internet
Skills for Online Searching
Evaluation as an ongoing process, "how to's."
of evaluation
Hands on SearchBank databases
Online Public Access Catalogs (*OPAC's*)
Classification Systems, Subject Headings

Assignment 2 in class
Hands on Catalist/ SUNY Connect, SENY Search
Assignment 1 due

Week 3: ONLINE SEARCHING: <u>FIRSTSEARCH</u>

2/2   OCLC *FirstSearch* (*WorldCat*)
      Reading: Chapter 5 p.73–93

2/4   FirstSearch **databases and documentation**
      Choosing appropriate databases
      Assignment 2 due
      Search strategies and limiting results
      Hands on practice *FirstSearch* databases
      Assignment 3 in class

Week 4: SEARCHING / EVALUATING THE INTERNET
      Assignment 3 due
2/9   Search **tools: Directories/Subject catalogs**
      Search Tools Chart

2/11 **Search tools: Search engines**
      Five criteria for evaluating Web pages
      Bookmarks
      Hobbes' Internet Timeline V 4.0
      Web reviews, rating sites, and Internet evaluation   =
      http://www.isoc.org/guest/
      Hands on practice WWW, Evaluation Exercise
      zakon/Internet/History.HIT.html
      Assignment 4 in class

Week 5: MORE ABOUT THE INTERNET
      Reading: Chapter 7: p.117 –20
2/18 **E-Mail and discussion lists**
      Assignment 4 due

2/23 **Subject sources on the Net**
      DISCUSSION: *Ten Internet Myths*
      Future developments/ questions
      DISCUSSION: *Surfer Beware*
      Course review
      http://www.epic.org/reports/surfer-beware.html

Final Final projects (in class exercise)
Final Exam (All Assignments due)

2/25 Final evaluation project (due by 3/4)
    Course evaluation (due by 3/4)

ASSESSMENT METHODS
Class will meet for 5 weeks, twice weekly for 80 minutes. The final exam
will consist of a multiple choice exam and research/evaluation project due
one week after the last class. There will be readings, exercises and written
assignments and time for hands on practice. Due to the importance of class
participation, demonstrations of electronic resources, exercises and group
work, attendance in class is required and will affect your grade.

Like any skill, searching electronically takes practice. Students are
expected to spend time outside of class reading, completing assignments,
and practicing using the tools introduced in class.

The final grade will be computed in the following manner:
Participation and assignments 70%
(In class exercises, groupwork, homework, quiz (es)

Multiple Choice: 15%

Final Project: 15%–20%

Part III
The Present Tense:
The Diffusion of the Internet
into the Work Flow of
Academic Librarians

The Internet and Work Flow: Impact and Inferences

Marilyn Rosenthal and Marsha Spiegelman

Within recent years, as academic institutions have embraced educational technology, librarians have witnessed the integration of the Internet into information services. Innovations wrought by the World Wide Web, e-mail, listservs, electronic resources, and online courses have dramatically altered the academy, but nowhere have they had more impact than in the library. In the wake of these advances, librarians scramble to cope with new dimensions in information technology and adjust to the accompanying metamorphosis. The insatiable desire for data from an ever-changing online environment has created an unprecedented need for instruction, triggering new models for learning and teaching. How have professionals gained the necessary skills to adapt, and what training may be necessary to negotiate the information continuum? What processes exist to facilitate the transfer of this knowledge? What organizational modifications are necessary to ensure its inclusion in the course of library services?

Background

As digital libraries emerge, no longer is the Internet in the library questioned but, rather, its presence is assumed and demanded. Concepts such as electronic publishing, distance learning, and virtual collections, part of the current vernacular of higher education, exemplify the convergence of information and technology and signal a paradigm shift in library services. From electronic acquisitions and cataloging to computerized reference searching, library functions have been redefined. In their traditional roles as providers of bibliographic instruction, librarians have taken on the responsibility of incorporating the Internet into the existing setting and creating a new framework for instruction. Recognizing its importance, they may seek to convert the conventional library into a learning organization, "an organization that is continually expanding its capacity to create its future" (Senge 1994, 4). Although institutional interest in this transformation has led many to reevaluate services and question priorities, little attention has been directed at the assimilation of the Internet into the work flow of the librarian.

This study grew from two areas of inquiry. The first nationally supported ACRL initiative, in the early 1990s, centered on an analysis of Internet learning and teaching in the metropolitan New York area reported elsewhere in this book. The second, a study performed by the authors in 1995, evaluated use of the Internet among academic reference librarians throughout New York State. The researchers sought to examine the usefulness of the Internet as a reference tool, as well as to identify Internet users, determine usage patterns, describe personnel behavior, evoke both positive and negative reactions to Internet use, and detect system strengths and weaknesses (Rosenthal and Spiegelman 1996, 53). The present research continues these themes with new emphasis on the diffusion of the Internet into the daily routine of librarians.

Purpose

The current project was undertaken to gather information on academic librarians' use of the Internet with the purpose of evaluating their perceptions of its influence on work flow and to ascertain attitudes about the overall impact of the Internet on academic librarianship. Information in different categories was collected for analysis. The goals were to:

- determine patterns of Internet use;
- review instructional models;
- identify training preferences;
- examine institutional support and response;
- analyze workload issues.

Methodology

This survey employed the technique of recording and analyzing data from a six-page questionnaire to which participants responded anonymously. In May 1998, multiple copies of the survey were mailed to members of the Metropolitan New York chapter of the Association of College and Research Libraries, reflecting the scope of the original initiative. To ensure an adequate period to analyze the data, a six-week time frame was allowed. Surveys received after that date were not included in the calculations, although participants' comments were considered. The data were gathered from eighty-three questionnaires, representing approximately 33 percent of those mailed.

Survey Design

Using elements from the previously mentioned studies, questions were grouped into categories from which six sections were created. Respondents were directed to select the single most appropriate answer to avoid ambiguity. Where more than one choice was applicable, specific instructions were provided. To profile the survey sample and determine degrees of Internet connectivity, the first section contained background questions regarding library position, and use and location of Internet access.

The second and third sections were designed to evoke responses related to Internet instruction. The second section queried participants' perceived levels of computer and Internet expertise, modes and motives for learning, institutional support, and further training requirements; and the third focused on teaching others. Librarians were asked to indicate categories of trainees, formats of sessions, and methods and delivery of instruction. In addition, subjects were asked to indicate the effect of Internet use on their weekly load of formal information instruction.

Section four measured the impact of the Internet on daily interaction. Those surveyed were first asked to select and quantify their most time-consuming Internet activity. Web searching, e-mail and listerv applications, and Web page creation, among others, were possible answers. They were then to convey the Internet's effect on workload, concomitant curtailment of responsibilities, and reason for any accompanying reduction. Next, inquiry was made into occurrence, if any, of decreased commitment to campuswide, professional, and library-related work. Librarians ranked, in descending order, the three most affected areas and noted whether released or compensatory time had been afforded to accomplish Internet tasks.

The fifth section elicited positive and negative reactions to the advent of the Internet as it related to public service. Reference librarians reported on resulting changes in quality and quantity of information exchange. Modifications in staffing and operation were queried.

Part six dealt with general attitudes toward this technology's benefits and drawbacks. Questions related to stress and institutional support, as well as factors creating the most frustration and satisfaction, were addressed. Equipment problems, lack of technical support, inconsistencies of the Internet, fiscal constraints, and technical illiteracy of patrons represented possible difficulties, whereas increased access to information, preference for electronic searching, networking capabilities, and rapid response exemplified causes for success.

The survey concluded with requests for summary comments on the integration of the Internet into library services. Furthermore, suggestions were solicited as to potential work flow restructuring.

Data Analysis

All sections of the eighty-three returned questionnaires were assessed quantitatively to create a total demographic profile. The results were tabulated and reported in percentage form. All blank or ambiguous responses in any category were not considered in the calculations of this study. The surveys were then divided into two groups: those whose workload had increased because of the Internet and those whose workload had not. For the purposes of this study, a participant who

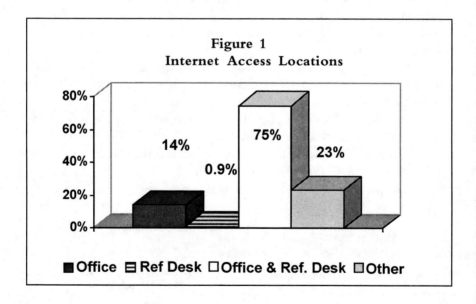

Figure 1
Internet Access Locations

checked "increased" in response to the question How has the advent of the Internet affected your workload? was referred to as W+, and one who checked either "decreased" or "no change" as W. Each group was separated further according to various components taken from the questions: reason for learning, teaching of students, teaching of others, increased workload of bibliographic instruction, reduction in commitments, increased stress, curtailment of responsibilities, and time spent on the Internet. Chi-square evaluations were completed using a significance level of .05. Finally, observations as to the effect of the Internet on library work flow were compiled and appraised.

Participants' responses to each of the three open-ended queries in the final section

Table 1
Participant Internet Training

Variable	Percentage
Computer expertise	
• Novice	13
• Intermediate	69
• Expert	18
Internet expertise	
• Novice	14
• Intermediate	75
• Expert	12
Primary mode of learning	
• Formal training	14
• Informal training	25
• Online or tutorials	1
• Self-teaching	42
• More than one mode	17
Received released time	70
Received funding	33
Need further training	83
Preferred method	
• Workshops	66
• Informal training	21
• Self-teaching	10
• Online or tutorials	3

were tabulated and aggregated according to similarities within each profile. Comments in part A were next categorized as positive, negative, or neutral, and then totaled as such. Finally, all sets of answers were compared and contrasted, and conclusions drawn.

Findings
Total Demographic Profile
Information relating to participants' backgrounds, gathered from section one of the questionnaires, revealed the following statistics. Ninety-eight percent of respondents were academic librarians from public and private two-year and four-year college and university institutions. Ninety-nine percent used the Internet in their positions as librarians.

All reported having Internet access in the following manner, as reflected in figure 1—14 percent in their offices, less than 1 percent at the reference desk only, 75 percent in both locations, and 23 percent in various other facilities such as classrooms, computers labs, home offices, and other library sites. Moreover, 94 percent offered access to patrons, whereas 5 percent did not.

Participant Training

Table 1 reveals key data related to participants' Internet training. When questioned about their computer expertise, 13 percent considered themselves novices, 69 percent intermediates, and 18 percent experts. In terms of Internet expertise, 14 percent rated themselves novices, 75 percent intermediates, and 12 percent experts. Respondents indicated primary modes for learning as follows: formal training such as classes and workshops (14 percent); informal training such as one-on-one, peer instruction, and consultation (25 percent); tutorials or other online training (1 percent); and self-teaching (42 percent). Seventeen percent included more than one category. Among the primary reasons for learning, 29 percent were excited by the wealth of information offered, 59 percent felt it was necessary for professional growth, 5 percent were directed to learn by supervisors and/or administrators, and 6 percent learned in response to patron demands. Although 70 percent received some form of released time to attend training, only 33 percent obtained funding. Furthermore, 83 percent believed further training necessary. In fact, in terms of best method for that training, 66 percent preferred workshops, 21 percent informal training, 10 percent self-teaching, and 3 percent tutorials or other online sources.

Instruction of Others

To determine the extent of Internet instruction across campuses, participants indicated to which groups the library offered training. Survey results, as demonstrated in figure 2, revealed that 62 percent provided it to students, 57 percent to faculty and administrators, 51 percent to librarians, 44 percent to nonprofessional staff, and 10 percent to others. A first set of questions was directed at nonstudent training. Fifty-nine percent noted that they were responsible for teaching nonstudents: specifically, 83 percent campus faculty and administrators, 56 percent other library personnel, 44 percent other librarians, 42 percent reference librarians, and 15 percent the general public. Sixty-three

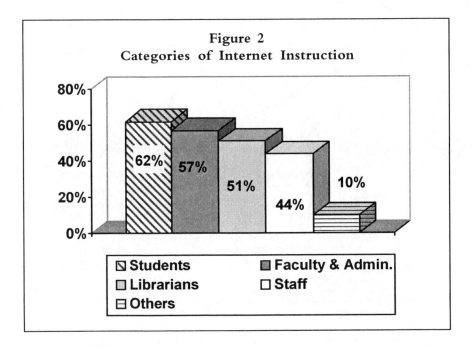

Figure 2
Categories of Internet Instruction

- ⧅ Students
- ▨ Faculty & Admin.
- ▤ Librarians
- ☐ Staff
- ⊟ Others

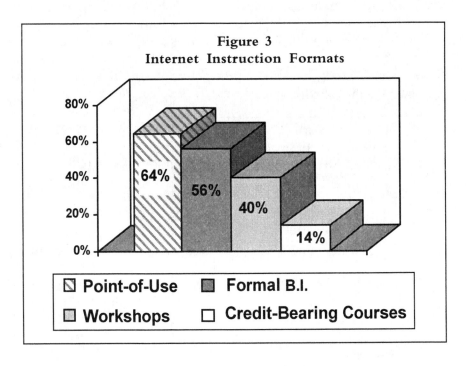

Figure 3
Internet Instruction Formats

- ⧅ Point-of-Use
- ▨ Formal B.I.
- ☐ Workshops
- ☐ Credit-Bearing Courses

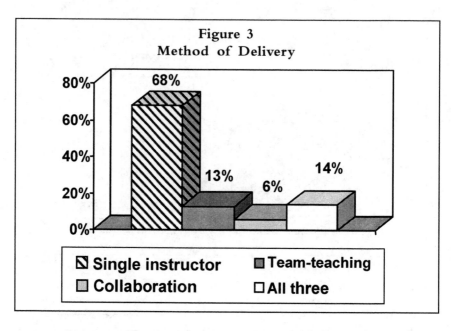

Figure 3
Method of Delivery

percent felt that follow-up and/or support for this type of instruction affected their workload somewhat, 19 percent not at all and 19 percent a great deal. A second set related to the teaching of students. As expected, a larger number, 78 percent, reported this task as part of their duties. Figure 3 illustrates that the most widely used formats were, in descending order, point-of-use instruction (64 percent), formal bibliographic instruction sessions (56 percent), scheduled library workshops (40 percent), and credit-bearing courses (14 percent). Although the primary mode of this instruction was either hands-on (54 percent) or demonstration (46 percent), the primary method of delivery was overwhelmingly by single instructor (68 percent), as displayed in figure 4. Other means included teamteaching (13 percent) and collaboration

Table 2 Reduction in Professional Commitments	
Activity	Percentage
Professional organization work	10
Scholarly writing and presenting	10
Professional reading	10
Other library-related work	10
Student-oriented activities	5
Department and/or campus committees	2
Volunteer work	2

with faculty (6 percent), with 14 percent employing all three. Surprisingly, only 60 percent perceived an increase in their weekly load of formal information instruction.

Internet in Daily Interaction

The pervasiveness of the Internet is evident with 96 percent affirming its use in their daily work. When asked to specify among suggested categories which activity had the greatest impact on their time, 62 percent selected e-mail and listservs, 31 percent searching the Web, 3 percent creating Web pages, and 3 percent other. Weekly use, queried by hourly time periods, was reported thusly: 0–5: 18 percent; 6–11, 40 percent; 12–16, 33 percent; 17–22, 6 percent; and over 23, 2 percent. Seventy-eight percent asserted that as a result of the advent of the Internet their workload had increased, whereas 21 percent recorded no change and 1 percent a decrease. Eighty percent, however, maintained that other responsibilities had not been curtailed in order to manage Internet activities. Of the 19 percent whose activities had been curtailed, 65 percent did so as a personal priority, 24 percent were afforded the opportunity due to staff increases, and 12 percent did so at the direction of a supervisor/administrator. When asked if it had been necessary to reduce commitments to activities and to mark, in descending order, the three most affected areas, 55 percent of respondents claimed no change. Table 2 shows that of the 45 percent remaining, reductions were made in the following categories: professional organization work (10 percent), scholarly writing and/or presenting (10 percent), professional reading (10 percent), other library-related work (10 percent), student-oriented activities (5 percent), department and/or campuswide committee work (2 percent), and volunteer work (2 percent). Yet, all told, only 18 percent stated that they were given released or compensatory time to accomplish Internet activities.

Impact on Reference Service

To ascertain the Internet's impact on reference service, questions were directed at the 80 percent of those surveyed who worked at the reference desk. Ninety-six percent agreed that the Internet increased access to information and 88 percent claimed that it improved the quality of service, but 85 percent affirmed that the accompanying workload was increased. Moreover, only 10 percent were assigned additional librarians to compensate for the additional work.

Overall Impact

Survey results reflected that institutional emphasis on educational technology influenced Internet use in the library in the following way: 51 percent a great deal, 43 percent somewhat, and 6 percent not at all. With regard to perceived increased level of stress, 54 percent responded affirmatively, and 48 percent negatively. In addition, 54 percent stated that their involvement with the Internet caused them to either work after hours or bring work home.

In reviewing the factors that created the most frustration in dealing with this technology, the choices selected in descending order were:
- ephemeral and inconsistent nature of the Internet;
- equipment problems;
- lack of technical support;
- fiscal constraints;
- technical illiteracy of patrons.

Similarly, factors that provided the most satisfaction were, in descending order:
- access to information not readily available at the institution;
- access to information from remote locations;
- opportunities for electronic networking;
- rapid responses to patron queries;
- preference for electronic searching.

W+ Profile

When asked their primary reason for learning the Internet, the 78 percent in the W+ group responded thusly: 30 percent were excited by the wealth of information offered, 59 percent felt it necessary for professional growth, 8 percent were directed by supervisors and/or administrators, and 3 percent learned in response to patron demands. Eighty-two percent had responsibility for teaching the Internet to students and 62 percent to others. In addition, 64 percent asserted their weekly load of formal information instruction increased. Forty percent felt the need to reduce their commitments to professional and/or institutional activities, only 24 percent had their responsibilities curtailed in order to manage Internet-related work. Resulting increased levels of stress were reported by 57 percent of the W+s. In terms of hours per week spent, the largest percentage, 39 percent, marked 6–11, followed by 36 percent with 12–16.

Table 3
Findings

Variable	W +	W
Reasons for Learning the Internet[1]		
• Excited by wealth of information	30%	41%
• Necessary for professional growth	59%	59%
• Directed by supervisors[2]	8%	0%
• Response to patron demands[2]	3%	0%
Teaching Responsibilities		
• Students[3]	82%	67%
• Others[4]	62%	50%
Increased Formal Instruction[5]	64%	21%
Reduced Prof. Commitments[6]	40%	6%
Responsibilities Curtailed[7]	24%	0%
Increased Stress[8]	57%	39%
Weekly Use in Hours[9]		
• 0–5	14%	33%
• 6–11	39%	44%
• 12–16	36%	22%
• 17–22	8%	0%
• 23+	3%	0%

Notes: Significance level $=.05$

1. $x^2=2.41$, df$=3$, p$=.299$
2. combined for statistical analysis
3. $x^2=1.84$, df$=1$, p$=.174$
4. $x^2=.830$, df$=1$, p$=.362$
5. $x^2=8.17$, df$=1$, p$=.004$
6. $x^2=7.62$, df$=1$, p$=.005$
7. $x^2=5.26$, df$=1$, p$=.021$
8. $x^2=1.85$, df$=1$, p$=.173$
9. $x^2=5.67$, df$=4$, p$=.225$

W Profile

Among the 22 percent in this group, only two reasons for learning the Internet were chosen. Those excited by the wealth of information represented 41 percent and those for whom it was necessary for professional growth, 59 percent. Sixty-seven percent of Ws taught students and 50 percent others. Only 21 percent, however, had increased their weekly load of formal information instruction. Interestingly, only 6 percent considered a reduction in professional and/or institutional activities necessary, although none reported curtailment of responsibilities. Furthermore, a majority (61 percent) claimed no increase in stress. The greatest percentages of weekly use amounted to 44 percent (6–11) and 33 percent (0–5).

Results of the chi-square of independence performed on eight variables related to increased workload and the Internet: reason for learning, teaching of students, teaching of others, increased bibliographic instruction, reduction in commitments, increased stress, curtailment of responsibilities, and time spent revealed three statistically significant findings. As disclosed in table 3, a correlation between workload and formal information instruction revealed that approximately two-thirds of the W+ category reported corresponding increases, compared to only one-fifth of the W group (p<.01). In terms of responsibilities, W+s were significantly more likely to have them reduced than Ws (p<.025). An even greater correlation established a direct relationship between increased workload and curtailment of professional and/or institutional commitments (p<.01). Although virtually no Ws lessened their undertakings, almost half of the W+s thought it necessary. On closer examination, it was apparent that the areas most affected were professional organization work, professional reading, and other library-related work, followed by scholarly writing.

The manner in which participants learned the Internet was found to be independent of increased workload. Whereas more Ws were excited by it, proportionally equal numbers believed it necessary for professional growth. In both groups, neither supervisory directive nor patron demand motivated many.

Findings revealed that, not surprisingly, W+s bore the greater responsibility for teaching students and other personnel, 82 percent and 62 percent, respectively. At the same time, the figures for Ws were 67 percent and 50 percent, respectively. Clearly, both groups were required to incorporate the teaching of this new technology into their instructional routines. Though not statistically significant, 15 percent more W+s were involved in student-centered training and 12 percent more in the training of others, explaining, perhaps, the perception of greater workload.

When asked to indicate weekly use, on the one hand, 6–11 hours was the most common answer for the majority of both groups (W+s, 39 percent, and Ws, 44 percent). On the other hand, the second most selected time period for W+s was 12–16 hours (36 percent), but 0–5 hours for Ws (33 percent). In fact, 11 percent of W+s spent more than sixteen hours per week on Internet activities, yet no Ws used it that extensively. Though not proven statistically, it is logical to assume that the more time spent on Internet activities, whether for e-mail, Web searches, or Web page creation, the greater the workload.

Perceived increase in stress was found to be independent of increased workload. Indeed, 57 percent of W+s experienced it, as did 39 percent of Ws. Although it may seem evident that increased workload causes increased stress, it is important to note that more than one-third of those reporting no increase in workload still experienced Internet-related stress. Certainly, it is a meaningful factor for consideration.

Comment Analysis Results

When asked in part A to comment on the manner in which the Internet had had the greatest impact on work flow, W+s reported nearly twice as many negatives as positives. Among the positives were: greater access to additional resources, improved professional relations, communication and collaboration, source of quick answers, and more interesting work. Negatives included: its encroachment on time due to e-mail, system inconsistencies, student help, training, preparation, instruction, and interruptions; increased pressure; and supervisory demands. Increased interlibrary loan transactions and changes in reference desk procedures were considered to be neutral.

Within the W group, negatives represented approximately one-half the number of positives. Greater access to information was the most common positive reaction to part A, followed by improved professional relations, communication, and collaboration; increased efficiency; and improved service and instruction. Expanded workload and time expended on e-mail and technical problems accounted for negative replies. No neutral comments were noted.

Statements of W+s made in response to part B as to possible restructuring of workload as a result of the integration of the Internet demonstrated an overwhelming desire for more staff, including systems, reference, and instruction librarians, and technical assistants. Additional time and reorganization of instruction were the next changes most requested, followed by a reduction in duties. Equal numbers sought product consistency, more collaboration, greater dependence on electronic communication, and additional training for all.

Ws, for the most part, required no restructuring of work flow. Of those who did, suggestions involved improved equipment, additional technical support, and standardized teaching hours, as well as more time to train faculty and to develop access tools.

Additional comments as called for in part C were minimal and mixed for both groups. Although W+s agreed that the Internet opened up a world of information, among their cautionary remarks were the need for evaluation and standardization, filtering, better hardware, greater technical support, increased computer literacy and training, and, again, more time. Not surprisingly, Ws comments reflected the integral nature of the Internet in academic librarianship.

As expected, those with increased workloads presented more negative comments with respect to the Internet's impact on workload than those whose workloads did not increase. Actually, they account for two-thirds of W+ responses. In contrast, positive replies represented an equal fraction of W remarks. Similarly, one-third of W+s viewed more personnel as the key to work flow restructuring, whereas an equal fraction of Ws were satisfied with current conditions. Ultimately, W+ additional comments disclosed a great deal of frustration, whereas Ws expressed gratification. An examination of all the surveys, however, revealed common threads. Within part A, discerned were the benefits of greater access to resources, improved professional interaction, and enhanced instruction and the liabilities of time consumption, technical problems, and demands of e-mail. Part B displayed shared desires for changes in training and instruction programs and reallocation of commitments. Finally, part C uncovered a mutual belief in the usefulness of Web-based materials with a recommendation for critical assessment and standardization.

Discussion : Mandates for Transition from a Traditional Library to a Digital Library

Results of the survey indicate five mandates that must be recognized to make the transition from a traditional to a digital library.

• *Further Internet training is considered by librarians to be essential. Academic institutions should support continued professional development through the creation of in-house training or the provision for outside education.*

A majority seek to improve their expertise even though they describe themselves as either intermediate or expert users of the Internet. Librarians recognize their expanding roles as enhanced service providers and understand the urgency to adapt. With the growth and popularity of Web-based distance learning and research, "The advice and skills of an Internet-savvy librarian become all but essential," according to Steven Gilbert (1995, 59). With this in mind, administrators must continue to furnish adequate time, funding, and resources to that end. Even though many respondents were given the opportunity to attend training, few received compensation. What form this training may take will vary. While participants, for the most part, either taught themselves or received one-on-one informal instruction, they prefer formal workshops as the model for future learning. Areas of study should go beyond conventional Internet topics such as e-mail and search strategies and encompass related and advanced skills like web page design and basic networking principles. Many individuals may need to further hone their basic computer knowledge so they are able to give instruction in downloading, saving, and printing documents. Possibilities exist for cooperation among library personnel and computer experts on campus. For their part, librarians must remain proactive in obtaining necessary proficiency by attending programs beyond their own discipline, as well as library conferences and continuing education courses.

• *To integrate electronic information into the learning process, libraries must restructure information instruction.*

The high level of point-of-use and single-instructor demonstration classroom modes reported in the research suggests inefficiency and the importance of developing a coherent information literacy structure. To avoid the pressure and increased workload that are an outgrowth of limited long-range strategic planning, a two-pronged approach must be established that will make libraries the center for teaching and learning activities. First, this dynamic environment requires updated teaching styles that foster active and hands-on learning through the use of electronic classrooms, teamteaching, and curriculum-based assignments. Second, librarians should institute models that are neither teacher nor classroom centered but, rather, are free from the traditional constraints of time and location. Anecdotal accounts have demonstrated that drop-in sessions have not succeeded, but universities are currently incorporating computer-assisted packages, Web-based tutorials, and online courses into existing programs of information education. The advantages garnered from these efforts ultimately out-weigh the initial work necessary for their creation. Thus, issues of increased workload may be addressed.

• *The electronic library requires the building of new partnerships and the nur-turing of these new collaborations. In today's environment, campuswide alliances are needed to support the digital library.*

Expressions of frustration caused by equipment problems, lack of tech-nical support, fiscal constraints, and technical illiteracy of patrons ne-cessitate communication and cooperation between academic library departments and computing services. Librarians still require help in areas related to systems, computing, network, and other technical con-cerns. At the same time, as information specialists, they can provide insight into user information needs and participate in network design.

It is equally important to foster interdisciplinary relationships with other faculty. Already an outgrowth of electronic communication, as denoted in the research, these connections must not be thwarted by increased workload.

"Technology is certainly a force for creating a needed cli-mate of collaboration and partnership as both groups strive to attain the institution's educational mission" (Rapple 1997, 46). Shared initiatives may take the form of learning communities that involve several academic disciplines or curricula that require print and Internet resources, Web-based courses, and other interactive media projects. Ties that enhance librarians' leadership positions on campus increase broad-based support for library goals, includ-ing additional materials, hardware, and personnel, as well as the restructuring of duties. Assuredly, results of the survey make it evident that the expanded workload at reference has not been matched with supplementary staffing.

• *Librarians must take greater responsibility for the management and direction of Internet activities.*

Internet activities have had an appreciable impact on time, some of which may be within a librarian's control and some of which may not. Findings revealed that although users felt e-mail and listservs extended opportunities for communication and collaboration, too much time was expended on these tasks. Web-searching and Web page design also accounted for time spent on the Internet, as did group and individual instruction. Although much of this may be a job-related requirement, it is incumbent upon the librarian as a professional to ascertain where alterations may be made. Opportunities for self-determination exist, for example, in cutting back on nonessential e-mail and listservs, creating online tutorials, and allocating specific Internet tasks to individuals or teams to avoid duplication. Clearly, it is impossible—and decidedly undesirable—to eliminate essential services such as teaching and reference work. To ensure positive work flow restructuring, librarians must take an active role in its formation.

• *Professional status must be maintained and adherence to recognized levels of staffing and funding affirmed.*
Professional status is defined through participation in professional organizations, scholarly writing and presenting, academic reading, department and campuswide leadership, and other library-related work. Analysis of the research, however, indicated a statistical significance between increased workload and reduction in professional commitments. Rather than reduce their work-related responsibilities, librarians opted to cut back on those very achievements that delineate their professional standing. As librarians are viewed less as educators and more as resource managers, the administration finds it easier to chip away at this status. The application of certain industry models of management, a current theme in the academy, may have a deleterious effect on the library organization. The bottom-line approach does not allow for all the intangibles of library service. Certainly, what librarians do cannot be measured, and administrators should not accept the HMO paradigm. Although librarians should be flexible and open to new models of organization, they also must guard against attacks on faculty status and work toward the application of current ACRL minimum standards of staffing and funding for the various types of college and university libraries (ALA 1997).

Conclusions
Debate about the Internet in libraries has shifted from questions of access, merit, and efficacy to those of work flow integration and management. Availability, use, and overall impact have risen dramatically since 1995. Then, access, if any, was generally limited to the reference desk; and its future as a research tool was unclear. Today, multiple points of utilization including patron workstations are the norm, and its acceptance is no longer in doubt. At the same time, expressions of satisfaction and consternation remain constant. Problems related to training, support, and inconsistency still linger.

In 1998, academic librarians have conveyed varying perspectives as to the Internet's impact on their work flow, but there is an undeniable sense of the vortex of change. If one librarian noted, "It has not created more or less work but rather it has changed the way I do my job," many more experienced "increased responsibilities," "more work," or "decreased work flow because of the need to work harder to learn Internet resources." According to Joanne Euster, "given the dramatic changes academic librarians have experienced in the last decade, it is unfortunate that there is so little breathing space from one change to the next." She continues, "Most perplexing, it often appears that so-called changes are in reality only added responsibilities" (Rapple 1997, 48).

By-products may be detected in others' remarks. Along with increased urgency that "certainly adds pressure to work in addition to traditional reference," the Internet has evoked a "desperate need for standardization of protocols." In addition, comments pointed to the difficulties stemming from its ephemeral nature. "Consistency," demanded one respondent. "Our system changes often. I am floored by the constant changes required by the Internet—new programs, databases, . . . a one-credit course is being almost completely revised each semester." "I feel as though I am always running behind it," complained another.

A concurrent theme is insufficiency of time. One participant quipped, "Can I clone a twin?" Whether to "keep up with new Web sites and changing technologies," "plan curriculum for courses and workshops," "prepare pathfinders," or "spend time with students," those surveyed are aware of the capacity of the Internet to "expand to fill all available cracks, much like air or water." Respondents, evidently, are voicing what Jim Dwyer (1997) refers to as the "very noticeable lack of discussion of the service aspects of the digital library" (2).

Despite the pitfalls they may encounter, most praised the advantages produced by the Internet. On the whole, the wealth of additional resources outside the library was considered its primary benefit. "Better communication and access to information" echoed in such comments as: "It's provided me with an efficient tool to disseminate information and obtain it" and "Personally I love using the Internet for reference and think that we now have a great deal more information available to us than we used to." One went so far as to say, "All reference or research questions now begin with Net searches." Some indirect consequences may be inferred: "The quality of service that can be provided has greatly improved," "liaison with academic departments and library instruction classes have improved," and "increased efficiency and productivity" have been accomplished. These observations reaffirm that "Librarians have been pioneers on the Internet, aggressively exploring its resources and sharing what we find" (Still and Alexander 1993, 138). They have always endeavored to achieve what Peter Senge (1994) refers to as personal mastery or "the discipline of personal growth and learning" (141).

Characteristics of the stereotypical library often evoke images of constancy, tradition, inflexibility, and order. In reality, a central thread in academia over the past few decades has been a continuum of permutations that has not produced the promise of Pat Battin's "discontinuous future." In the 1970s microfiche was touted as the answer; in the 1980s, the paperless society; in the 1990s, combinations of print and media; and finally in the 2000s, the digital library. Every succeeding innovation, heralded as the prevailing panacea, was pledged to render obsolete its predecessor. In fact, however,

> Each new technology resulted in increasing heterogeneity of media and format, complexity of access, increased expenditures, and a chaotic spectrum of choices. No formats, media, or communications technologies disappeared or superceded each other; rather, they continued to appear in new combinations and evolving functionalities (Hawkins and Battin 1997, 28).

Findings from this research illustrate the effects of this latest metamorphosis on the professional lives of academic librarians. "Their traditional role of assisting and instructing users will continue as, seeking to forestall user alienation, they endeavor to put a human face on information technology" (Dwyer 1997, 5). Predictions of an electronic library without walls or professionals neglect to factor in patron isolation, lack of skills, and the need for mediation. In truth, the universe of information available through the Internet has burdened the librarian with greater workload, stress, and responsibility, but issues of training, time, and support have not been addressed. Without cohesive planning, participants experience a lack of control and direction, coupled with feelings of insulation and disorganization. To meet the demands of the growing information infrastructure brought on by the Internet within the framework of the academy, the principles of the learning organization may be considered in the restructuring and redefinition of work flow.

According to Gephart et al. (1996), "The distinguishing characteristics of a learning organization include a learning culture, a spirit of flexibility and experimentation, people orientation, continuous learning at the systems level, a knowledge generation and sharing, and critical, systematic thinking." Because librarians already value many of these concepts as professional ideals, they may find this a meaningful approach to coping with change. Euster suggests four conditions necessary for successful organizational transformation: a clear statement of the essence of the needed change along with a means of measurement; suitable mechanisms for implementation; sufficient funding; and restructuring to accomplish the objectives (Rapple 1997, 48). At any rate, a shared vision is a vital first step in creating a "common sense of purpose, vision, and operating values" (Senge 1994, 208).

The diffusion of the Internet has irrevocably altered the library. It has, as one individual stated, "helped bring a new respect for libraries and librarians." Whether through the transformation to learning organization or an alternate design, change is an inescapable, but not altogether adverse, consequence. As librarians contend with the ramifications, they may be forced to reassess priorities, but they must not lose sight of their fundamental role as intermediary between patron and information. According to another respondent, "The Internet is an integral part of what we as librarians do and must know. The technology has changed. We need to adapt in order to continue to do what we have traditionally done." Assuredly, this study demonstrates the need for requisite work flow restructuring in order to compensate for increased workload.

References

American Library Association. (1997). *ACRL standards & guidelines.* Available online at: http://www.ala.org/acrl/guides/index.html [1998, July 28].

Dwyer, J. 1997. *Service perspectives for the digital library.* Available online at: http://alexia.lis.uiuc.edu/~sloan/e-ref.html [1998, July 17].

Gephart, M. A., V. J. Marsick, M. E. Van Buren, M. S. Spiro, and P. M. Senge 1996. Learning organizations come alive [CD-ROM]. *Training & Development* 50(12):34. Abstract from: Information Access File: Business ASAP Select Item:19045456 [1998, July 23].

Gilbert, S. 1995. Technology & the changing academy: Symptoms, questions, and suggestions. *Change* 2(5):58–61.

Hawkins, B. L., and P. Battin. 1997. The electronic library: New roles for librarians. *Cause/Effect* 20(1):22–30. Available online at: http://www.cause.org/information-resources/ir-library/html/cem9717.html [1998 July 17].

Rapple, B. A. (with J. R. Euster, S. Perry, and J. Schmidt). 1997. The changing role of the information resources professional: A dialogue. *Cause/Effect* 20(1):45–51. Available online at: http://www.cause.org/information-resources/ir-library/html/cem971a.html [1998 July 17].

Rosenthal, M., and M. Spiegelman. 1996. Evaluating use of the Internet among academic reference librarians. *Internet Reference Services Quarterly* 1(1):53–67.

Senge, P. M. 1994. *The fifth discipline: The art & practice of the learning organization.* New York: Currency Doubleday.

Still, J., and J. Alexander. 1993. Integrating Internet into reference: Policy issues. *College & Research Libraries* 5(3):138–40.

Learning Teaching and Learning the Internet: The Practitioner Perspective

Charlotte D. Moslander
Jayne B. Johnsen-Seeberger

Learning Teaching and Teaching Learning
Charlotte D. Moslander

My experience of learning and teaching the use of the Internet has proceeded in cycles of anticipation, preparation, practice, exploration, and teaching. The pace at which these cycles proceeded, and sometimes overlapped, has increased rapidly over the years.

At first, I did not think of the Internet as anything special—just another new information technology to be learned. To put my experience into perspective, I graduated from library school in 1969 without ever having touched a computer.

In 1979, without any hint that library automation was on my particular career horizon, I attended the Library Association of the City University of New York's Institute on Information Science. I was so fascinated and excited by what I learned there that I enrolled in Pratt's courses on Basic Information Science (1981) and Data Base Searching & Services (1982).

The terminal on which we did our lab exercises was a Hazeltine 2000, which I promptly dubbed "Hazel," much to the consternation of the lab supervisor, who thought I was being overly familiar with a very expensive piece of equipment. For some of the labs, I begged for—and was granted—time on a nearby public library's DECwriter, which had no monitor.

Anticipation

Sometime during those years, I became acquainted with an Apple IIe. It was love at first spreadsheet. A job change added online database searching to my job description, so I took the DIALOG: Beyond the Basics workshop in 1987. I already was using the OCLC ILL subsystem daily as part of my job. I was quite comfortable and adept at using the telephone lines to communicate with mainframes at remote sites. I knew what the parts of the computer were called, what an acoustic coupler was, what the word *modem* meant, and even some basic computer science theory.

In the early 1990s, rumors of things called e-mail and gopher came to my attention. I was convinced there was new reference territory to be explored, so I attended the NYSERNet (New York State Educational Resources Network) Conference 1992: Network Access—Training Issues for the Library. That was where I discovered that my institution had missed out on a chance to get connected to the Internet for free. Needless to say, I took all the handouts I could get (especially the one that listed the libraries in New York State that already were connected to the Internet via NYSERNet). This set of handouts included the colleges in our area that drew from the same potential student pool as we did. I delivered them to the associate vice president who was most likely to be interested in that information. Before long, each of the major segments of the school had a community address *@transit.nyser.net.*

The library's associate director had a computer and a modem at home, so she became familiar with the applications available to us first. After she had taught me how to use telnet, I promptly logged on to a library in Spain and looked up "biblioteconomia." The second thing I did was telnet to the catalogue of the university that had closed my library school and looked up "library science." I was very enthusiastic about this new-found ability to answer the question Does X library have y? by telnetting to that library's catalogue instead of looking up the requested item on OCLC, then having to go through all those codes.

Now faculty members who wanted to gain access to university or other research-level libraries while they were traveling could be much better informed about what was available and where. The public service librarians could make whatever arrangements were necessary to get them access to the most useful institutions. I took my knowledge and my enthusiasm out to the reference desk and tried to gain converts among my colleagues, with mixed results. After all, a lot of information was still much easier to find by using books and journals.

Preparation

The professional journals began to provide information on library-related listservs. I read the instructions very carefully, and soon I was receiving regular communications from Collib-L, Serialst, and Circplus. After a while, I even got up the courage to use the reply command. My library had a community computer (an IBM PS/2) that was used for everything not related to OCLC, so checking my e-mail was sometimes a challenge. The Apple IIe had been connected to a Kodak Datashow and was being used for instruction. Suddenly, I was the "Internet expert" among the public service librarians. I was being called on to teach my colleagues how to do things I really had not yet mastered myself. Sometimes people asked me to teach them how to do things I had not even tried yet. The information society was upon us, and I, at least, was getting breathless from trying to keep up.

When we got a new, faster community computer, the instruction room's Apple IIe was retired in favor of an IBM. Now we could do formal in-service instruction in our bibliographic instruction classroom, and we did. I found out by experiment how long it can take to download a file, so I did not try to demonstrate that the afternoon I taught my colleagues about gopher, Archie, and Veronica. I also started a loose-leaf binder titled Gopher Tunnels, in which I filed clippings and photocopies of articles about useful gopher sites. As more and more library catalogues became publicly available, their telnet addresses were added, and the binder received the formal title of Electronic Pathfinders.

Adaptation and Inventiveness

The next equipment upgrade put a computer in every office. Actually, I already had one: I had adopted "Granny Apple" and hooked her up to a noisy 24-pin Okidata printer that nobody wanted. Alas, her telecommunications software was not compatible with our NYSERNet service. This took some of the pressure off the community computer and, in my case, provided an out-of-the-way place in which to do database searching.

Unfortunately, the institution had declared a moratorium on the purchase of new modems and the installation of second telephone lines. With the help of the systems librarian, an "orphan" modem, a very long telephone cable, and a little adapter that allowed two telephone cables to be attached to the same jack were found, and I entered the era of the "clandestine modem." This involved stretching telephone cable across the office floor. My office mates learned to walk carefully and watch where they were going. I also had to try very hard not to lose my temper when one of my colleagues did not notice I was online, and picked up the telephone on his or her desk.

Awkward as it may have been, this arrangement came in handy when a disgruntled graduate student was favorably impressed by my use of the Internet. I logged on to the Dartmouth server, gained access to the Veterans Administration's PILOTS database, and presented her with a list of citations that were directly related to her thesis topic.

Most of my teaching still involved instructing public service librarians and other faculty members, as we did not yet have public access to the Internet in the library. Meanwhile, I was learning how difficult it can be to import and export files over an old telephone system that routes every call through a PBX. We still had a text-only connection when the World Wide Web was spun. If the screen said [link], I read the instructions on the bottom of the screen that told me how to [tab] [tab] [tab] [enter] to follow that link and how to use the arrows on the keypad to move back and forth.

I tried to teach this to a couple of colleagues, but the "computerphobe" said it was too much trouble, and the other one had Windows Everything at home and found [tab] [tab] etc. cumbersome compared to [point] and [click]. (I was still using Granny Apple for everything except telecommunications. Database search results were being downloaded to the IBM, because Granny did not have a hard drive.

One day, Windows arrived on our screens. I do not have good hand-eye coordination at the best of times, so pointing the mouse, then making it hold still while clicking presented a challenge. It did not help any that everybody else seemed to know instinctively which end was which. As far as I was concerned, the cable was the tail. The librarian who corrected that misconception should be commended for her tact; she did not even smirk.

Practice

I was quite comfortable with [tab] [tab] [tab] [enter]. I didn't like [point] and [click]. Who needs pictures on computers anyway unless they are illustrating text? I can read. The computerphobe and the public service librarian who had a computer at home felt otherwise. They were happily pointing, and clicking, and discovering new and useful Web sites. The Electronic Pathfinders binder grew to two volumes. My colleagues were generous about teaching *me* now, but I had to figure out for myself that I could make the mouse hold still by holding it down with one hand while clicking with the other. More than one adult learner was relieved to hear about my coordination problems and how I solved them. One memorable student exclaimed, "You mean you hold this (phrase deleted) down with one hand and poke it in the eye with the other?" Teaching the mechanical skills sometimes has to precede the intellectual work.

An internal institutional grant funded a pilot program to put public access Internet stations in the library. Now there were bundles of blue cables curving over doorways, snaking along the edges of stairwells, and popping out of walls. More new computers arrived and were set up. And we waited. And waited. And waited. Suddenly, in April, everything was turned on. It took the students about half an hour to discover those workstations and to start asking us to help them find information in Web sites we had never heard about, much less seen, before. Thanks to commercial advertising, they were convinced that everything was available, for free, on the Internet.

Exploration

The "learning" now took the form of exploring as many sites as possible and bookmarking the most useful ones, as well as learning how to navigate within those sites. It was with relief that I discovered that I was no longer the computer expert of public service. My coordination had improved to the point where I could point and click with only one hand on the mouse. Years of reading science fiction began to come in handy. I had taken many imaginary trips through "wormholes" in space and time, so I had no difficulty with the concept of an Internet gateway, although I preferred the image of a window.

The students understood my explanations when I told them that they were sitting on one side of a window and looking through it at material on a server that might be hundreds or thousands of miles away, and that the distant server, not their desktop microcomputer, controlled what could and could not be done with the words and images on the screen. I also discovered—and immediately began to teach the students— that a message that *the document contains no data* in response to a print command might not be accurate. If a print preview showed that there really *was* something to be printed, the print command from that screen would produce a printout. Frustrated students seemed to enjoy my telling them how to trick the computer into doing what they wanted it to do. (Where are the Three Laws of Robotics when we need them?)

The full-time public service librarians began to use our existing subject and searching strengths to explore the Web and to try to keep one step ahead of our clientele. I was frustrated by search engines' apparent inability to do any Boolean operation but "or." When another librarian told me about Excite's power search capability, I was convinced that the competition must have something like that. Fortunately, the professional literature was publishing useful how-to articles written by people who were way ahead of us, so some hints were picked up there.

It was back to taking the time to read the instructions on the help screens. Sure enough, +word +word +word and (word word) were found to work. This operation was shared immediately with frustrated students and faculty members whose searches were producing hundreds, sometimes thousands, of hits, most of which were not useful.

Our understanding of, and facility with, the use of Boolean operators made the librarians look like geniuses. I found myself explaining again and again that, to a librarian, information is information, no matter how it is packaged, and that the computer is a rather stupid assistant that happens to be able to sift through enormous amounts of data very quickly.

It cannot think.

It has no imagination.

If somebody does not tell it to truncate, it will not truncate.

If you do not tell it exactly what you want it to look for

(this *and* that) (this *or* that) (this *not* that), it just does not know, and

It is not going to ask, either.

Many people became very fond of power search.

Teaching

Questions about who was responsible for teaching students to use

Internet resources began to be raised at library faculty meetings. I was very quiet during those discussions because I already had included appropriate Web sites in many of the classes for which I provided library instruction. The students, especially the graduate students, were eager to do as much work as possible at home.

The fortunate ones who were in education and nursing needed to be introduced to an ERIC that was searched differently from the ERIC they found on the library's terminals. Others needed a PubMed that they were trying to search without having a copy of the MeSH "black book." The Internet was another reference tool that these students could use to get the information they needed, and my philosophy was that I was in an ideal position to teach them how to make the best use of it, even if it meant providing technical support over the telephone. I also let them know that they were going to be charged a considerable amount of money for every article they requested from any document delivery service connected to an online database. I reminded them that their tuition had prepaid their access to much of this material via the library's periodical collection and interlibrary loan service. Another public service librarian observed that sticker shock had accompanied Internet access.

The fact that we now had access to our catalogue and several indices, including one that offered selective full-image retrieval via the Internet confused some of our clientele. If they could get a copy of an article for free when they were using ProQuest Direct, why could they not get the same service when they were using PubMed?

I went back to the window image, only now it was an image of the screen on a Visiphone that autodialled one number for PQD and a different number for PubMed. Two different servers answered the telephone. Each server had distinctive rules. All that technical reading I had done over the years was paying off in the coin of simplification.

Most of the library's clientele did not know what an ISP was, much less an IP address. They were used to getting everything for free in the library, so they did not understand why they would have to pay for something they found by using a public computer located in the library, just because they found it on the Internet. I felt as if I had stopped having to run just to keep up. Sometimes I was a bit impressed by how much I knew.

The computer seems to have the same mystique now that the printed page had for earlier generations. Students have to be taught that anybody can put up a Web site and publish anything on it that they want to publish. Students (and others!) usually do not realize that the material in the library has been selected out of what is generally available because someone who knows something about the subject has recommended it.

I had to learn what .com, .org, .edu, and their kin meant, then immediately give that information to students so they could understand what agenda the owner of a Web site might have. Term paper time arrived, and with it, quite a few students who had obtained material by using the Internet now had to cite their sources. Yes, there is a book that provides this information, but students who were told to use MLA or APA style wanted to find the information in the approved publication manual. It took imagination to apply a rule that was written for a gopher site to one that was on the Web. Often it also took a patience and reassurance to persuade a student who wanted to do everything perfectly that it was all right to call the person who was teaching the course and ask for guidance. Learning and teaching were taking place simultaneously, but at least the publication manuals were familiar territory (for me, at least). I think a few of the students saw the new formats as marked: "Here be dragons . . . ."

When one of the deans asked that a librarian do a workshop on evaluating Web sites for the faculty, I felt lucky that I did not have to teach it. I did remember seeing an article in some issue of *LJ* that came in handy, but another public service librarian had seen a better one somewhere else. I have since found a third one, which I photocopied and put into my "Internet—Instruction" file.

I am not in an academic library anymore, but the learning and teaching cycle continues. The latest thing I have had to learn is how to search the New York State legislature's gopher site. This involves backing away from the Internet and learning how the laws are arranged and what the legislature calls its products. So far, it looks chaotic, but I have managed to find some useful material for people with questions. I am just glad I do not have to teach anybody how to do it yet because I have not formulated what I am doing into anything I can express; all I know is that it seems to work.

I now have Internet access at home, so the preparation, practice, and exploration parts of the cycle have become easier because I am working in a more relaxed environment, with much less competition for the computer. Sometimes I am surprised by how much I have learned in the past few years. I still do not know how to create a home page or establish links on a Web site, but that will have to wait until I figure out how legislative sites are arranged and how they can be searched most efficiently. Now, what is a chapter, and how does it relate to the consolidated laws? It is easier to do this with books and pocket parts, but the Internet is less expensive.

Considering the Cycle of Teaching and Learning the Internet

Jayne Johnsen-Seeberger

I have just spent a little over an hour at my favorite Greek restaurant re-viewing this contribution and found myself thinking how long I have been coming here. Twenty-three years. It has no terminals and no monitors, just quiet, grapevine-draped lattice, and dependable, savory food. It is a place I use to slow the pace of my life, to recalibrate, and to put things in perspective.

I woke up this morning at 5:00 a.m. By the time I left for one of my jobs at 8:45 a.m., I had already desktop published, laser printed, e-mailed, listserved, faxed, and done some preliminary research via the Internet to use for a class I am taking and several I am teaching. I can work around the clock—but do I want to? For a person who values making eye contact, this kind of relentless electronic dialog can be as draining as it can be efficient. When do I pay bills? When do I do wash? When do I talk to my family? When do I get to really read? All very good questions, but to be flip about the impact of the Internet belies the effort involved in keeping up with professional developments.

This is the sober reflection of a person who works as an adjunct reference librarian and instructor at three different institutions and who produces two specialized newsletters from home. A person who has a clue as to how to learn about and teach the Internet on the run. Adjuncts have intrinsic value in this learning/teaching process. Adjuncts are relied upon to rapidly evaluate and disseminate accurate and useful Internet information to colleagues and students. We are considered teaching faculty at many colleges and universities, augmenting the skills of less numerous full-time faculty and providing fresh ideas from outside institutional boundaries. We make our own loops, which we are fully in.

Many adjuncts work and teach the Internet at several institutions, contributing a vital cross-fertilization of information and teaching methodology to the profession. Because we are so mobile a group and are usually teaching in a rapid turnaround environment, we are quick to pick up Internet details and techniques and explore and experiment with new ones. Many of us have several e-mail addresses and have computers at home, which keep us interconnected, facile, and current. We are an innovative and highly skilled group. For me, learning the intricacies of the Internet is an everyday affair, and the vitality of this learning process has everything to do with being an adjunct as opposed to a full-time employee. The Internet has impacted the way I work at these institutions and at home. However, I have found it must be controlled or it will devour every morsel of time that you have.

What Are You Really Looking For?

Twenty years ago, as a reference librarian I had key reference books and sections of the collection memorized, especially useful if an entire class would start to trickle in with an assignment. Now I search for sites that mesh with print and other media resources. Twenty years ago, Medline did not suffer fools who entered without meticulous presearch preparation and frequent clock/price checking; now Medline is free. I have seen a person's eyes start to glaze over when I begin to tell them what is available to them and how they should start. The vastness of resources boggles anyone who cannot organize his or her task before putting fingers to keyboard.

Five years ago, when I started learning about the Internet as an adjunct reference librarian at a small coeducational institution on Long Island, e-mail; ftp, Telnet, and gophers were alive and well. One full-time librarian was considered the expert, and I pumped her every time I was on the desk for hints about how she found information. It was very convoluted and mysterious, and I took detailed notes on how she got from all point As to all point Bs. I believe what makes librarians special is our relentless curiosity, and it was probably this quality that finally pushed her over the edge to where she held a training class for all reference staff. She taught the entire reference group by giving us a brief history and overview of the Internet and some search techniques for the various text-only search tools. From then on, I was on my own, so I would sometimes test myself by searching the Internet when I knew the answer was in a reference book on our shelves. Dual searching helps uncover overlap as well as inaccuracy. Meanwhile, I signed up for a SuffolkWeb account and took an HTML class, two events that made exploring and creating on the Internet from home possible. I turned fifteen years of desktop publishing experience into a new skill by learning how to distribute newsletter information via a listserv and taking stabs at Web page design for information transfer to classes.

By the time our Internet maven returned from a sabbatical, we had all become "experts" out of necessity. In fact, some of us had even begun to specialize in art, business, or education sources. The World

Wide Web, which had been an infant when she left, transformed into an important reference tool. Survival on the front line of reference desk service meant being adept with print and digital tools and being able to create specialized source lists for library instruction classes; I was including Internet sites in my class pathfinders and bibliographies. When Windows 95 was installed and the library went from CD-ROM databases to online access, students were stymied. Databases they had come to know and love looked and acted completely different. This transition happened so fast, many times we figured things out together.

At my workplaces, several main icons launch the student into the OPAC, the library page on the Internet, or the CD-ROM database window. Depending on the question, I can start students searching where I see the greatest chance for their success. Recently, two of my institutions invested much time and effort into library Web page redesign. Library pages in general have become more organized and offer more resources, but in the rush to offer more and more, I find students becoming more confused and disoriented by the architecture of frames, lists, bullets, and artwork. As I visit other library Web sites, I can see format changes are being grappled with elsewhere as well. The best sites offer readily apparent navigation paths, logical arrangement of resources, interactive student learning tools, and comprehensiveness on some unique subject. Sometimes these sites can do all this and look good—but that is a bonus.

Is the phrase "hunt and peck" applicable when learning the Internet? I think, in looking back over five years of discovering sites, engines, and filters, that this old-fashioned term is much more fitting than the term "surfing." Of course, surfing the Internet sounds much more fluid and carefree, as if you really do not care where you end up. What a lark. But I have found that most people are not surfing aimlessly, they are looking for something specific.

Changes for Clarity

Although I always knew that teaching people how to use indexes and making them aware of various reference resources was an important part of each and every job, incorporating databases and the Internet into Internet lessons made me change my teaching style. I became less passive and more aggressive. I found that most classes held a broad range of Internet expertise. I began using an advanced student as the "demonstrator" connected to the projector while I canvassed the class explaining, repositioning mice, restating and answering questions. This method was developed after I entered one class prepared to teach a group of public librarians. The class patiently listened as I launched into the foaming waters of Boolean logic. I looked into thirty pairs of eyes for glimmers of recognition and received none. The class, one of seventy like it that summer, was actually composed of public library patrons who had submitted tickets and been picked by lottery. This singular event taught me that teaching requires mental agility—and professorial daring. By the end of class, the weak were helping the strong and the strong were helping me. We were searching for sites containing jobs for senior citizens, patent law sources, html guides, and bed-and-breakfast information.

In teaching classes, I work backwards from the objectives of the class to design the class's structure and assignments. Readings are current and Internet searching is focused and topical. If students see a flaw in my logic, the floor is open for discussion. I do expect discussion and sometimes inject a politically sensitive topic to nudge students into reacting and contributing. I want students to explore all information resources, including, but not exclusively, the Internet. As far as I can tell, some of the best information still comes from personal contact with people who know something. A professor once asked me to find the top ten baby names in 1954 for a business marketing class. After searching many different types of sources for more than an hour, I called a librarian at the Brooklyn Business Library who laughed and then pulled the answer from his vertical file in thirty seconds.

I ask questions of my students to get an initial feel for where they are. I ask questions to assure myself that they understand the points of the class. But mainly I ask questions because that is the spark that ignites imaginations. I use real-life situations to help people understand the usefulness of information gathering and skill evaluating, outside class.

From Filter, to Teacher, to Teaching How to Filter

Twenty years ago, I searched, found, and presented the golden information on demand, sometimes using both expensive reference indexes and databases that are even more expensive. I even created an in-house database when finding internal corporate information became mired and inefficient. Maintaining order, control, and access were key.

Next, I became a teacher of bibliographic methods. I would stand in front of classes and describe in great detail how to get into the OPAC and the databases—step by painful step. At the end of my classes, my students could gather information till they turned blue. As long as they felt they could complete the current pressing class assignment, I knew they felt in control of their destinies. I felt I had taught them thoroughly and well.

However, I began to observe two things. Many students, even given an assignment deadline of the most grievous weight, were gathering information far past a reasonable threshold, whereas others were sitting at a terminal and producing results using only the Internet. Databases were so plentiful and searching had become so user friendly that library users would just keep searching forever for that last perfect phrase that would dovetail into their paper. The first group was searching for information nirvana; the second for pizza delivery–like data.

I am now in my present phase. I am teaching library users how to filter for themselves. The tasty information fish I drop in people's laps these days is meant to spark an excitement for the sport of very selective fishing. Instead of having to be eternally grateful to me, it is far better to have them learn to fish for themselves and throw back the ones that do not meet their own exacting criteria. With an individual or a class, a search strategy is formulated, sources gathered, evaluated, and weeded and then—the ecstasy of closure. I show them how my brain is tracking down the desired information, why I am picking one path over another, why I would chose one source over another, why I would backtrack.

Finding or Making a Home

When I began teaching the Internet, I found people had trouble grasping the enormity of this communication medium. It was helpful to introduce them to a stable vantage point from which they could get their bearings, such as a large search engine, library, or company. Then any explanations I offered fell into place.

The people to whom I teach the Internet these days still need to center themselves first in order to go out foraging for information, but they are doing it for themselves using a wide range of tools. This need for a home base has triggered a surge in sites that can be customized, from search engines to personal planners to news filters. Library Web pages can offer the same centering function if they keep the student in mind.

The institutions I teach at are all beginning to teach library/information instruction from the home base of a self-styled library Web page on the Internet. This current state has evolved after years of separate terminals for OPACs, databases, and the Internet. When kinks are ironed out, with one fluid motion, I will be able to teach many sources from a single lead page.

Is this a wonderful thing? Yes. Is the process tricky to navigate? Yes. Are the results hard to judge beforehand? You bet. But the final outcome is that librarians are now fully in the loop of information transfer and fully responsible for the image and information they make visible and available to the larger academic community.

In designing library Web pages, librarians who are technically savvy must also be alert. If they are not, they create library Web pages that are very beautiful to look at, but very ugly to use. If these pages are to be used for teaching as well as searching, considerable thought must be given to the way information is organized, visually and textually. The aim must be the creation of a page that conveys information clearly and elegantly, meshes seamlessly with the curriculum of the school, and offers access to the widest variety of alternative information sources at other schools.

Through the Web page, we must impress the audience with several themes:

• Learning is not a timed event, that it is continual and valuable.

• Students will be learning content in their curriculum that overlaps and interconnects.

• They may learn more cooperating with several people than alone.

• Students are gathering knowledge and building their own; this gathering and building changes how they think about topics. It lets their decision-making ability mature over time.

• Information and knowledge can come at them in many different and valid formats.

A colleague and I have an ongoing debate about whether librarians should be filters, navigators, guides, or teachers. She asks herself how far a librarian should go in providing information to students, how much of the assignment should we do for the student before we hold back. I always answer, "As much as they want." As I help students with assignments, I am explaining just what they are clicking, what pathway they have selected, and where they may want to go. They are going to remember this search process over the final content. They will remember this process when they sit at another terminal far from me and my maddening ways. They will start to see familiar steps within unfamiliar databases. They will start to map out paths for themselves, and they will start to evaluate as they hunt. Will I be teaching them about currency, authority, scope, bias, and other criteria from reference classes? I will—because I believe a student who is armed with this fine mesh net will be able to make the best decisions. I personally prefer to live on a planet with people who are making very good decisions.

Immersion without Drowning

Overall, being in front of a class is the best immersion I know. You research, you prepare a syllabus, you keep current. If you do not, you will suffer humiliation and angst.

As course support is developed for library home pages, there will be more cooperation among full-time and adjunct librarians so that material is complementary and does not overlap. Library Web page content should be value added and not just links to links. Let us not forget that links must be continually checked to maintain the credibility of your site. Librarians must ask themselves if this is the business in which they want to be. Creating this kind of material also means "linking" up with the professor and teaching in consort. The collaborative links with professors are worth just as much or more than the links on the Web page. It is the interpersonal connections that make the Web links worth something.

Assignments must evolve with research tools. The array of tools offered by a library, such as full-test databases, should be part of information instruction class assignments. Offering advanced databases and then hesitating to teach ways and means of access to them is contradictory to someone who is desperate for information.

Virtual libraries are wonderful to explore and teach from, but I still would like to see specific libraries act as subject clearinghouses for Internet sites, much like ERIC clearinghouses specialize. I would like to be able to go to one central business clearinghouse or one regional clearinghouse so that I would not have to bookmark several "mother lode" sites. I think eliminating redundancy in library sites should be a major objective of librarians. The time could be better spent teaching students how to use this new medium.

The Next Phase—Bundling, Thin Servers, and the Community

At the same time libraries are designing efficient and attractive Web pages, they are getting well-priced bundles of databases. Library Web pages combined with database bundles are going to make efficiencies of scale the norm. Strong bargaining units composed of schools, public libraries, and county networks will create well-knit banks of research tools and application software.

As an adjunct, I am sometimes able to take free classes that are offered to me as a job benefit. I have taken several school media specialist classes, which have allowed me to compare the services and structure of high school libraries versus college libraries. A technologically advanced high school near where I live was the focus of a recent assignment I was given. The database icons are on the Windows 95 desktop alongside the production and communication tools. Windows NT and Fortress help control this array, but the benefits to students far outweigh the risks. School librarians and network administrators are in agreement that offering students complete interconnected access throughout the building enables them to become better researchers, process information more creatively, produce more polished and well-substantiated assignments, and become more resourceful and generous with personal knowledge.

I am curious as to why a high school can operate so open an environment and the colleges I work at cannot. I asked the director of one library, and he said that students would be taking up all the machines with e-mail, chat groups, and word processing and not research. When I asked if it was a matter of not having enough terminals, and if having more terminals might allow students to use everything, he said that having additional terminals would probably correct the balance. To provide the interactivity that students need, the future may hold lots of cheaper dumb terminals connected to a powerful off-site server. Ironically, as libraries start to offer clients at-home access, many will feel constricted by the separate room—separate tools environment currently in use. They will opt for working at a home computer where all their tools are at hand and flipping between multiple sites and applications allows them to use limited time more efficiently.

As purchasing decisions are removed from the daily task list of school librarians and administrators, said one vice principal, teachers can return to teaching. As a librarian and a teacher, I think I will find myself teaching students to concentrate less on how they produce and more on the quality of what they produce. They may decide to concentrate a little more and produce a product that will be sought after as useful to the larger community.

A patron recently confided to me that he felt that each new technology was designed to keep people apart. I see his point, but I find I am talking (by whatever channel) to more people about more things, especially because I move among three libraries each week. Some information gathering I do is completely unrelated to libraries, but I feel it must provide me with additional insight that I will be able to recycle somewhere along my path. Letter writing never kept people apart, why should e-mail? The difference is that there are so many ways to communicate with people. In the next few years, will I be a distance learning consultant to students from my home? Will they seek me out and ask me for help—after entering a log-in and password? I am hoping people will sometimes need real face-to-face discourse like a cool drink after the dry spell of isolation.

Bringing in the Sheaves

What will the Library of Congress do with the forty-four (40 gigabytes each) discs of Internet activity that it has just added to its collection? I am also hoping that besides functioning as an interactive sculpture and time capsule, it will allow metadata researchers to ascertain what people use most and why.

In the end, the reason we gather is to sow again. There needs to be harvest, there needs to be an offering of something new created from raw materials. Information from the Internet must be used to create something unique and valuable. I impress upon students that they are finding information to make decisions. They must use personal criteria that allow them to quickly incorporate this information into their work. The quality of the information they select will impact their product, which, in this interconnected world, will be quickly and publicly judged. I do not want students to be net fodder; I do want them to survive and prosper using information wisely.

New Librarians, New Experiences

David J. Franz
Emily Contrada Anderson

Between Gutenberg and Gigabytes: A New Librarian Makes the Leap
David J. Franz

The biggest challenge I face every day is making people feel comfortable with computers. PERIOD. There is a broad cross section of the public that shies away from them, from middle school students to senior citizens, from the wealthy to the poor. Students walk into the library looking for a card catalog because their schools still tenaciously cling to theirs. I explain that the electronic catalog has superceded the old cards. I try to explain the merits of electronic searching and the benefits of keyword searching versus strict subject searching. They look at me as if I have grown a third eye. They look down. "Huff."

Impatiently, they give the computer a whirl. Then they huff around some more. Then I give up and drag them to the section they need to browse in the stacks. Another young girl walks in. She needs magazine articles and asks for the *Reader's Guide.* I show it to her. I also try pushing the neat-o, whiz-bang, full-text-providing, periodical-indexing/abstracting database that is updated daily, and even spits out graphs and pictures on our neat-o, whiz-bang, laser printer. She remains decidedly unimpressed. "I'll just use the guide please. I'm in a hurry." Frustration sets in.

Public reference librarians have always been teachers and judges. All day long, we decide who are the gung-ho independent learners ready to master advanced Internet searching strategies and who simply need the information handed to them. My mission is clear. I try to turn the reluctant library user into the proactive library user. Remembering that all people learn differently and at different paces, I prefer to teach the Internet in short, one-on-one courses. For those who are computer virgins, I have to step back from all of the accumulated knowledge that I have built up over the years and look at the process with new eyes.

Atari

I admit I had an unfair advantage. I grew up in the age of Atari and Michael Jackson videos. The early 1980s. We did not want Beanie Babies or Tickle Me Elmos; we wanted the coveted Atari 2600 game machine so we could play Pong and Pac-Man. Even my forty-something uncle had to get one. I even made a train-shaped wall hanger out of wood with the lone word "ATARI" routed deep in the grain, a seventh-grade-school woods project. Another arts project yielded a linoleum relief outline of the ubiquitous joystick complete with firing button. Thousands of block prints could be made, in every color, declaring the obsession of a young lad. I loved playing video games.

For my birthday, during the sixth grade, my grandmother purchased an Atari 800. Unlike the simple game machine, this one had a keyboard and could be programmed in the BASIC language. I quickly taught myself how to make my own video games. I even published a program in my junior high-school newsletter that was a variation on Space Invaders called Teacher Attack. How that one got past the censors I'll never know, but I was an ambitious kid. I cannot recall ever having much difficulty learning how to manipulate computers. I was never afraid of them. It was all intuitive. To tinker with them seemed natural.

The first time I saw a modem in action was when friends of my mother had started a "marketing" business. They supposedly gave out free cruises to random homeowners. In actuality, they programmed a TRS-80 to dial sequentially through the phone book, then play a prerecorded message announcing that the owner had a chance to win a free cruise. It was crude, but I was amazed at the automation. I soon got my own modem.

Within weeks, I was dialing local bulletin boards, setting up accounts, fooling around. At thirteen, I had decided to set up my own BBS. The Bare Bones BBS operated on weekends, evenings only, for a few months. The short life span was due in part to my parents. They could not stand the telephone ringing every twenty minutes or so all through the night.

One book and one television show fueled all of this intense fascination. I read *War Games* no less than five times, and I am proud to say that I never watched the movie. The main character is a computer whiz who breaks into government computers. The show "Whiz Kids" also featured a computer whiz who used his skills to solve crimes. I never even came close to stardom; but I did manage to obtain a reservoir of technical experience that I now regularly draw upon in my day-to-day duties as a reference librarian and computer jockey.

Absence

During high school, I lost all interest in computers. I became a successful athlete and had no need to spend time online or programming. I did not want to be a nerd. I passed successfully through four and a half years of undergraduate humanities classes from 1989 to 1994 and never used the Internet, saw the Internet, or even heard of the Internet. All those years I used the electronic catalog and a few indexing services on Silver Platter. While researching my thesis for my history major, I used paper indexes, microfilm, and government documents. On several occasions, I stumbled into the computer labs only to find word-processing programs and spreadsheets—no Internet.

During those undergraduate days, I collected eighteen credits in education. The connection between computers and education stopped at word processing and running programs. The Internet as an information-gathering tool was never approached.

Resurrection

After deciding not to teach, I decided I would become a librarian. My experience as a reference assistant at a large historical society convinced me that I would enjoy helping people find resources, and directing their quests. I enrolled in an MLS program. Desiring to be well prepared for classes, I studied the Dewey Decimal System. All fired up, I also began playing with the Internet, which had just begun to be publicized in the popular press and at the county library.

My first encounter was with gopher. I can barely remember it. However, what I do remember is pressing numbers that indicated choices on a long list of possible destinations. A New York site organized information according to the Dewey system. Pages were grouped by subject, press a number, scroll down, press a number, another subcategory, press a number, and so forth. It was an endless chasing after the wind. Most infuriating were the mesmerizing slashes, asterisks, question marks, and other characters that flashed at the bottom of the screen to indicate that the computer was fetching the requested information.

At that point, I failed to see the usefulness of the Internet. It took forever to find anything, though the process of hunting was fun. I was getting hooked. I was amazed by the "You are connected to Washington University at St. Louis" message that flashed on the screen. I felt like I was getting away with something.

I could not believe it did not *cost* anything. Library patrons are still amazed by that simple fact and it is one concept they seem to grasp easily. When I explain it to them, I describe it as a local phone call; the person they call then places another free call on a second line to the next town and so forth. The first person can talk to the person on the end in San Francisco for free as long as all agree to hold the phones together at the same time. Simple visual diagrams help, too.

In the fall of 1994, I began taking classes at Rutgers University. I believe it was the first time that all classes would have some Internet component built into the curriculum. My first visit to the computer lab brought me face to face with the World Wide Web in all its technicolor and sonic glory. I absorbed everything: http, telnet, and then those links—click, click, click, rapid fire like the old Atari joystick button. In a few hours, I traversed the world by mouse.

I liken the newbie searcher to any of the characters in a computer game. Essentially, you learn to move your character through a maze of disasters and treasures. With every game you play, you learn more about the maze. You learn to survive, you learn the signs of danger, what good moves should look like. The further you move along, the farther you want to push the envelope. It is all-absorbing.

When I teach people the Internet, I tell them to view it as play. "Just play around." They have to get comfortable with it. I am greatly dismayed by those who approach the screen and wait for something to happen. The Internet does not happen; you make the Internet happen. It is not a passive activity. This is ever more true now that interactive forms and pull-down menus are built right into the basic fabric of most Web sites. Even children, who are assumed to know how to use the Internet, fail to understand that they have to refine their search skills through practice.

Some folks turn away, failing to see the potential. They would like to plug in a few names in a search box and find their long-lost friends. Well, sometimes they find them and sometimes not. I whip out my little scratch pad and illustrate what the computers are doing. This is how they are connected. This is how Yahoo works. This is how you get their file on our computer screen. Sometimes it works. They begin to understand. The simple correlation I stand by is that folks who have learned to understand how computers work tend to learn the basic concepts of the Internet quickly, much as I did.

Throughout the MLS program, I observed the great struggle play out in the computer lab. The techies would sit down for about a half-hour to complete their electronic bibliographies. Hours later, I would peer in. Again, the folks without a strong background in computers languished.

What I See Today

I watch the kids pour into the library after school lets out. There they go, dashing to the terminals. To the chat rooms they go. And there they stay. These kids are raised on AOL. Spoon-fed. They are not learning as I did. They have plug-'n-play peripherals, keyword searching on meta-indexes. From what I observe, I can tell that few of the average kids have ever learned to program. Their logic is lacking. They approach any search engine; type in a few keywords, and then wade through a long list of results. What they see on the screen is what they believe is available to them. They do not visualize the structure of Internet or understand how search engines work. When I offer help, they shush me away and proudly declare they know how to use the Internet.

Typically, when I approach a child and ask, "Did you find what you were looking for?" the child replies, "No, there's nothing here on the three-toed sloth." I suppress a grin. Then I proceed to show him how I would search. "There are many organizations concerned about endangered species. What I would do is search for the Web site of an organization, then search within that Web site for information on the three-toed sloth by using the keyword 'sloth'." We found a few paragraphs deeply hidden in a database. I try to explain that not all of the best information is ever picked up by a search engine. Work from the general to the specific.

I was taught a valuable adage in my reference classes. Identify the organization or agency responsible for, or most concerned by, a particular subject and you will be well on the way to finding valid answers. When I reveal this bit of wisdom to those learning the Internet, I see proverbial lightbulbs flashing brightly. "Oh, that makes so much sense!" Instead of paging through useless AltaVista results for "breast cancer," I demonstrate my point to one patron by plugging "american cancer society" into Yahoo. "There, see that! The ACS has pulled together all the reliable Web sites." The patron happily continues for another hour. She will be back.

My suggestion to curriculum developers everywhere: don not simply insert "and any relevant information from the Internet" into your syllabi. Basic computer literacy demands more attention than that. Wherever the ability to drive a car is seen as a basic life skill, the secondary schools provide a driver's education program. The ability to search the Internet effectively is becoming a basic life skill. Schools at all levels should integrate a pure computer literacy component into their curriculum. Even if a school is not wired for the Net, it can begin by teaching the way computers work and the way information is stored and retrieved.

Getting the MLS: A New View
Emily Contrada Anderson

One by one, the catalogs arrived—glossy, new and filled with promises. It was the summer of 1996, I was 44 years old and on a quest. The problem was, I did not know the object of the quest. I had been working as an RN for more than twenty years in a variety of interesting and challenging positions. Now, however, the health care environment was in the throes of upheaval, thanks mainly to fiscal constraints imposed by managed care. My own job was evolving from challenging to day-to-day dullness. My position involved review of medical records for patients in a home health care agency. Reviews focused on utilization (monetary) issues and quality of care issues. I had daily interaction with fellow nurses, discussing cases, planning care, and evaluating the outcomes of care using CQI techniques. Much of the work involved teaching on both an informal and formal basis. After two years, however, it had become routine, no longer a challenge.

When I looked around, I saw family, friends, and colleagues busily buying computers and trying to get on to the Information Highway. Nursing journals were adding special columns devoted to nursing and "The Net." At work, there was talk of requiring all the field nurses to use laptop computers for documentation of nursing visits. This, plus the PCs mysteriously appearing on everyone's desk, had set off a near panic. Computerization committees were hastily formed and then withered for lack interest (or heightened fear of the unknown). I plunged into the fray with the purchase of a PC for home, using it only for word processing, too afraid to touch any other buttons. Soon, it was relinquished altogether to my husband.

Add to the mix the fact that today's consumers of health care seem better informed than the practitioners. My colleagues and I had begun to notice that lately, everyone was an expert. With even eight-year-old children surfing the net, anybody could pick up information from countless "dot coms." It used to be that being a nurse conferred on you this mystical power of knowing. You would field telephone calls and conversations on supermarket lines from friends, family, and the lady down the block about everything from child care to how to get blood stains out of tee shirts. Of course, there were positive and negative aspects of this. You would limit both your answers and to whom you answered. Now, we had more of the type of questioners who already know (or think they know) the answer, they just want to test you and your knowledge. This was getting tiresome!

As a nurse, I needed not only to keep abreast, but also to get ahead of the pack to reclaim my mystical powers. So what to do? Going back to school was an obvious choice. The appropriate course of study was not that apparent. I already had an MA and did not want a Ph.D. in nursing. My investigation into nursing doctoral programs showed that most programs were research based and my interests lay with something with practical applications.

Back in the 1980s, before PCs were invented, I had enrolled in a diploma program at New York University to learn computer programming. Rather quickly, I realized this was not for me and gave up midway through. It was not until Windows replaced DOS that I even thought about computers again in a less threatening way. This experience led to the realization that, for me, learning how to use computers could best be accomplished in a hands-on, seat-of-the-pants method. Formal classroom settings, focused just on learning the keyboard functions of computers, would be just too intimidating. What I did need that formal setting for was to learn how to extract information from the little devils and how to judge whether the information was worthwhile.

While investigating various schools and programs, I also read the want ads for all different kinds of careers. Somewhere along the line, I started thinking about an MLS degree. So many years ago, I had learned to read and I grew up with a love of books. I was the kind of kid who always had a book, with a backup in case I was near the end of the first one and might finish it before I could get home. I read everything and I read all the time. The thrill of expectation on my first visit to the library, my very first library card, my adult card—these feelings I can summon up as if it were only yesterday. And the kind library ladies of my childhood who took me by the hand, literally and figuratively, to all the new worlds represented by the contents of the shelves. All those books to read—what if I finished them all? Would there be nothing left to read?

The ultimate thrill of those days was my very first paying job—as a page. Oh, the indescribable joy of being on the "inside" of that wonderful world. I do not know that I ever consciously thought of becoming a librarian. Nursing had a hold on me from when I was very small because I had a knack for nurturing—my dolls, my sister's dolls, our pets, the neighborhood kids. This kind of nature is integral to a successful nursing career and that was my preordained major in college.

For the next twenty-five years, I worked my way up the ladder in the profession in clinical and administrative roles. After I obtained a master's in nursing administration, I began to specialize in continuous quality improvement and utilization management. Now, reading ads for librarians and information specialists, I found lots of indecipherable jargon such as MARC, OPAC, RLIN, and Nexus Lexis. Wow—this was as mystical as PTCA, TAH-BSO, and RAST. All the librarian and information specialist positions called for computer knowledge. I began to view the MLS degree as a chance to learn about computers and as a gateway to knowing where the information was, how to access it, and, most important, how to judge its worth.

I sent for the catalogs of the four schools closest to both home and work, and compared tuition, classes schedules and travel considerations. After I narrowed the choice down, I became obsessed with weighing the pros and cons of returning to school. Unfortunately, it appeared that the pros were outnumbered. My anxieties all stemmed from my age—I was convinced that I would older than not only be all the other students, but the instructors as well. Everyone would undoubtedly be smarter than I was. Besides, I had not taken notes for real since 1981, the same year of my last formal exam and research paper.

On the pro side was my desire to get a greater return for the investment I had made on my own PC by using it for more than just word processing. I wanted to learn e-mail, and above all, I wanted to move out of my illiteracy of the information opportunities on the Internet. Throughout my nursing career, I was always involved with teaching something to someone—patients, families, new nurses, peers. Teaching methods could be enhanced with computer skills, and curriculum could be improved with access to this new world of electronic information.

Finally, I saw my colleagues at work, frustrated and fearful with these new electronic challenges, and took it upon myself as a personal mission to conquer these strange new worlds and then teach others the necessary skills to gain access. I was on a mission for nurses and nursing. Information is power—if you know where the answers are and can find them, you are in control of the situation. Consumers of health care today are not only well versed in the current health care literature, but savvy users of the Internet as well.

As my fellow baby boomers age and interact more frequently with health care providers, they bring with them the same inquisitiveness, tenacity, and need for answers they brought to all their causes of the 1960s and 1970s. Information on the latest cancer treatment protocols at Memorial Sloan Kettering, to take one example, is available online at its Web site. I know that helpful tidbit now. I did not know it when I started this course of study, and that was the information gap the MLS would help fill.

My application for admission was quickly accepted, but my own dithering resulted in my missing several open-house conferences and the start of the fall semester. Finally, at the last minute of the last day to register for the spring 1997 semester, I met the dean, was advised, and registered all in one hour. Things sure had changed from my graduate and undergraduate days when registration took a full day of waiting on a million endlessly long lines for a tedious manual process to be completed. Maybe computers are not completely bad after all!

I had kept my enrollment in the program secret from everyone—family, friends and colleagues—because my expectations of failure were so great. Perhaps the biggest part of that fear was my very first class. I sat near the door to make a quick getaway. To my complete surprise and joy, more than half the students were either my age or maybe about ten years younger. Only a handful of students were actually "kids," and many of the younger students were teachers working on school media certification. This proved to be the same proportion in all my subsequent classes.

Unfortunately, that early, good feeling was completely obliterated by the very first words spoken by the professor in that very first class: "If you're here because you love books and like to read, you're in the wrong program." It took all my willpower to stay seated. Inside, I was dying because underlying all the brave talk about information and computers and saving the nursing profession was the secret knowledge that I *did* love to read and I *did* love books, and if I could not make it with sophisticated information technology, I could be a librarian in a small town. You know, just deal with kids before they became more computer literate than I did, say up to age five.

After I decided to tough it out, it went from bad to worse when our professor compelled us to "Go around the room and tell us a little about yourself." I sat in a sweat agonizing over what to say without sounding pompous or stupid or both. Somehow, I stumbled through, red with embarrassment. Much to my chagrin, I found that this tortuous routine was part of every first night of every class. They never did this back in my day! In retrospect, my fellow sufferers and I realized that these short introductions served to break the ice and enabled us to more easily start conversations with each other after the class. We all seemed to have similar fears and anxieties associated with being older students embarking on second careers.

My long-suffering husband met me after classes that first, horrible night. He had been encouraging me for months, reassuring me about how much fun school would be. I got into the car that night and screamed: "Fun? You thought this would be *fun*? Honey, you couldn't be more wrong!" To his credit, he sat still for this verbal abuse and has been a rock of support ever since.

The rest of that semester is a blur. I have only vague memories of topics such as historical trends and developments in library science, computer-based information systems, bibliographic control, and the functions of the catalog. I had registered for both the introductory class and the cataloging classes (back to back on the same night—not something I would recommend even to an enemy). My wrists and hands ached constantly from note taking; my eyes blurred from reading and burned from looking at the Xerox machine innards while copying endless articles that remained largely unread because there just was not time.

Many nights, I cried myself to sleep, and then had nightmares about MARC records. During the semester, I finally had to come clean with my colleagues and family who were worried about my physical deterioration, crankiness, and lack of participation in stuff such as my own birthday. I was met with incredulity ranging from "Why would you ever want to be a librarian?" to "Have you memorized the Dewey Decimal System yet?" After they got over their bemusement, almost everyone was supportive.

No one at work seemed threatened by my return to school. Maybe because it was not an advanced degree in nursing and no one felt the need to justify her own decision not to pursue higher education. In addition, on the plus side, my relationship with students of all ages was very positive. Friendships formed and team effort became the rule of the day. No matter our ages or backgrounds, we were in this agony together and sharing was the only pathway to survival.

This was the complete reverse of my experiences in graduate school for nursing. Through the entire six years it took to complete that degree, I made few friends, never participated in class because it was not expected, and used the library only rarely. Times and adult students sure have changed. Now, I live in the library, have tons of new friends, and participate in classes to the point where I annoy myself.

Each of us brings something unique from our past lives and work experiences. These elements enhance problem solving and the learning process. Many of my classmates already work in libraries or are doing internships. They bring real-world experience and solutions that supplement the "book" learning imparted by our professors. The faculty also comes from solid, real-world backgrounds in libraries. It is akin to learning bedside nursing techniques from an experienced bedside nurse versus someone who has never bathed an incontinent adult patient. There is no substitute for hands-on experience as being the best teacher in any field.

The biggest logistic problem and greatest challenge has been the amount of computer work required, not just for OCLC in cataloging class, but for basic searching, e-mailing professors, and other purposes. The logistics were difficult because I had planned to do my work at home. However, my chosen school has such state-of-the-art equipment that it was necessary, and actually better and easier, to do the work at school, even though that meant being there just about seven days and nights each week.

Another challenge was electronic technology in use in the library. The last time I visited a library for school, the card catalog reigned. Now, there was this strange thing called OPAC. I sweated through my first few sessions with this new monster as well as a class assignment based on its use. Talk about a learning curve! Next, came Power Point, and then being required to hand in assignments on a disk. Sounds so easy and elementary now, but a few short months ago, I was so afraid of hitting the wrong button I would have anxiety attacks over the simplest function.

Just to increase the gut-wrenching fear of failure, I took a class in designing Web pages. Here again, the camaraderie among students made a difference. Every one of us represented a different skill level with technology. We all looked out for each other, nurturing along anyone who seemed stuck at a particular point.

Many more hours than I could possibly have anticipated were eaten up by assignments. I joined a study group for exams and it reminded my of my undergraduate days, just before the nursing boards. A group of us sat around answering review questions, prompting the others, devising aids to memory, etc. It was a tremendous help then and now.

Somewhere in my second semester, as I struggled in the computer lab, cursing and yelling and close to punching out the monitor, something I did not only worked, but I could replicate the actions and make it work again. There it was, my very own Web site with five linked pages and flashing, scrolling messages and other hot stuff. Wow—I had arrived! Things finally came together for me. My mantra switched from Why am I doing this to myself? to I can do this and be good at it.

The true turning point was when I began to bring the things I had learned in class back to the job. I joined the hated computer committees and dragged friends with me. When it came time to orient the new staff, I put my usual lecture onto Power Point. Word got around about my new expertise, and I became the resident go-to person for computer-related stuff. Need a graph or some clipart—see me. I encouraged my colleagues to try—to use the PCs at work and then to go home and wrest from their kids and spouses control of the mouse and, above all, not to be afraid.

We nurses have always handled hi-tech equipment in all aspects of our jobs, from computer-controlled intravenous devices to bedside cardiac monitors. There was no reason to allow this piece of equipment, the PC, to render us helpless.

My first activity was to create and present a Power Point presentation for the nursing staff on the basics of the Internet—what it is, some definitions, how to access it, search engines, etc. I prepared a formal proposal to establish a system to train the trainer to bring Internet searching skills and computer skills to all our staff. I used a survey of the staff to ascertain their use of information sources for work and their computer knowledge. I also evaluated the small collection of medical and nursing books located in our agency. Using the skill and knowledge gleaned from my courses in reference and collection development, and the results of the survey, I made formal recommendations for purchases to bring our little library up to date.

This past summer, I took an advanced reference course in which I had the privilege of working on a project to create a reference service for the Catholic elementary and high schools in the Brooklyn and Queens Diocese of New York. This experience was an opportunity to give back to the same community that had given me my love of books and learning. It was a chance to work on something totally different from nursing, yet with a nurturing component.

That course and another I am currently enrolled in, made use of WEB-CT. Basically a tool for distance learning, it makes communication with instructors and fellow students quick, easy, and efficient. No matter the time of day or day of the week, we can share ideas, solve problems, and commiserate. This tool is directly transferable to my nursing career because continuing education is soon to be mandated in New York State as it already is in many other states. Many nursing journals offer continuing education online, which I now know how to access and use effectively. Most regulatory agencies have their own Web sites and access to them keeps me on the cutting edge.

The other day, I excused myself from calling back an acquaintance, another nurse, by explaining that I would be online later. She asked, "online? Where—the bank?" It took me a few seconds to realize the reason for the miscommunication and when I explained, she laughed and said she envied me because she had no idea what her kids were doing on the Internet for hours each day, but she was too scared to learn. I added her to my nurturing list. Hey, I even have my sexagenarian mom surfing the web!

Early on in the program, I pigeonholed my goal and concentration as medical librarianship. As time went on, I realized that this circumscribed role was not necessary. I have taken as many different classes as possible to become as diversified as possible. With only two classes left, I am firm in my commitment to remain within the nursing profession. Perhaps I can create a new specialty that will concentrate on the education of nurses and nursing students in how to access the information they need for their professional growth and success.

So far, I have evaluated a collection and made recommendations for purchase. I have made cogent arguments for Internet access for staff at my job. Issues such as censorship, electronic versus print, and copyright are meaningful and important to me. Whenever I find myself at a PC, playing the keys like a piano, without flinching, I have to stop and remind myself of the hard road I have struggled along to reach this level. Then I smile and tell my husband, "You were right, it has been fun."

Part IV

Preparing Librarians to Teach the Internet

Somewhere between a Fire Hose and Loneliness: Use of the Internet as a Teaching Tool with MLS Students

Heather Blenkinsopp

rinking from a fire hose was the metaphor used to describe the overwhelming onslaught of information from the Internet when I first became an active member of the online community. I have not heard this phrase used in a while. Perhaps we are all so accustomed to being overwhelmed that we no longer need to conjure up pictures to help us describe our reaction to the flood of data that has become an integral part of our professional and personal lives. Drowning has become the norm.

However, the analogy holds true, at least for a computer service manager who was intrigued by the concept during a recent discussion. Now even the computer techs have come to value librarians for their "Web-wiseness." We, as librarians, have become inextricably entwined with the technology that allows us to find information, to chat with friends, to connect with colleagues on the other side of the country or on another continent, and to book our occasional getaways from the rat-race life of the library.

Internet Usage and Loneliness

In a recent flurry of newspaper articles, experts have debated whether Internet usage leads to greater levels of loneliness and depression. A Carnegie-Mellon study, which followed 169 average Americans in Pittsburgh over a two-year period, found that the folks who used the Internet, even for moderate amounts of time, were more depressed and lonely after two years than they were when the study began (Harmon 1998). This finding was surprising because we had assumed that we were increasing our sense of connection by using the Internet. No one questioned what was happening to our psyches by spending long periods in front of a computer monitor. Other experts quickly retaliated: the study was flawed, no control group, there was not a large enough sample to be representative, and other factors.

Flawed or not, the study does raise interesting questions about the usefulness of the Internet in connecting us with the outside world and about the value of the Internet in general. There are societal issues seen in questions about the effects of long-term usage, especially for those in developmental stages of life. There are the questions focusing on priorities for increasingly elusive personal time. The personal space pits one's need to keep up with the fast-moving information revolution versus the need for quiet, contemplative, reflective time required to maintain lasting relationships.

For librarians, the questions of what else we need to be teaching students about the Internet emerge. Beyond the search strategies and the mechanics of navigating the Net, past the merits of print versus electronic sources, behind the shimmer of the glossily spinning Web pages, what do we need to be saying about the Internet and the knowledge it provides? Have we had the time to reflect on the potential effects involved in using the Internet? For most academic librarians, probably not.

Reading about the Carnegie-Mellon findings developed my thinking about my own experiences in working with, learning, and teaching about the Internet. In many ways, I could empathize with those participants who felt more disconnected from life while logging on to the Internet. I found that I could spend several hours in front of the terminal with nothing more tangible to show from the effort than myriad printouts that would be recycled in a month or so. I now limit my at-home connection time to early mornings.

Net adventures that get out of control seem less intrusive if lived out while the first cup of coffee is still perking. I gave up on chat rooms when I realized that no matter what the listed topic of discussion, at some point the room would be monopolized by teenagers using the kind of computer terms that were too reminiscent of work to be fun. Yep, those Carnegie-Mellon social scientists were on to something here!

However, in the middle of negative rumination, small glimpses of wonderfully human connections began to appear in my head. There were all those librarians who stepped beyond their own hectic existence to respond to a frantic plea on one list or another to help us with a pressing problem here at our library. There was the thrill of being able to eavesdrop on the online conversations of Bronte fans when I was reading a biography of Charlotte. There were the individual students who stopped me as I floated by the terminals on my way to another access services crisis. Sometimes a few moments offered by a librarian to help a student past a navigational obstacle yielded professional reward to the librarian.

Cataloging for the Non-cataloger

The experience that seemed to be in direct contrast to the findings of the Carnegie-Mellon study involved a classroom setting with library science students and an assignment that went in directions none of us anticipated. Last year, I unexpectedly found myself teaching a required bibliographic control class to thirty-three library school students at Long Island University's Westchester Campus. Only two of the students felt they would definitely seek a career in cataloging. The majority of the students were headed toward public services positions in public, school, and, to a lesser extent, academic and special libraries.

Many of the students expressed outright fear at having to learn about bibliographic control, which seemed much too technical and was discussed in terms so foreign that it might well have been in a language other than English. At the time, my experience included ten years in two acquisitions departments of medical college and academic libraries along with six years of interlibrary loan expertise at the academic library.

The time spent in technical services had given me a broad understanding of bibliographic control principles, which I felt comfortable passing on to future librarians. Granted, I learned some of the details as the class progressed, often barely a few steps ahead of the students. Students even vied for the honor of having the "stumper of the week" question that sent me researching for an answer. But generally, they received a sound foundation of the basics of bibliographic control. What I could not provide for them was the ongoing discussion of hot issues currently facing catalogers. Nor could I paint a picture of the daily life of a cataloger to help them understand catalogers as something other than intimidating receptacles of incomprehensible technical knowledge.

At the same time, I was involved in a college implementation committee working to ensure that all of Mercy College's undergraduate students were at minimum competency levels in the areas of critical thinking, quantitative reasoning, writing, oral communication, and information literacy skills when they reached graduation. The committee was asking professors to integrate competency-skill building activities into their class assignments. There had been some resistance from faculty, who felt that the content of their discipline did not lend itself to these activities.

The bibliographic control class offered me the opportunity to design an assignment that would connect my students with the real world by cataloging ideas. The assignment also offered me the challenge of incorporating competency skill-building activities into a highly technical and specialized course content. The Internet called out as the perfect vehicle for this type of assignment.

Internet as a Teaching Tool: The Use of Discussion Forums

I am a great fan of listservs, or discussion groups, on the Internet. What better way to stay current than to exchange ideas with people from around the world who are interested in your favorite topic? For my class assignment, the idea of connecting students with actual catalogers via a listserv seemed appropriate. AUTOCAT is an active list with professionals from a variety of libraries. They have different daily experiences, and all discuss contemporary cataloging issues.

The first part of the bibliographic control class assignment was to sign on to the list and to begin reading the messages. This activity posed an almost immediate and completely unexpected problem. When the assignment was announced in class, several hands shot up. "What's e-mail?" A later survey revealed that nine of the thirty-three students had no prior experience using e-mail. Of the twenty-four students who had used e-mail, only five had ever subscribed to a listserv.

My assumptions about the level of Internet proficiency were wrong. I had not paid enough attention to the fact that half of the class was returning to classroom instruction after a long absence. In addition, slightly more than 20 percent of the students were taking bibliographic control as their first class in the library school program. The establishment of several e-mail workshops, with individualized assistance, solved the problem.

After they had overcome any technical or mechanical problems, the class then began to read about real-life cataloging issues on a daily basis. At first, both the number of daily messages from the list and the content of each missive overwhelmed many. Gradually, as we progressed through the textbook, the content became clearer. As threads of discussion developed, the students followed topics of particular interest to them. To ensure that everyone was able to sign on, I asked students to print out and bring into class a message that struck their fancy. We then discussed some of the concepts included in these messages. Though highly instructive, this first part of the assignment allowed for only passive participation in the discussion process. Not wanting to create a class full of lurkers, I had constructed a second part to the assignment: they were to ask a question.

The class experienced trepidation at the thought of asking a "stupid" question of the experts. They hesitated. Then one brave soul posted her question—and immediately was "flamed." The other students could see in glorious living detail, paragraph by paragraph, how one of their colleagues was living out their worst nightmare. We spent some class time talking about the possible causes of a "flame," of how the Internet in its facelessness lent itself to miscommunication and misunderstandings.

I regaled them with stories of several brilliant "flames" I had caused over the past few years by posing what had seemed a harmless query. We spoke of the irony of questions causing such a furor in a profession where the driving passion is to assist people with questions. Then I sent an explanatory message to the list, asking for patience and encouraged mentoring of the students. Our savior arrived in the form of one of the list moderators.

The moderator publicly set the ground rules for responses to our queries. "Flames" were not to be tolerated; all queries were to be treated with respect. He went one step further to ensure the success of our assignment. He offered to filter the assignments before they went to the list as a whole.

Lessons Learned: Language and Electronic Expression

The students learned as much about online communication from the questions he returned as they did from the list responses. One student tried to send a message in all capital letters, which was how she always typed because her skills were not good and capital letters alleviated odd typos. The moderator returned the query with an explanation that words in capital letters representing online shouting. The student certainly had not intended to shout.

Another student used a term that meant one thing in real life and another in Library Land. The ambiguity would have set off a discussion that had nothing to do with her question. Through the filtering process, the students discovered nuances of electronic communication that none would have thought to question before.

The responses from AUTOCAT participants to their queries were equally instructive and enlightening. The questions ranged from queries about the technical specifics of cataloging rules to broadly ranging inquiries about the cataloging profession. Each student received at least three responses. The highest response rate of thirty-four replies was the result of a series of questions that dealt with reasons for entering the cataloging specialty and the importance of the work that catalogers do.

Many students were amazed at the rapidity of early responses when they received a reply in only a few hours. Respondents took their mentoring potential quite seriously. Answers often included specific information plus a referral to additional online or print resources. In several cases, AUTOCAT members even suggested follow-up questions that students should examine.

Several students, motivated by the professional interest shown by the respondents, took their questions to other lists or embarked on real-life interviews with local librarians. A number of students who asked questions related to problems in libraries where they worked were able to translate the responses into actual practice to help solve the problems.

One student changed her mind about the nature of the problem she posed about shelving series as a series or breaking up the series to shelve the volumes with like subjects:

> The original question was about visual appeal and led to many other questions. The visual aspect is important but takes a back seat to the real process of searching. I am still intrigued about the importance of browsing and the autocatters' responses indicating that children do not browse in the way adults do.

The student who received only three responses analyzed the distribution of types of institutions represented by AUTOCAT readers over a week's time. Based on the results, she realized that her question was posed to a different audience than she had assumed. She began an investigation of other lists where subscribers would be more likely to respond to her question.

To complete the assignment, students wrote a report on their question and the responses they received. They included background information on why they posed the question and what they would do with the responses. The report included a summary of the responses received from AUTOCAT and each student's analysis of the responses.

A five-minute oral presentation summarizing the report for their classmates was also required. Many students thought their questions were too basic to be of interest to anyone other than themselves or perhaps their classmates. Because of this and because of a desire not to clog an already busy list, students requested private responses to their questions.

The class was surprised when AUTOCAT readers began requesting summaries to the list. Some of their student questions had touched on topics that professional catalogers were facing in their own libraries. Although a summary for the list was not part of the original assignment, students indicated that they would like to participate in this follow-up activity. After the class received instructions on summary formats and content priorities, several students did indeed send response summaries to the list and received appreciative responses from the AUTOCAT subscribers.

Connection to the Profession

For some of the students, the AUTOCAT assignment was their first venture into professional connections. Did the assignment succeed in its goal of providing greater connection via the Internet? Were catalogers now viewed as having a dimension? Were the students drowning at the fire hose? The conclusion of each AUTOCAT assignment report included a critique of the process. I will let some of the students speak for themselves.

> I enjoyed this process more than I thought I would. I still have not gotten over my aversion to computer labs. Being a novice with e-mail, I encountered numerous technical problems. I would have enjoyed this project more if I owned my own computer. It was difficult to make time specifically to go read my e-mail. Hopefully, with experience and my own computer I will learn to love e-mail.

What I found most interesting was my personal response to AUTOCAT. To be quite frank, when we first started reading the listserv, I found it boring and somewhat unbelievable that people were really that obsessed with things like labels . . . . I now have a great desire to find a listserv for children's librarians, for there are many questions and situations I would like to address.

Though there were some negative comments in response to some of the questions, it is a part of the learning process to accept and use all types of critiques to format an answer and improve the next search strategy. It is also a great way to interface with other professional colleagues.

I found that being part of the listserv added tremendously to my understanding and appreciation of this topic. More importantly, I feel strongly that having to pose a question to the list increased my interest in the daily participation of AUTOCAT, knowing that soon it would be my turn. Finally, receiving responses from my peers and future "coworkers" was an extremely rewarding experience and developed a sense of community I had not yet experienced.

The listserv added another dimension to the class. It contributed to the ongoing cyber technology that librarians must be at ease with. It was reinforcement of class topics but on a different level. It complimented the lectures and readings with a current slant of how professionals seek each other's help. If you missed an article from a trade periodical, chances are it would be mentioned. The downside was the time involved in reading the e-mail.

In essence, you are inviting the catalogers out there to improve their field through their relationships with potential catalogers. And if we don't all join their ranks, then we have certainly stood in their shoes for a moment, and will leave with a profound feeling of respect for what they do.

Connector or Isolator?
Based on the experience with the bibliographic control class, I would say

that the Internet has great potential for connecting students with professionals, in whatever field, who can add to the knowledge that learners acquire in the classroom setting. The Carnegie-Mellon study, though initially alarming but open to debate, may offer an indication of the limits of the Internet in human interaction. The Internet has its place in the academic world but needs to be tempered by concurrent human contact. The library school students' experiences bore out the need for that extra human touch. They were most impressed by the generosity and graciousness of the librarians with whom they came in virtual contact. What set the experience apart for them was the consistent willingness of professionals to go beyond the minimum, and even the norm, to be of assistance.

From the moderator to the respondents, each librarian became a teacher in addition to the instructor he or she saw in the classroom each week. Without the dedication of these professionals, the Internet assignment would certainly have been shallower. The assignment would have been another assignment instead of a glimpse into the world of their colleagues.

The library people were what gave the shimmer to the e-mail Web. Perhaps this is where our role with the Internet lies. Librarians as the antidote to Internet depression and loneliness? It is a thought.

Reference

Harmon, A. 1998, August 30. Sad, lonely world discovered in cyberspace. *New York Times*, 1–1, 1–22.

Librarians Helping Librarians: An Annotated Listing of Internet Resources for Instructional Use and Professional Renewal

Harriet A. Hagenbruch and Irina Poznansky

It is hard to believe that as recently as the beginning of the present decade many, regardless of profession, had never heard of the Internet. In the past several years, the Internet has become a household word as increasing amounts of people go online. In a recent article, Elizabeth Weise (1998) cited a report produced by the Commerce Department that indicated Net traffic is doubling every 100 days. More than 100 million people access the Net now. Clearly, something this big will ultimately affect every aspect of librarianship, including the way we communicate, do business, and gather information.

Early in the development of the Internet, some librarians realized its potential as a research tool, while at the same time they recognized the need to harness something powerful and chaotic. These librarians were innovators who organized resources, gave training sessions on the Internet, and incorporated the Internet into their teaching and reference work. However, other librarians did not follow the same path in their use of the Internet, nor did they embrace the Internet with equal degrees of enthusiasm. As the Internet evolved, librarians began to teach and learn it. The recent proliferation of librarian-produced tutorials is evidence of Internet influence on instructional options. This article focuses on the best of the available instructional materials, so those librarians can examine the structure of the materials and integrate them into their teaching. A secondary purpose is to provide review sources for those who want to revisit aspects of the Internet.

Librarians in academic settings have produced some of the best Internet tutorials, and their work is dominant in the listing. In addition, other educators and Internet product companies have created a number of well-designed instructional materials on the Internet. Yahoo indexed many Internet tutorials (Access: http://dir/yahoo.com/ Computers_and_Internet. Netscape's *New to the Net* (Access: http:// www.netscape.com/netcenter/newnet/) and Earthlink-Sprint's *Using the Net* (Access: http://www.earthlink.net/internet/) are among the many commercially prepared Internet tutorials.

The authors selected listed resources for annotation based on specific criteria, not all applicable to each site:
- authoritative source;
- recommendations from librarians constructing Web pages;
- breadth and depth (or both) of information pertinent to review or instruction about Internet;
- currency (where relevant);
- ease of use (user-friendly interface, straightforwardness of language, and arrangement of page);
- citation frequency on gateway sites;
- excellence of instructional use of the Web to teach the Web.

The listing is composed of six sections. Within each section, some sites are quite broad, grouping many different sites on related topics. These "entry sites" are listed at the beginning of each section. Other sites focus on narrow areas and function as ends in themselves. The listing is divided into these sections for ease of referral:
- Basic Background: Includes sites that present definitions of Internet terminology, historical background of the Internet, and searching techniques;
- Evaluation of Internet Resources: Includes sites providing criteria for evaluation of Internet resources;
- Evaluating Information Sites: Lists sites that provide criteria to evaluate the sites themselves;
- Keeping Current: E-mail and Newsletters: Provides venues to keep current;
- Organizing Information on the Internet: Presents sites demonstrating logical subject organization;

- Constructing Web Pages: Focuses on selected sites providing HTML tutorials, elements of a Web site, style, and form

Basic Background: Terminology, Timelines, and Tutorials
Explore the Internet (Library of Congress)
(Access: http://lcweb.loc.gov/global/explore.html).
The Library of Congress's guide to the Internet includes *Learn about the Internet*, which includes search tools and guides prepared by Library of Congress reading room and subject specialists. There is a comprehensive listing of online tutorials. The Library of Congress does not endorse these tutorials and the listing contained many that appear on other collections of tutorial links.

Kathy Schrock's Guide for Educators
(Access: http://www.capecod.net/schrockguide/)
Kathleen Schrock, Technology Coordinator, Dennis-Yarmouth Regional School District, maintains this site. It is a "gateway" site providing subject access to various Internet resources. The intended audience is teachers on the elementary or secondary level. However, there are sections of particular benefit to any librarian seeking to learn more about the Internet. Three relevant areas include Internet Information, Slide Shows for Training, and Critical Evaluation Tools. The latter section collates many sites that will be described in a later section. The site is updated daily.

The History of the Internet
(Access: http://ftp.isoc.org/internet/history/)
The Internet Society's collection of Internet histories includes those written by creators of the Internet, as well as two time lines (Hobbe's and PBS). Eighteen links on the history of the Internet function as a comprehensive picture as seen from distinguished viewpoints. The Discovery Channel prepared another time line (Access: http://www.discovery.com/DCO/doc/1012/world/technology/internet/inet1.html), which begins in the 1940s when the first civilian portable telephone was invented (1947.) It functions best as a quick overview.

Glossary of Internet Terms
(Access: http://www.matisse.net/files/glossary.html)
Matisse Enzer of Internet Literacy Consultants produced a site for defini-

tion of Internet terminology. The glossary is arranged alphabetically: one clicks on a letter to find a term. One such search yielded a surprising fact about the term *listserv*: the word is now a registered trademark with L-Soft International, Inc.

InterNic 15-Minute Series: Tools for the Internet Trainer

(Access: http://rs.internic.net/nic-support/15min/)
Tools for the Internet Trainer was developed in 1996 by InterNIC and LITA (Library and Information Technology Association). The need to train the trainer was the basis for the development of the series, which contains forty brief lessons on Internet-related topics. The topics include Internet History, Electronic Mail, and Indexing & Search Services. What makes it useful for a trainer is that each module, designed as a mini-slide presentation, may be downloaded in either HTML or PowerPoint format. This site was last modified in August 1996 and discontinued in March 1998. However, it is maintained due to many user requests. There is a link to the *Com Series*, which targets the business community.

World Wide Web Workbook

(Access: http://www.fi.edu/primer/setup.html)
This site, produced by the Franklin Institute of Science, in Philadelphia, is geared to the Internet novice. The workbook was intended for a class application where all computers were configured alike. It explores topics (hypertext, Web graphics, interactivity, and others) by providing a series of simple exercises that are a systematic guide through the basics of the Internet. Especially amusing is the little Spot (friend of Dick and Jane) image that leads you to a variety of information, including Spot's personal home page. The suggested educational hot list of sites (primarily related to science) at the end of the workbook is worth exploring.

Welcome Back to School: The Electronic Library Classroom 101: A Class on the Net for Librarians with Little or No Net Experience

(Access: http://www.sc.edu/bck2skol/bck2skol.html)
Welcome Back to School was developed by Ellen Chamberlain, Head Librarian, University of South Carolina, Beaufort, and Miriam Mitchell, Sr., Systems Analyst, University of South Carolina, Columbia. Originally distributed as a listserv in 1995, it has been revised

several times and consists of a collection of thirty lessons targeted toward librarians and other information professionals. Lessons include information on: The History of the Net, Usenet: The Wild Side, and Internet Security, in addition to lessons on mailing lists, basic Internet tools (telnet, ftp, and Web browsers). There are pointers to help librarians research the Net in several academic subject areas. At the end of each lesson, there is an assignment and a bibliography of related online information. An addendum includes a compilation of Ask-an-Expert sites.

A Guide to Getting Started on the Internet: The Help Web

(Access: http://www.imaginarylandscape.com/helpweb/welcome.html)
The Help Web by Imaginary Landscape is user-friendly, well organized, and intended for Internet novices. It includes help on a large variety of Internet-related topics such as indexes, and search engines. The site can be searched by scrolling through the Site Guide or by performing a keyword search through the Help Web by Keyword. (A Panic Button is included to help the frustrated user.) Humor, graphics (images hand-rendered by Corky and Holly Siegel), and interesting quotations enhance the appeal of the site. Of special interest is a list of online resources under the heading Common Concerns that consists of topics such as: Children and the Internet Dealing with Internet Spam and others.

Exploring the World Wide Web

(Access: http://www.gactr.uga.edu/exploring/index.html)
Brad Cahoon originally designed this tutorial, from the University of Georgia Center for Continuing Education, for a one-day workshop. It is intended for the novice and includes such basic concepts as exactly what elements make up the Internet as well as what the World Wide Web is and how it works. Topics cover the Netscape Navigator browser, Web sites, HTML, and others. A demonstration page shows hypertext as it appears on a terminal.

An Introduction to the World Wide Web

(Access: http://www.usyd.edu.au/su/course/)
This site is a Web-based course from the University of Sydney, Australia. The opening page explains that the course assumes no knowledge of the World Wide Web. The viewer automatically starts with

Module 1 to learn basic terminology and concepts. After completing the first Module, he or she will be able to judge whether to select another module or to move to independent exploration. A short multiple-choice quiz at the end of each section helps the student to assess progress.

University at Albany Libraries Internet Tutorials
(Access: http://www.albany.edu/library/internet/)
Laura Cohen maintains the *Internet Tutorials* site. Basic knowledge of a Web browser is necessary. The course consists of sections that include Basic Internet, Research Guides, Search Engines, Subject Directories, Netscape Navigator, Communicator, and Software Training. Included under Search Engines and Subject Directories is a section on Boolean Searching on the Internet, as well as How to Choose a Search Engine or Research Database.

Internet Navigator
(Access: http://www.lib.utah.edu/navigator/navigator.html)
This site is sponsored by the Spencer S. Eccles Health Science Library and the Utah Academic Library Consortium. It is funded by a Higher Education Technology Initiative grant. The tutorial (which contains six modules) is intended for students to navigate effectively and access essential information resources. The use of simple graphics signals the viewer to proceed at one's own pace or go back when needed. Each module, with the exception of the sixth on file transfer protocol, which is considered optional, ends with a quiz or assignment. Only those registered for the class can submit a quiz.

Finding Information on the Internet: A Tutorial
(Access: http://www.lib.berkeley.edu/TeachingLib/Guides/Internet/FindInfo.html)
These online tutorials present the substance of the Internet workshops offered year-round by the Teaching Library at the University of California at Berkeley. The progression from beginning information to advanced search is logical. The viewer has a choice of proceeding in order or starting anywhere in the outline by clicking on the desired section. On any page, one can click on the Glossary of Internet and Netscape Jargon for a definition of terms one will encounter. Particularly outstanding are the charts that depict the search strategies associated with each search engine.

Evaluating Search Tools
Annotated Guide to WWW Search Engines
(Access: http://www.ciolek.com/SearchEngines.html)
Dr. Matthew Ciolek and Irena Gotz, consultants in Asia Pacific Research Online, mounted their research results on this site. Although the document keeps track of information retrieval facilities of significance to researchers in the field of Asian studies and social science, it also provides an overview of general options with search engines. However, the site does not give detailed instructions on how to use a particular search engine.

Understanding WWW Search Tools
(Access: http://www.indiana.edu/~librcsd/search)
Jian Liu, Reference Librarian, Indiana University Libraries, developed the site in 1995 and has updated it twice; a new version is in progress. The main objective of the site is to present a comparison of major search engines by characteristic (size, content, currency, speed of searching, ease of use, and other aspects). There is a full listing of different search engines with details on their use. Worth noting is "Guide to Meta-Search Engines" (1998).

Evaluation of Selected Internet Search Tools
(Access: http://www.library.nwu.edu/resources/internet/search/evaluate.html)
The evaluation site, from Northwestern University Library, reviews a number of commonly used Internet search tools. Each review describes the search engine by characteristic (database size, search features, retrieval results, brief comment). Direct links to each search tool are provided as well as links to other sites such as Search Engine Watch and Getting the Most Out of Guides and Search Engines.

Evaluating Information Resources
Evaluation of Information Sources
(Access: http://www.vuw.ac.nz/~agsmith.evaln.htm)
Alastair Smith maintains this site, which lists links to sites containing criteria for evaluating Internet information resources. Although intended for librarians to use as a resource guide on this particular topic, it is in itself a valuable tool. The site is part of the WWW Virtual Library which contains several related sites, grouped under *Informa-*

tion Quality (Access: http://www.w3.org/vl/) site was last updated in November 1998.

Web Sites for Educational Uses: Bibliography and Checklist

(Access: http://www.unc.edu/cit/guides/irg-49.html)
Carolyn Kotlas maintains this site on behalf of the Institute for Academic Technology. It consists of a bibliography of resources that discuss how to evaluate information on the Internet. Links are provided to each site and, at the end of the document, there is a checklist of questions for evaluating Web sites. This site was last updated in December 1997.

Bibliography on Evaluating Internet Resources

(Access: http://refserver.lib.vt.edu/libinst/critTHINK. HTM)
Nicole Auer, Library Instruction Coordinator for Virginia Polytechnic Institute and State University, developed and maintained this extensive bibliography. Originally prepared for a regional conference in the state of Wisconsin, the list includes print as well as online sources pertaining to evaluation of Internet resources. This site was last updated in October 1998.

Techman's Techpage: Evaluating Information on the Internet

(Access: http://thorplus.lib.purdue.edu/~techman/evaluate.htm)
D. Scott Brandt, Technology Training Librarian at Purdue University Libraries, wrote this article (1996), which focuses on the importance of discrimination in Internet usage. It provides the distinction between evaluated sources of information (typically found in books and scholarly journals) and the numerous sites available on the Net. At the end of the article, the viewer is advised to "check, check, doublecheck" when using the Internet as a research tool.

Evaluating Information Found on the Internet

(Access: http://milton.mse.jhu.edu:8001/research/education/net.html)
Elizabeth Kirk, Electronic and Distance Education Librarian, of the Milton S. Eisenhower Library, Johns Hopkins University, in Baltimore, maintains this site. It starts with an interesting comparison of information found on the Internet as opposed to traditional evaluations by librarians and experts in the field. The site includes discussion of the basic criteria used to evaluate print resources and extends the criteria

to evaluation of information on the Internet. Detailed and logical, this document can serve as a basic guide to any research librarian. It includes a link to the copyright Web site.

Library Selection Criteria for WWW Resources

(Access: http://www6.pilot.infi.net/~carolyn/criteria.html)
The information contained in this document was first published as an article by Carolyn Caywood (1996). This site lists several criteria that are particularly related to Internet resources. For example, under the section: Access, she lists questions to ask, such as "Is it stable, or has the URL changed?" and "Must you use software to download it?" Under Design, she lists, "Can you find your way around and easily locate a page from any other page?" The main sources for the criteria are based on the author's personal experience of what works.

Evaluating Web Resources

(Access: http://www.science.widener.edu/~withers/webeval.htm)
This site is the seventh in a series of modules produced by Widener University's Wolfgram Memorial Library and focuses on the evaluation of resources on the Web developed and maintained by Jan Alexander and Marsha Tate, reference librarians at Widener. The document includes a PowerPoint presentation on The Web as a Research Tool. A text version is available as well. Like several of the other sites listed above, this presentation demonstrates how criteria used for reviewing print translate to evaluating material on the Web. The site calls attention to an article written by Jan Alexander and Marsha Tate on this same topic (1996). A brief bibliography of other related resources is included.

Keeping Up-to-Date: E-mail and Newsletters
The Weekly Bookmark

This e-mail newsletter presents reviews about "new and newsworthy" sites on the Web in more than fifteen categories. Readers submit sites and the editor make final selections. All submissions are welcome and carefully reviewed. Subscribers to this free newsletter will receive each issue first. Issues will be made available online at URL: http://www.weeklyb.com. /. To subscribe, use the form available in the site.

Free Pint

Free Pint is a free e-mail newsletter produced by information consultants in the United Kingdom that informs the viewer about access to Web sites considered outstanding. It contains a variety of "tips, tricks and articles." Now, it is sent every two weeks to more than 10,500 people involved in the information professions. To subscribe, use the form at URL: http://www.freepint.co.uk/ or contact enquiries@freepint.co.uk.

Blue Web 'N Update

This newsletter keeps readers up-to-date (on a weekly basis) about new additions to the Blue Web 'N site—a site that provides access to listings of Blue Ribbon Web sites for K–12 education. These outstanding sites are arranged by grade, subject area, and other factors. To subscribe, either enter your e-mail address online at URL: http://www.kn.pacbell.com/wired/bluewebn or send an e-mail message to majordomo@lists.sdsu.edu. The site is sponsored by Packard-Bell.

The Scout Report

The *Scout Report* is a publication of the Internet Scout Project, located in the Department of Computer Sciences at the University of Wisconsin-Madison. It is sponsored by the National Science Foundation. The primary goal of the site developers is to offer the latest and best Internet resources to members of the education community. A team consisting of librarians and various subject specialists contributes to this endeavor by sorting through a vast number of sites and selecting those they consider outstanding. This is accomplished on a weekly basis. The *Scout Report* is available on the Internet or as a weekly e-mail newsletter. To subscribe, access a form at URL: http://www.scout.cs.wisc.edu/scout/report/index.html.

Organization of Information on the Internet

The above sites focus on learning the Internet itself. However, librarians sift through the vast array of information and organize it in a logical way in order to help their patrons. The following sites present the best Internet resources for organizing information.

Beyond Bookmarks: Schemes for Organizing the Web

(Access: http://www.public.iastate.edu/~CYBERSTACKS/CTW.htm)

Beyond Bookmarks, a comprehensive collection of organization links compiled by Gerry McKiernan, Science and Technology Services Department, Iowa State University Libraries, encompasses categorization types that are international in scope. *Schemes* includes sites that are organized with many categorical modes, including: alphabetical, numeric, the Universal Decimal Classification, the Library of Congress Classification System, the Agricola Subject Headings, ACM Computing Classification, Medical Subject Headings (MeSH), and many more.

Argus Clearinghouse
(Access: http://www.clearinghouse.net)
The *Argus Clearinghouse* archives librarian-rated, selective topical guides. A Digital Librarian Award recognizes the work of academic (and other) librarians who have prepared high-quality resources indexing Web content by subject. The criteria and the ratings on each criterion (from one to five checks) for each guide are displayed.

INFOMINE
(Access: http://lib-www.ucr.edu)
The University of California, Riverside Library, maintains INFOMINE as a subject-sorted collection of scholarly Internet resources.

Librarian's Index to the Internet
(Access: http://sunsite.berkeley.edu/InternetIndex/)
Carol Leita maintains the 43-subject area index. It is updated daily. Each subject area is further divided into subtopics, which lead to the annotated resources selected for quality by librarians.

Constructing Web Pages
About HTML with Style
(Access: http://www.webreference.com/html/#tutorials)
This site consists of a series of tutorials (six as of October 15, 1998) produced by Stephanos Piperoglou, Mecklermedia Corporation, that are designed to teach the viewer how to create Web pages. The tutorials begin with the basics of HTML and gradually include more technical aspects of Web page design. All of the tutorials contain basic examples and, in addition, offer links to other related sites. Other tutorials will be added in the future.

A Beginner's Guide to HTML
(Access: http://www.ncsa.uiuc.edu/General/Internet/WWW/ HTMLPrimer.html)
The National Center for Supercomputing Applications, University of Illinois (Urbana-Champaign), developed this three-part guide to learning HTML. It serves as an introduction and does not offer in-depth training. Part one includes terms to know, basic HTML, and the markup tags that permit one to construct a basic Web page. Part two concentrates on character formatting, and the difference between a relative and an absolute path name. Part three focuses on images and tables. The appendix links various style guides and other resources on HTML.

Introduction to HTML: Table of Contents
(Access: http://www.cwru.edu/help/introHTML/toc.html)
Eric A. Meyer, Hypermedia Systems Manager, Digital Media Services, and Case Western Reserve University prepared this tutorial. It is intended for people who have never written in HTML. The author seeks to provide users of this guide with everything they need to set up a basic, functional Web page. All the terms and concepts are simple and straightforward. There is a multiple-choice quiz after each chapter, and if viewers wish to repeat what they have learned, the Tag Summary in the appendices provide this opportunity.

HTML Crash Course for Educators
(Access: http://edweb.cnidr.org/htmlintro.html)
Andy Carvin, author, and producer of *EdWeb: Exploring Technology and School Reform,* designed this tutorial. It is designed primarily for teachers, but it can serve as a valuable tool for anyone who wishes to learn the basics of HTML. There is a link to an interactive quiz at the end of the lessons. A participant has the opportunity to post a self-designed Web page on the Interactive Doodler to see how it would look on a browser This tutorial is also available in French.

Writing HTML: A Tutorial for Creating WWW Pages
(Access: http://www.mcli.dist.maricopa.edu/tut/)
Alan Levine, Instructional Technologist at Maricopa Community College, developed this site. It is a project of the Maricopa Center for Learning and Instruction. Like the previous site, this course is intended to help K–12 teachers learn how to create their own online activities and

exercises to use in the classroom. It is useful for anyone seeking to learn basic HTML. The tutorial consists of fourteen basic-level lessons and nine advanced lessons. The lessons cover the steps for writing HTML files and provide illustrative examples for creating Web pages. The tutorial is available in Spanish and Icelandic, courtesy of professors at the institution.

Web Wonk: Tips for Writers and Designers
(Access: http://www.dsiegel.com/tips/index.html)
David Siegel, the head of an Internet design firm, created *Web Wonk*. This site has information from a professional designer related to the creation of Web page design, rarely found in librarian-developed sites. The author's purpose in creating the site is to make the viewer "a better communicator on the Net." Siegel includes Designing Text Ergonomically, Practice and Principles, Perspicuity...the English Language in Cyberspace, and Use Images and Use Them Well, among other topics. The site provides a link with another site: Dr. HTML. One can have a site page evaluated for spelling, correct HTML, live links, space taken up by the page, and correct commands.

The Elements of Web Style
(Access: http://www.bluehighways.com/style.htm)
Karen G. Schneider, author of the column "Internet Librarian in American Libraries," created this site. She wrote this style guide while she was director of the U.S. Region 2 New York Library. Although intended for employees of Region 2 of the United States Environmental Protection Agency, this guide is useful for anyone who composes HTML documents. It contains nine elements of Web style for composing a Web page. These elements provide information for would-be Web authors and are useful for assessing other Web sites.

Conclusion
There is a wealth of information on the Internet to assist librarians with little Net experience. In fact, the amount of material is overwhelming to some. Midcareer librarians exploring the various sites available, including many suggested in this article, need to develop a plan of exploration. Information overload can be avoided by proceeding in a logical order (from a narrow focus to a broad one) and trying to concentrate on one topic at a time. The Internet is constantly changing, and we are all learning as we share our knowledge with others.

References

Brandt, D. S. 1996. Evaluating information on the Internet. *Computers in Libraries* 16: 44–46.

Caywood, C. 1996. Selection criteria for World Wide Web resources. *Public Libraries* 35: 169.

Liu, J. 1998. Guide to meta-search engines. *Business and Finance Division Bulletin* 107: 17–20.

Tate, M., and J. Alexander. 1996. Teaching critical evaluation skills for worldwide resources. *Computers in Libraries* 16: 49–52.

Weise, E. 1998, April 16. Net use doubling every 100 days. *USA Today*, A1.

Professional Development Resources for Internet Instructional Expertise

Patricia O'Brien Libutti

nstructional librarians need opportunities for renewal and creative growth as educators, perhaps more in this time than other times. They are confronted with rapidly changing information needs and the pressure to use the Internet to fulfill demands quickly. They must assess accurately their learners' questions, which may include developing appropriate instruction for students in distance education courses (Estabrook 1999). The demand for information available on the Internet makes necessary an instructional librarian's "current awareness program." This article is a review of the spectrum of resources for librarians to develop expertise in Internet instruction.

Definitions Used for Instructional Expertise Resource Review
For the purposes of this article, "instructional expertise in Internet education" was operationally defined as:

> the array of skills and concepts (conceptual, assessment, technical, design, evaluation, scholarly, and social skills) needed to conduct effective classes to higher education students, staff, and faculty about Internet function, operation, search, and evaluation of resources.

At this moment, thought about what constitutes expertise in Internet instruction is evolving. Several relevant areas of knowledge and skill appear to be important, as seen in the wide variety of instructional and learning behaviors reported in this volume by practitioners. Therefore, this working definition includes conceptual mastery, technology competency, assessment and inquiry skills, instructional skills, and scholarly and social skills.

The expertise in this area needs more precise definition; however, the field is in a state of exploration and experimentation with new methodologies that match Internet instructional possibilities. Figure 1 was derived from the behaviors reported in this book, as well as from an examination of the literature on instruction and information literacy. Resources examined were related to the areas in the figure, as well as the behaviors used as examples. As with any evolving perspective, this competencies listing is intended as a tentative summary and is as malleable as similar efforts.

The conceptual mastery of current thought on information literacy standards and learning theories (adult education, technology education frameworks, and information-seeking behaviors) is the basis of the choices made by the librarian. The behavioral examples in figure 1 assume that conceptual frameworks underlie instructional choices. Assessment and inquiry skills include skills in individual and group needs assessment as they relate to Internet instructional proficiency. Instructional competency includes the mastery of Internet search protocols, search engine operation, and the ability to sequence and structure class sessions for articulated learning outcomes. Technology competency includes the use of instructional technology and the ability to troubleshoot mechanical difficulties with the machinery used. Scholarly competencies include reflection and logical examination of sources. Social competencies include collaborative and outreach skills important to the development of an instructional program. Many of the articles in the volume provide behavioral examples of tasks in each of the competency areas.

Also important is the terminology used to describe those providing instruction in academic libraries. The title "librarian" is intended to refer to the instructional librarian throughout the rest of this article. Many librarians other than those designated as instructional librarians by their institutions are called upon for point-of-use instruction. It is likely that the instructional function will increase in the library. The use of the term *librarian* matches current practice, as well as simplifying the text.

Resource Search Methodology

Resource selection proceeded by initially examining the literature on Internet instruction and Information Literacy from 1994 to1998, using these and related terms. A content trend analysis provided themes and likely resource areas to conduct further searches. The most likely sources for resources (library schools, professional associations, schools of education, higher education professional associations, library discussion group lists, and academic libraries) were searched, using Internet for location of relevant resources. The resulting resources were reviewed, prioritized, selectively annotated, and arranged by type of resource. A complementary article in this volume (Hagenbruch and Poznansky) focuses on the resources prepared by librarians to review resources on Internet education.

The Place of Information Literacy in Professional Development for Instructional Expertise with Internet Education

Information literacy is juxtaposed with Internet education as central conceptual frameworks for current library education. Bonnie Gratch Lindauer (1998) reviewed many information literacy competency statements and prepared a *Compilation of Core Information Literacy Competency /Outcomes for Undergraduates*. The synthesis of the many documents indicated that common threads appearing in the information literacy standards aimed at instruction students who could:

- develop effective search strategies;
- locate and retrieve information sources;
- analyze and critically evaluate information;
- organize and synthesize information;
- use/apply information;
- (develop) awareness and attitude formation about information and information technology.

Each of these student competencies needs to be specified by tasks and instructional behaviors for the instructor teaching particular aspects of Internet use or Internet information assessment (Fitzgerald 1997). Emerging needs may be a trigger for a librarian to pursue a topic or competency. Fitzgerald's article addresses several areas important for curriculum design. She lists the common sources of misinformation, including:

- hardware and software problems;
- lack of central authority;

Figure 1: Competencies for Instructional Expertise in Internet Education

Assessment & Inquiry Competencies: The Instructional Librarian

Reflects an understanding of a student's expressed information need.

Recognizes the appropriateness of Internet as the venue for search inherent in a query.

Assesses the student's proficiency with Internet use, then helps develop the student's questions into query language useful with search engines.

Extends questions into language leading to related topics for use in searching Internet for relevant sites.

Provides conditions for a student to individualize an inquiry and direct it appropriately.

Provides a framework for students to rearticulate inquiry in the light of new information, refining questions.

Instructional Competencies: The Instructional Librarian

Demonstrates the efficacy of search protocols with Internet, using and comparing search engines.

Helps the student read the Internet screen by facilitating the decoding of electronic text.

Presents and requires evaluation of the information gathered in an Internet search: using similar standards for evaluating print re-sources. May have students examine the presentation of informa-tion on particular sites.

Helps the student distinguish among results of differing Internet searches.

Ensures the application of location descriptions (URLs) through required navigation of selected topical sites.

Ensures the student navigation process: demonstrates review strategies (e.g., looking at history screens).

Technology Competencies: The Instructional Librarian

Demonstrates a knowledge of Internet search strategies through hands-on application gathering different formats of information (voice, visual, textual) and showing the storage for such information.

Is able to use demonstration equipment: LCDs, video projectors, etc., for whole-class demonstrations.

Figure 1. (Continued)

Structures the learning environment so that use of hands-on activity for students is a part of the class.
Recognizes and provides opportunities for operation of computer s and peripherals effectively.
Is able to troubleshoot technical problems with Internet searching, recognizing the nature of the problem.
Can use multimedia applications with Internet, and structures such experiences in class sessions.

Scholarly Competencies: The Instructional Librarian

Helps students recognize the nature of the information gathered (quality of preprint, possibly drafts)
Requires that the student examine opinions by formulating a strategy to gather other perspectives on the topic.
Models reflection on diverse points of view gathered from Internet searches on controversial topics, holding onto ambiguity and tension while examining evidence.
Requires the examination of individual pieces of information gathered and facilitates the development of a pattern of inquiry across all information examined on a topic.
Models metacognitive strategies (thinking about the thinking) to regulate information behaviors while using Internet (keeping track of sources, using "tangents" effectively by examining related sites, using the history screen to examine the track of a query).
Demonstrates proper citation of electronic sources.
Prepares instructional Web page for students to visit postclass for review and revisiting of topical links.

Social Competencies: The Instructional Librarian

Collaborates with teaching faculty in the development of the session so that the scholarly intent of the course is aligned with the particular Internet training.
Involves teaching faculty through proactive activity.
Is involved in academic community activities so that use of Internet can develop as response to needs.
Seeks external support for Internet program development, in coordination with colleagues and faculty.

- data malleability;
- the removal of information from context, which is most important for those teaching critical thinking for Internet use.

Fitzgerald suggests several skills be developed in students, including:

- adopting critical consciousness of all Internet interaction;
- establishing prior knowledge through wide browsing, searching, and reading;
- evaluating arguments;
- comparing and contrasting related pieces of information (15).

The use of the Internet crosses many information literacy competencies, such as "selection of appropriate electronic resources," "develop effective search strategies," "analyze and critically evaluate information sources," and "awareness and attitude formation about information and information technology." To see a comprehensive set of information literacy sites on the Internet, consult Grassian's compilation of information literacy Sites (*College & Research Libraries News Online*, Feb. 1999:http://www.ala.org/acrl/resfeb99.html).

Preparation for Information Literacy and Internet Instruction

Woodsworth (1998) notes that librarians who have skills that exceed five years in acquisition most need training to keep abreast with technology, including the Internet. Instructional expertise needs the same bolstering, because methodologies using Internet as a delivery medium offer rich possibilities for sound pedagogy and self-directed learning. Instructional expertise development exceeds theory awareness and must incorporate extensive practice with the variety of learners present in the current library environment (Marchionni and Maurer 1995). A unique experience happens each time one steps into the classroom to teach and, one hopes, to learn from the learners.

A librarian may or may not have taken formal bibliographic instruction courses, depending on the time in the profession and the opportunity in particular library schools. Loomis and Fink (1993) describe the needs for training for the future:

> Regardless of who provides instruction, more resources
> for training must be allocated. Librarians must be trained not
> only in the content of the lesson plan but in the teaching
> methods, such as hands-on instruction and group discussion

methods that are fundamental to teaching in the virtual library. Teaching in a lab setting introduces a whole new set of instructional challenges. . . . Librarians also must be trained to use the increasingly complex instructional technology-LCD's, multimedia projectors, ethernet adapters, and such that bring the virtual library into the classroom. Training must address not just mechanics but affective issues as well (62).

This depiction of training needs is true today and is addressed for current MLS students in a variety of ways. User instruction courses include the current technology, instructional design, and Internet experience for current instructional demands in libraries. An inspection of all course offerings posted on Web pages of library schools linked with ALISE (http://www.alise.org/schools.html) revealed that some, but not the majority, had such specific courses in user education or bibliographic instruction at the MLS level. The University of Buffalo, the University of California at Los Angeles, Indiana University, and Rutgers University are among those who do have such courses.

Library In-house Preparation for Librarians
Some libraries have developed systematic programs for in-house preparation of librarians for Internet use and instruction, as reported in the article on Columbia's Internet Training Program (ITP). Currently, Columbia University Libraries offers training modules to "build your own program." The handouts and resources are available at http://www.columbia.edu/cu/libraries/inside/internet/.

Librarian, Teach Thyself the Internet
The titles of many Internet training texts, such as Barclay's (1996) and LaGuardia's (1996) how-to-do-it manuals indicate that the expertise may be expected to be gained on the job. Instruction texts for library research courses (List 1993, 1997; Bazillon and Braun 1995) illustrate the active attention to the competencies needed on the job. By the mid-1990s, many resources for Internet training proliferated on the Web for self-instruction (Weissinger and Edwards 1994, 1995).

Instructional Managers: Additional Responsibilities, Additional Training
Librarians who have managerial responsibilities for instructional pro-

gram development, such as information literacy coordinators, are those who face managerial tasks for instructional programs. The models for managing library instruction programs are often seen as an emulation of current corporate practices (total quality management, team management, and collaborative practices, as reported in Koval-Jarboe 1996, and Mattesich and Monsey 1992). Librarians in this position must implement ways of interacting with their colleagues and teaching faculty in modes that are similar to a coaching nature than a hierarchical structure.

Information literacy coordinators face the essential need to form collaborative relations with schools, corporations, and differing constituencies, as outlined by organizational practitioners (Bergquist, Betwee, and Meuel 1995) and librarians (Raspa and Ward 1998). These issues are related to the development of instructional Internet expertise in practitioners by the exercise of managerial skills. The *Hot Topics in College Library Management* videotapes produced by the Continuing Education Committee of the College Libraries Section address aspects of instructional issues from a managerial standpoint (http:// bertrand.bucknell.edu/hot/). Study questions accompanying each videotape in the series are provoking and help one gauge a direction for oneself.

Competencies Needed for Internet Instruction
A librarian has demonstrated basic skills in instructional design and delivery by preparing and delivering class sessions that are pedagogically sound. Internet instruction, as is true for any subset of instruction for information literacy, may require differentiated competencies. The array of competencies for Internet instructional expertise is as malleable as any other set of competencies being proposed in this arena of thought. The development of such competencies is likely to provoke discussion about the spectrum of skills needed in Internet instruction.

Assessment for Professional Development Directions by the Librarian
A librarian is in the best position to lead self-development through self-reflection (Schon 1983). The reflection is grounded in daily practice. Some tools for reflection are class evaluations, as well as peer discussion topics and supervisor's evaluations. Various tools are used for class evaluations, ranging from after-class surveys to in-depth in-

terviews with students. Two sets of assessments for current MLS students may be useful in assessing one's own currency. Syracuse University's *Information Technology Literacy Requirements* (http://istweb.syr.edu/design/academic/degrees/grad/literacy_requirements.html) and Emporia's *Diagnostic Examination* (http://slim.emporia.edu/program/DIAGNOS/diag981.htm) can be used to assess gaps in information literacy or technical proficiency.

Some methods of assessing gaps in competencies exist in the formal documents prepared by library associations on essential librarian competencies. Recent compilations of competency listings for information literacy (Oberman, Gratch, and Wilson 1998, http://www.ala.org/acrl/nili/integrtg.html) feature *The Information Literacy Initiative*, with accompanying literature and examples. The Special Library Section has prepared another competencies listing, titled "Competencies for Special Librarians of the 21st Century" (http://www.sla.org/professional/comp.html). These competencies are both professional and personal, and serve as a self-review of an instructional librarian's proficiencies. The Continuing Education Committee, College Libraries Section of ACRL prepared the videotape *User Education in the Electronic Age* (http://bertrand.bucknell.edu/hot/study1.html). Study questions on the user instruction tape can help librarians assess institution-specific issues for Internet and information literacy instruction.

Professional Development for Instructional Expertise: A Spectrum of Options

Exemplary Internet Instructional Program Sites in Libraries

Web-based instruction centers. Teaching centers in libraries and colleges can be examined for organization, resources, and specific instructional delivery. The Web-based Instruction Resource Center, maintained by Ann Scholz-Crane (http://crab.rutgers.edu/~scholzcr/cil/) presents the viewer with instructional modules used to teach students the basics of keyword searching. The site contains links to other library sites with Web-based instruction, development resources (HTML guides, graphics and color, software tools, and other resources) to create Web pages.

Colleges have collated links to examples of higher education examples on the Web. Maricopa College has more than 600 examples of instruction using the Web on its site, demonstrating the diverse ways instructors can integrate the Web into educational planning. Maricopa also maintains an online workshop: "What a Site! Finding, Evaluating, Sharing, and Taking 'Em Home" for instructors using the Web (http://www.mcli.dist.maricopa.edu/tl/). One feature of the site is a critical appraisal of factors that influence decisions to use or not use the Web in instruction. The cases presented for not using the Web are useful thoughts to consider when planning an instructional delivery method. Many other examples of Web-based instruction can be found in LOEX (http://www.emich.edu/~lshirato/loex.html).

In-house Training: Benchmarking Instruction Programs in Academic Libraries

The most documented area of library education is that of in-house training, which forms the basis of many articles in library journals. *College & Research Libraries News*, May 1998 issue, lists five institutions as exhibiting best practices with information literacy" (http://www.ala.org/acrl/nili/integrtg.html). All sites in the *College & Research Libraries News* article have Web-accessible descriptions of their programs. They include, besides Ulster County Community College, the following:

- California State University-San Marcos (http://ww2.csusm.edu/library/ILP/);
- Florida International University (http://www.fiu.edu/~library/ili/);
- Pierce College-Lakewood, Michigan (http://www.pierce.ctc.edu/);
- University of Iowa, Iowa City (http://www.lib.uIowa.edu/info.html);
- University of Washington, Seattle (http://www.washington.edu/uwired/).

ACRL: College Libraries Section.
The Continuing Education Committee of this section prepared videotapes relevant to the needs of instructional librarians (http://bertrand.bucknell.edu/hot/study1.html). The page listing the tape links one to York College, which has its "eText on Information Literacy" for study (http: //www.ycp.edu/library/ifl/).

Other Instructional Programs Emphasizing Collaborative Teaching

The Instruction for Educators Committee, Education and Behavioral Sciences Section, ACRL, collated sites for a midwinter discussion group that had as its distinguishing feature the collaboration work of librarians and faculty. Dane Ward (1998), Wayne State University, collated these sites for an upcoming book on collaboration in instruction between teaching faculty and librarians. The site list includes:

* Project Renaissance from the University of Albany (http://www.albany.edu/projren/9697/hutech/projren.html);
* The University of Iowa's TWIST program (Teaching with Innovative Style and Technology (http://twist.lib.uiowa.edu/);
* Wayne State University Learning Community (http://www.langlab.wayne.edu/TLC/TLChome.html);
* The University of Arizona Teaching Technology Partnership (http://www.library.arizona.edu/partnerships/welcome.html).

Internet Instructional Design Materials Sites, Archives, and Products

LOEX (Library Orientation Information Exchange)

LOEX (http://www.emich.edu/~lshirato/loex.html) has existed since 1973 for the purpose of providing materials on loan to interested librarians. LOEX lists materials on the Web site that include instructional sites using Web-based instruction, online tutorials, handouts and tip sheet descriptions, and essays on bibliographic instruction. LOEX also links critical association sites that focus on instructional design.

ACRL: College Libraries Section

The Continuing Education Committee, College Libraries Section of ACRL, prepared the series *Hot Topics in Library Management* (http://bertrand.bucknell.edu/hot/). Study questions on the user instruction tape can help librarians assess institution-specific issues for Internet and information literacy instruction. Management issues for information literacy coordinators to examine are included.

ACRL: Distance Learning Section

This section (http://personal.ecu.edu/shoused/home.htm) has two links to materials useful for review of distance education materials and strategies over the Web for instruction: The Distance Education Clearinghouse and the Centre for Distance Learning. The latter link has European examples for course study.

ACRL: Instruction Section

The instruction section maintains links to Internet materials, methods, and developments (http://www.lib.utexas.edu/is). The *Internet Edu-*

cation Project is described. Peer-reviewed instructional materials on Internet teaching (about Internet, with the Internet) are linked, and full-text documents are included. Training resources bookmarks also provide a connection for instructional librarians with materials developed by others.

LIRT (Library Instruction Roundtable)

LIRT (http://Diogenes.Baylor.edu/Library/LIRT/) maintains a Web page of Internet Tutorials and Evaluation Tools. LIRT designates and lists The Top Twenty Instructional Articles annually and documents the activity of the Electronic Library Initiative Team. There is a section summarizing related instructional topic programs at ALA.

Courses and Workshops: Internet Instruction

ALISE (Association of Library and Information Science Educators) (http://www.alise.org/schools.html) was reviewed for library school continuing education options relevant for instructional librarians. The following categories emerged from examining the options:
* workshops;
* certificate of advanced study (which can also include the sixth-year program, specialist certificate, post-MLS certificate);
* conferences;
* institutes;
* seminars;
* university professional development (outside library school);
* nondegree courses.

Prevailing Professional Development Options and Internet Instructional Expertise

The majority of post-MLS options in library schools address technology concerns. However, there is little direct focus on Internet instruction. The predominant option is the Certificate of Advanced Study (or a variation of the term). This option usually includes a description of the individualized planning of a program of study. This option would provide instructional librarians the opportunity for relevant courses if this option is taken.

Most schools offer training in Web design in continuing education, as seen at The University of California, Los Angeles (Friday Forums), Drexel University, and The University of Michigan (Digital Toolkit). Several schools have pertinent programs or workshops for designing Internet education (e.g., Pratt: How to Conduct Internet Instruction for Libraries), Several schools offer multiple options of delivery. One example is Rutgers University, which offers distance education, in-house training, courses for credit, and workshops, with topics pertinent to instructional expertise. A Rutgers distance education course on information literacy modules, intended to help design Internet exploration, examines multiple information literacies. Several schools have overlapping programs with other divisions, as seen at The University of Missouri, Columbia, which combines library science and education. A few schools combine their offerings with those of a state agency or company (Colorado, Texas, and California).

Online Courses and Workshops for Internet Instructional Expertise

The Internet Guide: University of Toronto

This course, named as the "best information product designed by a librarian" by the Special Libraries Chapter of Toronto, is available by subscription. Gwen Harris and Sandra Wood developed the TIG (The Internet Guide). A demonstration of the course is available at http://conted.fis.utoronto.ca/tig/demo/. This product may be taken via e-mail and is updated regularly. It appears to be a "best buy" for training librarians, and is particularly suited for training when the campus is distant from library schools or conference sites.

ALA (American Library Association)

Several sections of the ALA have presented courses via teleconferences, audio-and videotapes, and regional workshops. One example of an online course to help teachers and school librarians is ICONnect. Examining the site for structure would deepen awareness of design for diverse groups (http://www.ala.org/ICONN/index.html). The material in this course would help academic librarians as well.

ASIS (American Society for Information Science)

ASIS includes a course catalog on its Web site that includes continuing education courses (http://www.asis.org/CE/). The courses are advertised as "in-house," which effectively brings the course to one's workplace. The content of the courses reflects an orientation toward technology in libraries. One course titled "Harnessing New Technologies for Collaboration" (seen in fall 1998) emphasized the social and technological sides of information work. Although the description states that is for information professionals at all levels, there is the caveat that the course is "for those who have some involvement or responsibility in upgrading . . . their organization's information infrastructure."

SLA (Special Library Association)

SLA 's page (http://www.sla.org) provides information on distance education courses offered in partnership with Pace. Topics that may interest an instructional librarian who has Web page design responsibilities (for fall 1998) include Creating Your Own Home Page, Advanced HTML, Writing Java Applets, and The Seven Keys to Highly Effective Web Sites.

Conference Proceedings on Internet Instructional Factors

ACRL (Association of College and Research Libraries)

ACRL (http://www.ala.org/acrl.html) presents significant links of value for librarians. Items of interest include the 1999 conference "Racing Towards Tomorrow" outline, with some of the invited papers available in full text (http://www.ala.org/acrl/prendex.html). Papers from the prior ACRL Conference, "Choosing Our Futures," are archived for retrieval (http://www.ala.org/acrl/papers.html). The Information Literacy Institute is described, with links to supporting documents and articles. ACRL sections have Web pages with relevant resources, described in an earlier section.

Internet Librarian '98

The most relevant part of this conference was the "Learning Track," listed in the program (http://www.infotoday.com/il98/il98.htm). Presentations are linked to the presenter's sites at their institutions. Relevant presentations included those in the learning track. Titles that are worth exploring include "Baby Boomers Teaching Generation X" (http://www.isr.bucknell.edu/monterey/boomer/), among others.

The Allerton Conference

The Graduate School of Library and Information Science, University of Illinois, maintains conference archives (http://edfu.lis.uiuc.edu/allerton/). There are numerous relevant papers for selective reading.

Online Journals and Instructional Design for the Internet
The American Association of School Librarians' page has a link to the online journal *School Library Media Research* (http://www.ala.org/aasl/journals.html), as well as a listing of "Information Literacy Competencies for K–12." The latter was an excerpt from the book *Information Power* (AASL and AECT 1998). The interest in K–12 programming would be most relevant for librarians working with freshmen (http://www.ala.org/aasl).

Other online journals pertinent to Internet instructional issues include the *Katherine Sharp Review* (http://edfu.lis.uiuc.edu/review/). *American Libraries Online* includes Karen Schneider's monthly column "The Internet Librarian," often relating to instructional issues (http://www.ala.org/alonline/). *Syllabus Magazine* has an online version and often features Internet instructional themes (http://www.syllabus.com/). *From Now On* (http://www.fromnowon.org/) is an educational technology journal with articles of interest to educators and librarians. In 1998, *From Now On* reprinted Phi Delta Kappa's article "Raising a Generation of Free-Range Students." "Current Cites" is a searchable database of articles in journals that provide relevant instructional leads (http://sunsite.berkeley.edu/CurrentCites/). A collection of electronic library journal links can be found at San Jose State University (http://witloof.sjsu.edu/prof/journals.htm).

Library and Information School Syllabi and Bibliographies
The librarian is able to access Web pages for syllabi and subject links due to the efforts of a variety of faculty/scholars. Syllabi to study for sequence of instruction, reading lists, and lecture notes, as well as prepared links to relevant resources are on content related to Internet expertise issues. These syllabi include the following samples:

Collaboration across Boundaries (http://syy.oulu.fi/collab/) is a syllabus prepared by Diane H. Sonnenwald, University of North Carolina at Chapel Hill, which incorporates cross-continental collaborative work using the Internet. Although the instructional librarian may not have a specific opportunity to use this model, the literature on collaboration is recommended for review.

Information Literacy Modules. Rutgers University. The modules were based on Bellingham Public Schools, Washington. Kay E. Vandergrift adapted the modules with permission from Bellingham Schools. The modules, seen in fall 1998, presented related literacies (visual, numeri-

cal, and textual) needed to use the Internet (http://
www.scils.rutgers.edu/de/decourses.html). New distance education
courses are listed at the URL for spring 1999.

Internet Access Issues for Libraries. Karen Schneider, University at Albany, SUNY. Her resources link important federal and state documents relevant to examining the Internet as a social force. Technology planning aids, such as the *Equipment Nuts and Bolts* (pricing lists), are reality checks (http://www.albany.edu/~ks9888/risp623t/syllabus.html).

The Internet: Communicating, Accessing, Providing Information. Dwayne Harapnuik, University of Alberta, California (http://
dte6.educ.ualberta.ca/tech_ed/). This course from the Education Division has an overview of relevant learning theories prepared by the designer of the course titled: "Inquisitivism or the 'HHHMMM???
What Does This Button Do?' Approach to Adult Education." This overview is perhaps the most concise, if not the smoothest worded, presentation of learning theory contributions to Internet education. The overview leads to a critical appraisal of assumptions about learning with technology.

Taming the Information Technology Jungle Home Page. Daniel Barron, University of South Carolina. More than 2,000 school library media created this page specialists' contributions, according to the credits (http://www.libsci.sc.edu/Dan/Dan.htm). Particularly important are the links collected and the syllabus itself. Look for "Classes I Like to Teach" in *Taming the Information Technology Jungle.*

User Needs and Behaviors in Theory and Practice. Charlotte Ford, Indiana University (http://php.indiana.edu/~ceford/L503.html) The assignments in this syllabus may help you design some for in-house study.

World Lecture Hall. Librarians can try "Education," "Distance Education," and "Library" for materials to examine for structure and sequence (http://www.utexas.edu/world/lecture/lis).

Other library school links of interest for professional development include *The Directory of Online Resources for Information Literacy* (http:/
/nosferatu.cas.usf.edu/lis/il) maintained by Drew Smith, University of Southern Florida. This directory includes major papers and links on information literacy, including LOEX.

Consultants: Seminars and Training
Many consultant groups offer Internet training for librarians, that pro-

vides models for instructional librarians. Library Solutions Institute, composed of librarians, provides a specific model (http://www.library-solutions.com/seminars.html). The instructional materials for sale are train the trainer books, with such titles as *All about Internet FTP* (Robison 1994), *Crossing the Internet Threshold* (Tennant, Ober, and Lipow 1994), and *Introducing the Internet* (Jaffe 1994).

Other consultants outside the library and information science fields have options that are relevant to the interested instructional librarian. Edward Tufte's seminars on visual information, based on his three books (1997, 1990, and 1983), are offered in major cities. Other workshops or courses that may be important depend on the librarian's mental map and imaginative linking of opportunities. Such topics as ergonomics, human-computer interaction, creative process, and right-brained drawing provide alternative experiences in processing information. A variety of information processing can lead to a richer instructional expertise base.

Collaborating with Colleagues across Institutions
ACRL: Association of College and Research Libraries Chapters

The added dimension of shared thought, continuing education, and topical planning activity across institutions provides joint presentations, such as ACRL/NY's Annual Symposium. The most recent symposium, "Changing Courses: Libraries as Learning Organizations," featured Dr. Deanna Berg as the keynote speaker on the topic of creating learning organizations. The concepts of Peter Senge, Chris Argyris, and others were applied in discussion and exercises. Continuing education opportunities in ACRL/NY have included workshops, such as "World Wide Web: Creating a Home Page" (prepared by Charles Greenberg, Columbia University).

Similar events occur in all forty-three ACRL chapters at regional conferences, as seen in their newsletters mounted on ACRL's Web page (http://www.ala.org/acrl.html). Several chapters (13) have newsletter links on the Web site, which occasionally reports on Internet instruction programs. Oklahoma's chapter has a newsletter that is downloadable in .pdf format. A recent issue focused on libraries and distance education, as well as presenting links to relevant sites. The Indiana ACRL chapter announced the theme of the annual conference, "Libraries and Lifelong Learning," relevant to all librarians seeking professional development planning options.

Peer Discussion: Mailing Lists

One of the most effective methods of self-education is dialogue with peers. Several discussion lists have specific focuses that involve technology, often Internet-related. NETTRAIN, CRISTEL-ED and Web4, among others, often focus on Internet instructional issues. NETTRAIN draws postings from a wide spectrum of Internet training scenarios. Academic, public, special libraries and corporate training situations are reflected in the contributions and questions on Internet instructional issues. NETTRAIN postings often include resources developed by trainers who list their URL for review.

To subscribe, send the message "sub NETTRAIN your name" to listserve@acsu.buffalo.edu." CRISTAL-ED (Coalition on Reinventing Information Science, Technology, and Library Education) has Web-accessible moderated discussions on instructional themes, such as "BI and Technology," "Repackaging the Library for the Web," and "The Future of the Book." On April 24th 1999, the CRISTAL-ED Mail List discussion moved its base from the School of Information, University of Michigan, to the Department of Information and Library Studies, University of Cape Town. To subscribe to CRISTAL-ED, switch off the "signature" feature of your mailer and then send an electronic mail to majordomo@lists.uct.ac.za with the message: subscribe cristal-ed .

The archives have been moved to: http://www.uct.ac.za/org/cristal-ed. Web4Lib (http://sunsite.berkeley.edu/Web4Lib/) focuses on issues for library Web managers and has content on training staff and users on the Web.

Understanding Diverse Viewpoints in the Academic Community through Virtual Connections

The collaboration effort needed to a user education program using the Internet requires the understanding of differing positions in the academic community. Librarians need the larger picture beyond personal contact with those involved in education programming (e. g., academic computing centers, student groups, teaching faculty associations, as well as individual faculty, all departments in a library, and instructional support services of all kinds). Scanning Web-accessible sources including *The Chronicle of Higher Education* (http://www.chronicle.com/) and sites of professional associations for teaching faculty (e.g., American Association of University Professors), and national associations for educational practice (e.g., the National Educational Association and the American   Association of Higher Education) helps maintain awareness of events that affect library instruction.

The American Association for Higher Education posted an article on distance education, citing the competitive edge that distance education courses presented to universities and colleges (http://www.aahe.org/bulletin/bull_1may98.htm).The National Education Association (NEA) has prepared a report depicting different situations in an information environment: "Education and Community: Four Scenarios" (http://www.gbn.org/Scenarios/NEA/Scenarios.html). Because librarians are involved in many institutions in the preparation of distance education resources and instruction, these developments in the larger sphere are important for practice and needed persuasion at the local level.

Other Links to Academic Community Members
The Library Support Staff Resource Center (http://www.lib.rochester.edu/ssp/) links offer a library of full-text articles, history of the field, educational opportunities, and job lines. This site is for library support staff and does not relate to instructional issues. However, academic librarians need to consider the relationship with the paraprofessional in the work setting, who often supports a user in need, as well as being a partner in instruction in certain situations (e.g., technology setup or assisting users). This site provides an instructional librarian with many opportunities for understanding the paraprofessional's viewpoints

Education Links Related to Instructional Design
The EdTech Web Ring has a component on learning theory, as well as model curriculum, design development, and faculty development, which belongs in an instructional librarian's conceptual toolkit (http://iml.umkc.edu/web-ring/edtech/). Links to formative technology standards for teachers in cooperation with NASA demonstrate the level of learning students coming into universities may possess (http://www.iste.org/Resources/). Higher education resources are linked at the NEA site (http://www.nea.org/).

McRel (Mid-continent Regional Education Laboratory) has an exhaustive listing of technology resources for instruction (http://www.mcrel.org). A thought-provoking link is ThinkQuest (www.thinkquest.org), which has a library of award-winning Web sites collaboratively produced by teams of children from ages 12 to 18. The content of these sites is educational material seen from a child's perspective. ThinkQuest Junior is also included. Librarians can see the levels of production of Web material in their incoming students, as well as the active learning methods employed by the children.

Summary and Recommendations

The continuing education options seen across the country do provide Internet awareness and tools for professional development on the topic of Internet instruction, primarily from professional associations and librarians themselves. They can be located online or on-site, in the field or in another arena. The instructional librarian can strategically plan both formal and informal options, with a view for professional growth across a career.

The library professional associations lead in the development of resources for Internet instruction. Practitioners share their experiences, working curriculum, resources, and ideas on the Web. Because these resources are rooted in practice and real-life situations, their authenticity is inspiring. The associations most involved with instruction have incorporated Internet instruction into their mission, to the benefit of all. Libraries have developed institution-specific working programs that can be examined for "fit" in another institution. These developments are some of the best resources found. Librarians have taken the traditional value of information sharing and extended it to resource sharing.

Library schools can offer needed specific courses on educational design for the post-MLS instructional librarian. The resources for creating instructional design workshops, seminars, and courses for instructional librarians in the field can be mobilized. They can build on the grass-roots collaborative work seen in institutions cited in this article and elsewhere in this volume. This area must be considered for academic courses replete with Internet-intensive education because the primary intermediaries in libraries of the future are likely to be instructional librarians.

Research on the effects of the differing professional development options as they provide for Internet instructional expertise is sparse and needs attention. The literature on adult education (androgogy) is replete with conceptual frameworks and results with specific populations that can be transferred to librarians for systematic examination of efficacy. A systematic evaluation of professional development opportunities would serve mature librarians. They would be the logical candidates for such research and should be asked for recommendations.

A final concern is the rapid overlap between teaching faculty and what is becoming "instructional faculty-librarians." This fusion of roles is likely to continue as the library assumes more instructional responsibility. The library was once a place where different learning experiences happened for a student precisely because the environment was different and learning was at one's own pace and direction. With the advent of the Internet and the emergence of information literacy standards, students are exposed to instruction in the library that is similar to what they experience in the classroom. The facilitation of a student to learn as he or she wishes is as important as instructional expertise. The library still needs to be "The Open Learning Place."

References

American Association of School Librarians and Association of Educational and Communications Technology. 1998. *Information power: Building partnerships for learning.* Chicago: ALA.

Barclay, D., ed. 1996. *Teaching electronic information literacy: A how-to-do-it manual.* New York: Neal-Schuman.

Bergquist, W., J. Betwee, and D. Meuel. 1995. *Building strategic relationships: How to extend your organization's reach through partnerships, alliances, and joint ventures.* San Francisco: Jossey-Bass.

Bazillon, R., and C. Braun. 1995. *Academic libraries as hi-tech gateways: A guide to design and space considerations.* Chicago: ALA.

Estabrook, L. S. 1999. *New forms of distance education: Opportunities for students, threats to institutions.* ACRL National Conference: Invited Papers (http://www.ala.org/acrl/estabrook.html).

Fitzgerald, M. A. 1997. Misinformation on the Internet: Applying evaluation skills to online information. *Emergency Librarian* 24(3):9–29.

Jaffe, L.D. 1994. *Introducing the Internet. A trainer's workshop.* Berkeley, Calif.: Library Solutions Pr.

Koval-Jarboe, P. 1996. Quality improvement: A strategy for planned organizational change. Perspectives on Quality in the Library. *Library Trends* 44(3):605–27.

LaGuardia, C. et al. 1996. *Teaching the new library: A how-to-do-it manual for planning and designing instructional programs.* New York: Neal-Schumann.

Lindauer, B.G. 1998. Compilation of Core Information Literacy Competency/Outcomes for Undergraduates. Available at: http://www.ala.org/acrl/nili/integrtg.html.

List, C. 1993. *Introduction to library research.* New York: McGraw-Hill.

———. 1998. *Introduction to information research.* Dubuque, Ia.: Kendall-Hunt.

Loomis, A., and D. Fink. 1993. Instruction: Gateway to the virtual library. In L. M. Saunders, ed. *The virtual library: Visions and realities.* Westport, Conn.: Meckler, 47–69.

Marchionni, G., and H. Maurer. 1995. The role of digital libraries in teaching and learning. *Communications of the ACM* 58(4):67–75.

Mattessich, P. W., and B. R. Monsey. 1992. *Collaboration: What makes it work.* St. Paul, Minn.: Amherst H. Wilder Foundation.

Raspa, R., and D. Ward. 1998. Information literacy: The collaborative imperative. *NCA Quarterly* 72(4):436–39.

Robison, D. 1994. *All about Internet FTP.* Berkeley, Calif.: Library Solutions Pr.

Schon, D. A. 1983. *The reflective practitioner: How professionals think in action.* New York: Basic Bks.

Tennant, R., J. Ober and A. G. Lipow. 1994. *Crossing the Internet threshold.* 2d ed. Berkeley, Calif.: Library Solutions Pr.

Tufte, E. 1983. *Visual display of quantitative information.* Cheshire, Conn.: Graphics Pr.

———. 1990. *Envisioning information.* Cheshire Conn.: Graphics Pr.

———. 1997. *Visual explanations: Images and quantities, evidence and narrative.* Cheshire Conn.: Graphics Pr.

Ward, D. Feb., 1998. "Web sites on librarian and faculty collaboration." (Unpublished handout distributed at The Education and Behavioral Sciences Section [ACRL] Midwinter Current Topics Discussion Group, New Orleans, distributed by e-mail on EBSS_L @UNCCVM.UNCC.)

Weissinger, N. J., and J.P. Edwards. 1994. "Selected online sources of information for Internet trainers." (Unpublished annotated bibliography prepared for ACRL/NY program: Six degrees of connectedness: Different views of who, what, where, and when of Internet training in academia. New York University, Bobst Library, May 25, 1994.)

———. 1995. Online resources for Internet trainers. *College & Research Libraries News* 56(8):535–39.

Woodsworth, A. 1998. Learning for a lifetime. *Library Journal* 123 (1): 62, 24–29.

Afterword

Theresa M. Maylone

After the words of authors as engaged, committed, and eloquent as those of the preceding articles, what is an appropriate afterword? The words that follow are, therefore, a continuation of the reflections provided throughout this volume. Although informed by my years as a practitioner, my reflections here are the ruminations of someone who has been privileged to oversee the education of new entrants to our field at a time exactly coincident with the diffusion of the Internet throughout our domain.

In the summer of 1993, the Palmer School offered a three-credit graduate course called "Electronic Resources of the Internet." The original intent was to offer one section, limited to twelve students—the number of workstations in the computer lab. After all, how much interest could there be among library school students for such an uncharted course in the middle of a very hot summer? That was quite a wrong assumption, as it turned out. We quickly added three more sections of the course, offered concurrently, at geographically dispersed locations. Not only would we offer the course, but we would literally and conceptually reinforce the meaning of "inter-networking" by making it possible for students in all sections to communicate with each other during class via the Internet.

One observable measure of the diffusion of Internet expertise in academic libraries is how ordinary such a course sounds today, only five years later. Applicants for entry-level academic library positions now are routinely asked at interviews for the URL of their personal Web page.

The Internet is neither the first nor likely the last great technological innovation to engage our creativity or entangle our frustrations. It is, however, the one that comes closest to being preemptive when viewed among the individual technologies of our recent professional past. By providing an opportunity to fundamentally alter how we practice our profession, the Internet has also presented us the opportunity to evaluate our roles as never before. As the authors in this volume have demonstrated, we are both teachers and learners; the institutions that employ us are, similarly, teaching institutions and learning organizations. Can we now, however, comfortably allow these labels to define and communicate the value of the librarian or the academic library? In the way that the Internet has taken down the boundaries of access to information, through our relationship to this technology have we not potentially also removed the boundaries that traditional labels have often made self-fulfilling?

Whether "potentially" becomes "actually" depends on our responses to the challenge. Clearly, the authors of the preceding articles see a spotlighted leadership role for the academic librarian as teacher, facilitator, coach, and consultant. How we (practitioners, library administrators, professional organizations, and schools of library and information studies) take advantage of the spotlight to sustain leadership seems to me to require first an honest appraisal of our situation and our values. I am neither wise enough nor arrogant enough to feel comfortable holding the crystal ball, but overseeing the education of others calls for both attention and reflection. As a consequence, I may have formulated a few significant questions that will help to focus the gaze of others into an always-uncertain future.

Is our experience in libraries with the Internet indeed unique, in relation to technology in general, as a tool or resource and in its impact and influence on our profession? Is the diffusion of the Internet having similar affects in other social institutions? Is teaching and learning the Internet in the context of the academic library different from learning and teaching it elsewhere? Because of the boundary-spanning nature of the Internet, are we now better able to interact with other disciplines, and inform and be informed by them?

Is our goal the virtual library? If that is not our goal, where are we going with our Internet experience? The articles in this book have detailed the diffusion of Internet experience in academic libraries. What further diffusion of that experience is possible throughout our academic institutions?

How do we learn what we know, and how do we teach what we learn? Does our learning, like that of those whom we teach, now depend less on method of instruction and accommodations to individual learning styles than on our attitudes toward learning itself? Do we learn because we have to or because learning is the greatest excitement on earth?

If tacit knowledge is that which practitioners know, is the current pace of our need to learn more and more faster and faster, making it impossible for us to internalize new learning such that it may become tacit knowledge and used in everyday practice?

Borrowing a description from social scientist and educator Donald Schon, can we accept that a "state of stability" in our organizations or in our knowledge is probably unattainable; rather, revision without end is more likely the norm?

This book, and this Afterword, is really about our love–hate relationship with technology and with what technology calls into question about our beliefs and practices. Educators and practitioners alike must continue to question our true tasks as we assess our relationship to known technologies and their diffusion. The asking of such questions is also the essence of research, a pursuit in which we all must continue to engage.

About the Contributors

Authors

Emily Contrada Anderson, RN, MA, is currently enrolled in the MLS program at St. John's University, Jamaica, NY. She is a utilization manager/quality improvement coordinator for the New York Hospital Queens Home Health Agency, Fresh Meadows. Her previous positions in nursing include staff nurse in adult and newborn acute care, school and occupational health nursing, and hospitalwide continuous quality improvement manager (e-mail: anderson@concentric.net).

Heather Blenkinsopp is head of access services at Mercy College Libraries in Dobbs Ferry, NY. Previously, she was assistant head of technical services at Mercy. She received her MLS from SUNY Albany and has a master's in human resource management from Mercy College. Heather is active in local professional organizations (e-mail:hblenkin@mercynet.edu).

Daniel J. Caldano is the user support specialist, Libraries Systems Office, Columbia University. He has worked in the LSO since the 1970s and has spent the past decade concentrating on staff training and Internet instruction. He was instrumental in setting up Columbia University Libraries' Internet Training Program and continues as one of its trainers (e-mail:caldano@columbia.edu).

David W. Carr is an associate professor in the School of Information and Library Science at the University of North Carolina at Chapel Hill, where he teaches courses in collection development and advanced social sciences and humanities reference. Dr. Carr's scholarly work emphasizes learning in cultural institutions. He has been a consultant at the Brooklyn Museum of Art, the Children's Museum of Indianapolis, and the Museum of Fine Arts, Houston, among other institutions. He is a recipient of the ALISE Award for Teaching Excellence. His essay "The Situation of the Adult Learner in the Library" was pre-

sented in May 1988 at the LOEX Annual Conference, and is reprinted in
this volume with permissions from both the author and the publisher of
the *Proceedings*, Pieran Press (e-mail:carr@ils.unc.edu).

David J. Franz received his MLS from Rutgers in 1996 and is a librarian at the Montvale Free Public Library, Montvale, NJ, since 1996. He
served on the Bergen County Cooperative Library System Reference
Committee from 1997 to 1998. He also served as consultant to the
Westwood Public Library in the development of its Web site (http://
www.bccls.org/westwood). David designed and maintains the Montvale
Library Web site at http://www.bccls.org/montvale (e-mail:
franz2eclipse.net).

Harriet A. Hagenbruch received her MLS from the Palmer School
of Library and Information Science, Long Island University, C.W. Post
Campus, and her MA in elementary education from Hofstra University. A former school library media specialist, she has held the position
of curriculum materials center/education librarian, Axinn Library,
Hofstra University, since 1989. Professor Hagenbruch has been an active member of ACRL/NY, having founded and continuing as chair of
the Education/Curriculum Materials Center Librarians, an interest
group. As vice-president of the Academic and Special Libraries Division of Nassau County Library Association, She cochaired a successful
conference in April of 1992 titled "Librarians as Educators: Defining
Our Role." (e-mail:libhah@office.hofstra.edu).

Roger T. Harris, a reference librarian at Fordham University at Lincoln Center, is author of *Our Town: An Introduction to the History of Columbus, Georgia*, which was supported by the National Endowment for
the Humanities. He was the recipient of a Fulbright teaching appointment in Aix-en-Provence, awarded by the Institute of International
Education. Mr. Harris received the MLS degree from the University
of North Carolina at Chapel Hill.

Dottie R. Hiebing is currently executive director of the Metropolitan New York Library Council (METRO). Ms. Hiebing has a master
of arts in library science from Rosary College (Dominican University)
and a master of public administration from the University of Denver.
Prior to joining METRO, she was director of the Central Jersey Re-

gional Library Cooperative in Freehold, NJ. She has also served as director of the Office of Library Development at the State Library of Iowa, as director of a public library system in Minnesota, and as a continuing education consultant with the Wisconsin State Library e-mail:hiebing2metgate.metro.org).

Jayne B. Johnsen-Seeberger has a BS in library science from West Virginia Wesleyan, where she minored in English and Biology, and an MLS from Long Island University with specializations in academic, medical, and school media libraries. Since graduating, she has held medical and corporate library positions. She has been editor of the ACRL/NY Metropolitan Area Chapter's newsletter, *Connections*, for five years. Ms. Johnsen-Seeberger currently works as a reference librarian at Dowling College and Suffolk County Community College, and is an adjunct instructor at Long Island University's Palmer School of Library and Information Science (e-mail: jbjs214@ibm.net).

Eleanor R. Kulleseid, director of Mercy College Libraries, was a school library media specialist and director of the Bank Street College of Education Library for many years. The research completed for her 1985 monograph, *Beyond Survival to Power for School Library Media Professionals*, has informed the author's subsequent professional activities in higher education. During the past decade, Dr. Kulleseid served on the boards of the Metropolitan New York Library Council (METRO) and the Westchester Academic Library Directors Organization (WALDO) dealing with issues of rapid and constant changes in communications technology, training, and delivery of instruction (e-mail:ekullese@mercynet.edu).

Patricia O'Brien Libutti is the Cybrarian at ThinkQuest, Armonk, New York. ThinkQuest is a nonprofit organization focused on developing children's collaborative use of technology to prepare curricular materials. She has worked as a consultant at the National Library of Education for the upcoming National Education Network. She prepared proposals for and received two ACRL Initiative Funds in 1994–1995. She chaired the Education and Behavioral Sciences Section, Association of Research and College Libraries, 1996. Dr. Libutti has held positions as a Librarian (education subject specialist, Fordham University Libraries), and as an educator (gifted education, art, and human relations, K–12). Her adjunct experience in higher education includes teaching courses in library science, Rutgers University, and educational technology, Fordham University. Her publications and presentations over the past decade focus on instructional roles of librarians in technology-rich scenarios, as well as ethical considerations of qualitative research on the Internet. Her Ph.D. is in educational psychology ,Temple University. Her dissertation on Peer Facilitation of Curiosity and Exploratory Behaviors influenced subsequent education and library work. Other educational background includes an M.Ed. in art education (Tyler Art School) and an MLS from Rutgers University. She edited *Librarians as Learners, Librarians as Teachers:The Diffusion of Internet Expertise in Academic Libraries* (e-mail: libutti@thinkquest.org).

Laurie J. Lopatin is a catalog librarian at Hofstra University, Hempstead, NY. She cataloged the Weingrow Collection of Avant-Garde Art and Literature at Hofstra University under a grant from the National Endowment for the Humanities. Ms. Lopatin has previously been a catalog librarian at Long Island University, Pace University, and Bloomsburg State University. Ms. Lopatin has published "The Series Authority File at Hofstra University" *(Cataloging & Classification Quarterly* [1995]) and "Not Left by the Wayside: A Case Study of the Creation of a Library for Troubled Adolescents of the Wayside Home School for Girls" *(Public & Access Services Quarterly* [1996]). She has also cocompiled several ACRL/ NY symposia bibliographies, including "Libraries: The Heart of the University?" which was published in *The Unabashed Librarian* (1996), and the annotated bibliography "The Book & the Brave New Library," which was accepted for publication in *The Unabashed Librarian*. Ms. Lopatin is president of the Academic and Special Libraries Division of the Nassau County Library Association. She also serves on the ACRL/NY Symposium Planning Committee and is a member of ALA, ALCTS, and AAUP. She has an MLS from Drexel University and an MS in information science from Long Island University (e-mail:libctljl@mail1.hofstra.edu).

David S. Magier earned a BA in linguistics from Cornell, and both the MA and Ph.D. in linguistics (with specialization in South Asian languages and linguistics) from the University of California, Berkeley.

He did field research for his dissertation "Topics in the Grammar of Marwari" on a Fulbright in Rajasthan, India, in 1981. After obtaining his doctorate in 1983, he taught in the Department of Linguistics at Berkeley. He then spent two years teaching in Pakistan and returned to the United States as professor of linguistics at Michigan State University. In 1987, he made a career shift and took the position of South Asia librarian at Columbia University Libraries, where he has worked since. From 1991 onward, he has held the position of director of area studies at Columbia Libraries (a division that includes area-specialist librarians for Latin America, Africa, Middle East, Russia/Eastern Europe, and South & Southeast Asia). Dr. Magier is a well-known Internet trainer and serves as a trainer and consultant to libraries worldwide (e-mail:magier@columbia.edu).

Theresa M. Maylone is assistant dean at the Palmer School of Library and Information Science of Long Island University. Among her recent publications is the spring 1998 "Qualitative Research" issue of *Library Trends*, which she coedited with Gillian M. McCombs (e-mail:tmaylone@phoenix.liunet.edu).

Patricia H. Carroll-Mathes, professor and coordinator of information literacy at SUNY-Ulster County Community College, has developed library programs there since 1971. Her commitment to instruction was recognized by ACRL with the 1997 Innovation in Instruction Award for the Collaborative Information Literacy Program. Credit instruction at UCCC, initiated in 1993, has evolved into a departmental program with multiple course sections taught by a teaching team with faculty from many disciplines. Information literacy is required for all students in degree programs. Both Dennis Swauger, professor of chemistry, SUNY-Ulster County Community College, and Richard B. Phillips, Ph.D., reference librarian and instructor of information literacy, Marist College, reviewed her article (e-mail:CarrollP@sunyulster.edu).

Charlotte D. Moslander has been a science fiction fan for forty-four years. For the last twenty-nine of those years, she has also been a librarian. Her avocation and her vocation merged several times during those years, most recently in enabling her to work comfortably in Cyberspace. While in library school, she worked for one year as a librarian trainee assigned mostly to the technical services unit of a public library. The following year, she was a library teacher in an elementary school. Since receiving her MS from Columbia University in 1969, she has held professional and faculty positions in public, special, and academic libraries, as well as teaching undergraduate library skills classes to adult learners, reviewing books and nontheatrical films, publishing a few articles and interviews, and indexing. When asked what kind of librarian she is, her standard reply is, "Darn good!" (e-mail:cdmoslander@hotmail.com).

Rona L. Ostrow is the assistant campus provost at Fairleigh Dickinson University, Teaneck, NJ. The former chief librarian of the Shanahan Library/Media Center (1994–1998), Dr. Ostrow received her Ph.D. from Rutgers, The State University of New Jersey, in 1998. Her dissertation is entitled "Library Culture in the Electronic Age: A Case Study of Organizational Change." Previously, Dr. Ostrow served as associate dean of libraries for public services at Adelphi University (1990–1994), associate professor (Library Department)/associate director of the technology-based Graduate Business Resource Center at Baruch College, City University of New York (1980–1990), assistant business reference librarian at the Fashion Institute of Technology Library (1978–1980), and as a librarian at both the Research Library and the Branch Library System of the New York Public Library. She holds an MS in library service from Columbia University (1970); an MA in English literature from Hunter College, City University of New York (1975); and a BA in English and comparative literature from City College, City University of New York (1969). She is a former chair of the New York City Section of the Association of College and Research Libraries, a former member of the METRO board of trustees, a member of the American Library Association (ALA), the Library Administration and Management Association (LAMA), the Library and Information Technology Association (LITA), the Association of College and Research Libraries (ACRL), and the American Association of University Women. She coauthored the *Cross Reference Index* (1989), *The Dictionary of Marketing* (1987), and the *Dictionary of Retailing* (1984), and has also published several articles. Dr. Ostrow has extensive experience in bringing information technology to college campuses and in training end users in its use. She coauthored *Six Degrees of Connectedness* (e-mail:ostrow@fdu.edu).

Irina Poznansky was born, raised, and educated in Moscow, Russia. She came to the United States in 1989. In 1990 she started working in Butler Library, Columbia University, and the same year enrolled in the master's program at Columbia School of Library Services. She graduated in 1992 with an MS with a major in information services. Since February 1993, she has worked as a resource center librarian in Teacher's College (e-mail: irina@edunet.tc.columbia.edu).

Debra Randorf is the librarian at Decatur Clearpool School, PS/IS 35, in Brooklyn, NY. She previously was librarian at the New York Historical Society (e-mail:nyhs3@metgate.metro.org).

Marilyn Rosenthal is associate professor, reference librarian, and head of interlibrary loan at Nassau Community College Library. Since 1991, she has been active in ACRL/NY as an executive board member, vice-chair and chair of the Long Island Section, and membership secretary. Ms. Rosenthal has been chair of the Long Island Library Resources Council Interlibrary Loan Committee and her campus's delegate to the SUNY Librarians Association, as well as a member of the SUNY/OCLC Resource Sharing Committee. In addition, she has assumed leadership positions in her department and on campus. Currently, she serves as a member of the College Executive Committee, second vice-chair of the Academic Senate, and president of the Women's Faculty Association. She has chaired other organizations, presented frequently at conferences, written more than a hundred book reviews for *Library Journal* and *Choice*, and published a book chapter and numerous journal articles. The enclosed article is an outgrowth of the spring 1996 *Internet Reference Services Quarterly* survey, "Evaluating Use of the Internet among Academic Reference Librarians," which she co-authored with Marsha Spiegelman. She received the SUNY Chancellor's Award for Excellence in Librarianship in 1996 (e-mail:rosent@sunynassau.edu).

Marsha Spiegelman is assistant professor, head of reference, and archivist at Nassau Community College Library. Since 1995, she has been active in ACRL/NY as an executive board member, vice-chair and chair of the Long Island Section. From 1994–1998, she served on the Executive Board of the Nassau Library Association, and is currently chair of the Long Island Library Resources Council Resource Sharing

Committee. As an active member on campus and in her department, Ms. Spiegelman has served as chair of Community Services Committee and is currently secretary of the College Grants Committee and chair of the Library Curriculum Committee. A frequent presenter at conferences, she has written a published book chapter and journal articles. The article in this volume is an outgrowth of the spring 1996 *Internet Reference Services Quarterly* survey, "Evaluating use of the Internet Among Academic Reference Librarians" which she coauthored with Marilyn Rosenthal (e-mail:spiegelm2sunynassau.edu).

Catherine M. Thomas has been the user services librarian in the Library Systems Office at Columbia University Libraries since 1991. She has coordinated the Internet training program for libraries' staff since its inception in 1992. She is the chief editor of SWIFT (the libraries' Web service for its staff) and a contributor to LibraryWeb (the libraries' Web service for its users). Prior to joining the Systems Office, Catherine worked as a serials cataloger for four years at Columbia University, and prior to that, for six years at the University of California, San Diego. She began her library career in 1978 as a serials acquisitions clerk at the University of Delaware. Catherine feels that her serials expertise has been invaluable in learning to cope with the Internet (e-mail:thomas@columbia.edu).

Jana Varlejs is an associate professor at the Rutgers School of Communication, Information and Library Studies (New Brunswick, New Jersey). She served as director of the School's continuing education program for library and information professionals from 1979 to 1993. Before joining Rutgers, she worked in public libraries in New Jersey and was a consultant at the state library agency in Massachusetts, specializing in outreach services. At Rutgers, she coordinates internships in a wide variety of organizational settings and teaches a course on designing information services for a pluralistic society. Her research has focused on library and information science faculty publication patterns and on librarians' continuing professional learning. As of 1998, she has been responsible for the continuing education chapter in the annual statistics publication of the Association for Library and Information Science Education. She has edited thirteen titles in a series of Rutgers SCILS symposia proceedings, of which the last was *Safeguarding Electronic Information,* in 1996. Recently, an exploration of the beginnings of the Rutgers MLS program has led to an interest in the history of information science. Her Ph.D. is from the University of Wisconsin-Madison and her MLS is from Rutgers (e-mail:varlejs@scils.rutgers.edu).

Anne Woodsworth was dean of the Palmer School of Library and Information Science at Long Island University from 1991 to 1998. She obtained her Ph.D. in education (higher education administration) from the University of Pittsburgh. Until she joined the educational side of the field in 1988, she held management positions in a variety of settings including director of two ARL libraries (Pittsburgh and York), personnel director of Canada's largest public library, head of reference at the University of Toronto, and, concurrently, for ten years until 1983, president of her own consulting company. With an undergraduate degree in fine arts, a second bachelor's and a master's degree in library science, she has also been considered qualified to be a reference librarian in a public library, in a science and medicine library, and a medical librarian in a hospital library. She has held numerous elected leadership positions such as president of the Association of Research Libraries and its equivalent in Canada. She has served on the Council of ALA and has been a member of its Committee on Accreditation. She will become president of the Association of Library and Information Science Education in 1999. At Long Island University, since 1991, she led the faculty through a transition that has resulted in the school introducing the full MS program in Manhattan, and establishing an undergraduate BS in information transfer and a Ph.D. in information studies at the C.W. Post campus of LIU. Woodsworth is the author of five monographs and more than sixty articles mostly on the effects of information technology on organizational structures and work. Her latest research focus is best reflected in a monograph published in 1993 titled *Reinvesting in the Information Job Family: Context, Changes, New Jobs, and Models for Evaluation and Compensation,* coauthored by Theresa Maylone (Boulder, CO: CAUSE in cooperation with the Association of College and Research Libraries and College and University Personnel Association. Professional paper series, #11)(e-mail:woodswor@phoenix.liunet.edu).

Reviewers

Nancy J. Becker is an assistant professor at St. John's School of Library and Information Science. Dr. Becker served as a mentor for MLS student Emily Contrada Anderson's contribution to this volume. She coauthored "Online Resources for Internet Trainers" (*College & Research Libraries News* 56(8): 535–39) with J. P. Edwards in 1995. Dr. Becker presented "The Significance of Service Learning for LIS Education" at the Association of Library and Information Science Educators (ALISE) program in 1999 (e-mail:nbecker@snet.net).

Susan Griswold Blandy is professor and faculty librarian at Hudson Valley Community College in Troy, New York. She is currently periodicals librarian, liberal arts liaison, and chair of the Academic Senate Planning Committee. She holds degrees from Oberlin, McGill University and the University at Albany (SUNY); and has published in the areas of library instruction, multicultural librarianship, assessment, and public relations. She teaches the Honors Course American Architecture in its Social Context and is president of the local chamber music presenting society. In 1989, she was awarded the New York State Chancellor's Award for Excellence in Librarianship, and in 1996, the New York Library Association Academic and Special Libraries Section "Spirit of Librarianship" (e-mail: blandsus@hvcc.edu).

Sarah K. Burns is head of instructional services for Pace University's Westchester campuses. She holds an MLS from the State University of New York at Albany, an MA in theology from Villanova University, and a BA in English from the State University of New York at Geneseo. Ms. Burns currently serves as adjunct professor in the Palmer School of Library and Information Science at Long Island University's C.W. Post campus. She is a member of the Association of College and Research Libraries, Instruction Section, and the METRO (Metropolitan New York Library Council) Bibliographic Instruction SIG (e-mail:sburns@pace.edu).

John P. Edwards is digital resources librarian at Teachers College, Columbia University. His involvement ranges across cataloging, Web site development, systems, and technology training for staff. In 1995, he coauthored "Online Resources for Internet Trainers, (*College & Re-*

search Libraries News 56(8): 535–39), with N. J. Weissinger (e-mail:jpe9@columbia.edu. URL: http://www.columbia.edu/~jpe9).

Sheryl Chisamore is a writing tutor at Ulster County Community College, Stone Ridge, NY.

Cecile A. Hastie has served as a reference librarian at Teachers College, Columbia University, since 1986, where she has also coordinated library instruction and services for students with disabilities. She was president of the ACRL/NY chapter during 1998. She also has contributed as vice-president and president of the New York City section of ACRL/NY during 1993–1994, as coeditor of the ACRL/NY newsletter, and as a member of the Symposium Committees for 1996–1998. Moreover, she has been an active member of the ACRL/NY Bibliographic Instruction group (e-mail:cah33@columbia.edu).

Lucy Heckman is a reference librarian (business–economics) at St. John's University Library. Prior to this position, She was catalog librarian at St. John's University, from 1977 to 1982. She is a member of the American Library Association and is secretary of ALA/RUSA/BRASS. She also is a member of New York Library Association and served as treasurer of the RASS Section from 1996 to 1998. Ms. Heckman was elected to Beta Phi Mu. Publications include *Franchising in Business: A Guide to Information Sources* (New York: Garland Publishing, 1989) and *The New York Stock Exchange: A Guide to Information Sources* (New York: Garland Publishing, 1992). In addition, she reviews books for *Library Journal* and *ARBA*. She is currently president of the ACRL/NY chapter (1999). She has contributed to the ACRL/NY chapter as vice-president (1998) and chair of the 1998 Symposium Committee, which prepared "Changing Courses: Libraries as Learning Organizations" (e-mail: heckmanl@stjohns.edu).

Jayne B. Johnsen-Seeberger: See About the Authors section.

Mary Kopala, Ph.D., is associate professor at Hunter College, City University, New York, in the Department of Educational Foundations and Counseling, where she teaches research courses. Many of her presentations at national and regional conferences have focused on the use of qualitative methods. She is actively involved in research, both quantitative and qualitative. She has written numerous book chapters and articles.

Dona McDermott is an assistant professor at the Center for Business Research, Long Island University, where she teaches Internet classes for students and has developed search engine presentations for the business community. She holds an MLS from St. John's University and is currently enrolled in the MBA program at C.W. Post. Ms. McDermott is a member of the ACRL/NY Symposium Committee (e-mail:dmcdermo@liu.edu).

Richard P. Phillips is a reference librarian at Marist College, Poughkeepsie, NY.

Marilyn Rosenthal: See the About the Authors section.

Dennis Swauger is a professor of chemistry at Ulster County Community College, Stone Ridge, NY.

Catherine Thomas: See the About the Authors section.

Bellinda Wise is a reference librarian and instructor at Nassau Community College (1995–present). She was formerly with SUNY Farmingdale (1990–1995). She is the ACRL/NY Long Island Section chair (1999), and has served on the ACRL Symposium Planning Committee (1994–present). She is a member of the ACRL/NY Long Island Bibliographic Instruction Discussion Group (1992–present), as well as a member of ALA, ACRL/NY, SUNYLA, and NCLA. In addition, she is a reviewer for *Library Journal* (e-mail:wiseb@sunynassau.edu).